Taste of Home

Vol. 2

WHAT CAN I BRING?

360+ DISHES FOR PARTIES, PICNICS & POTLUCKS

TASTE OF HOME BOOKS • RDA ENTHUSIAST BRANDS, LLC • MILWAUKEE, WI

1610 N. 2nd St., Suite 102, Milwaukee WI 53212-3906

Visit us at **tasteofhome.com** for other Taste of Home books and products.

International Standard Book Number:
Trade: 979-8-88977-171-5
Special Market: 979-8-88977-182-1

Content Directors: Ellie Martin Cliffe, Mark Hagen
Creative Director: Raeann Thompson
Associate Creative Director: Jami Geittmann
Senior Editors: Christine Rukavena, Simrran Gill
Senior Art Director: Courtney Lovetere
Art Director: Jazmin Delgado
Manager, Production Design: Satyandra Raghav
Assistant Art Director (Production): Jogesh Antony
Senior Print Publication Designer: Bipin Balakrishnan
Print Publication Designer: Mukesh Kumar
Print Production Artist: Akash Christopher
Deputy Editor, Copy Desk: Ann M. Walter
Contributing Copy Editor: Nancy J. Stohs
Contributing Assistant Art Director: Julie Wagner

Cover Photography
Photographer: Dan Roberts
Set Stylist: Melissa Franco
Food Stylist: Josh Rink, Ellen Crowley

Pictured on front cover:
Iced Raspberry Tea, p. 8; Loaded Twice-Baked Potato Casserole, p. 141; Spicy Chicken Wings with Blue Cheese Dip, p. 40; Lemon-Blueberry Pound Cake, p. 278.

Pictured on back cover:
Slow-Cooker Spinach & Artichoke Dip, p. 228; Colorful Cornbread Salad, p. 152; Buffalo Chicken Enchiladas, p. 137; Bacon Cheeseburger Slider Bake, p. 205; Fresh Strawberry Pie, p. 295.

Printed in China
1 3 5 7 9 10 8 6 4 2

P. 253

NEVER WONDER WHAT TO BRING AGAIN!

The best moments are the ones shared over good food. Whether it's a summertime barbecue, holiday potluck or game-day get-together, every invite comes with the same challenge: What can I bring?

With ***Taste of Home What Can I Bring? Vol. 2***, you'll never run out of ideas. Inside, you'll find more than 360 dishes perfect for every season and celebration—each one made to travel, share, and steal the spotlight on the buffet.

With everything from easy snacks, appetizers and salads to comforting sides, mains and desserts, this cookbook has it all. Find big-batch favorites to feed extra-large crowds as well as slow-cooker staples that come together without much effort. There's even a bonus chapter of no-bake cookies, bars and other treats that satisfy sweet cravings in a snap.

Every recipe has been perfected in our Test Kitchen, so you can cook with confidence knowing each dish has been tried, tested and loved.

You'll also find smart Test Kitchen tips, handy answers to common cooking questions, substitution ideas and simple ways to make every dish look party perfect. You'll even learn how to transport dishes with ease, keep food at the right temperature and add the simple finishing touches that make a lasting impression.

Take the guesswork out of entertaining and always arrive with the scene-stealing bite that has everyone talking. With ***Taste of Home What Can I Bring? Vol. 2***, it couldn't be easier ... or more delicious.

P. 304

P. 134

CONTENTS

GUIDE TO BRING-A-DISH SUCCESS

BRING YOUR A-GAME TO GATHERINGS WITH THESE EASY IDEAS

You know who they are: the mom who makes the perfect casserole for the church supper, the neighbor who contributes the best dessert to the block party, the guy whose appetizer receives cheers at the barbecue. Well, at *Taste of Home* we think it's about time you start counting yourself among these cooks!

With the 369 crowd-pleasing recipes in this exciting new collection, bring-a-dish success is as easy as pie. Simply follow these practical pointers, prepare a recipe from this book and become the life of the party!

PLAN AHEAD

Who has time to set a dinner on the table, let alone whip up dozens of cupcakes for a bake sale? You do ... with a little planning, that is. Be realistic about the time you have available, and choose a recipe that best fits your schedule. Look for MA throughout this book, and consider those recipes first if time is tight.

USE YOUR SLOW COOKER

When it comes to making and taking a dish to a get-together, slow cookers are ideal travel vessels. Not only do they simmer large-yield recipes on their own, but they also keep food warm on buffets. See page 220 for an entire chapter of slow-cooker greats.

TRAVEL SAFELY

All the recipes in this colorful collection travel well, but we recommend planning accordingly. A four-layer cake may not be the best option for a long drive. Sturdy cardboard boxes prevent slow cookers and casserole dishes from sliding around in car trunks, so ask your grocer for any clean boxes you could have. Secure lids with bungee cords.

THINK OUTSIDE THE BOX

Salads, dips and brownies are welcome at shared-dish events, but why not wow the crowd with a change-of-pace item? Consider something like Grilled Ribeyes with Blue Cheese Butter (p. 99), Burgoo (p. 184), or Orange Bavarian (p. 267).

BUILD A DIY MULTILEVEL TOTE

If you have more dishes than hands to hold them, use a cooling rack with folding legs. Fold out the legs and use the rack to create sturdy, stable levels inside a carrying tote without crushing what's below. You can also build layers by propping a sheet pan with ring molds or cans.

ENSURE A NO-SLIP TRIP

Place grippy drawer liners or silicone baking mats in the car before loading your food. The liners will keep dishes from sliding and contain any errant spills. An old yoga mat works well for this too.

KEEP A LID ON IT

Use a bungee cord, painter's tape or a thick ribbon to keep the lid of your slow cooker or Dutch oven in place. Secure the cord around the handles and over the top. Now you're ready to transport without risk of a mess.

BRING A SALAD

It's easy to serve a crisp salad even when you're far from home. Bring the fixings in a serving bowl along with the utensils. Toss it all together at your destination. Hold off on adding salad dressing or croutons until it's time to serve. Adding these too early can result in soggy salad greens or the croutons absorbing moisture and losing their crunch.

FROSTING IS GOOD GLUE

If you're transporting a cake to a special event, make it easier to tote with this little tip: Secure the cake (and cardboard cake circle, if you're using one) onto the presentation plate with a dab of frosting. This makes the cake less likely to slide around, even if you have to brake suddenly.

PACK A TOUCH-UP KIT

Make a little touch-up kit of decorations and frosting (just in case) to take with your decorated cake. Pack the items with a clean dish towel and offset spatula. Take the frosting in its pastry bag.

FOOD SAFETY TIPS

- If the party is outdoors, set up the buffet in a cool area—such as in a garage, in the shade of a building or under a big tree. Stash coolers in the shade to keep drinks colder.
- Have plenty of ice to pack around dishes to keep them cold. The food will taste better when it's properly chilled, and you won't have to worry about the risk of any foodborne illnesses.
- Likewise, keep hot foods hot. Hot foods should not be out at room temperature for more than 2 hours (less if it's hotter). Set chafing dishes, slow cookers, and grills or ovens to the low setting to keep food warm. Remember to pack an extra extension cord for buffets.

POTLUCK POINTERS

- Before selecting your recipe, ask the host if any guests have food allergies.
- Tell the host what you're bringing and stick to it.
- Bring a dish that is ready to serve or requires minimal setup or kitchen space at the party.
- Bring your contribution intact. Don't arrive with a slice of cake missing because your spouse wanted to sample it first.
- Bring food on/in a decorative serving piece. Leave that piece as a hostess gift.
- Share extra copies of your recipe.
- No time to cook? Offer to bring beverages, plates, napkins, plastic utensils, condiments or even a centerpiece.
- After the party, offer to clean up or do dishes.
- Leave leftovers at the party. Don't pack a to-go plate for home; take food home only if the host asks you to do so.

SNACKS & APPETIZERS

P. 47

P. 36

P. 11

CAPRESE SALAD KABOBS

OLIVE-STUFFED CELERY

My grandmother taught both me and my mom this appetizer recipe. We always serve it at Christmas and Thanksgiving. The stuffing is so yummy that even if you don't normally care for the ingredients on their own, you'll love the end result.
—Stacy Powell, Santa Fe, TX

Takes: 25 min. • **Makes:** 2 dozen

- 1 dill pickle spear plus 1 tsp. juice
- 3 sweet pickles plus 1 tsp. juice
- 6 pitted ripe olives plus 1 tsp. juice
- 6 pimiento-stuffed olives plus 1 tsp. juice
- 1 pkg. (8 oz.) cream cheese, softened
- ⅓ cup Miracle Whip
- ¼ tsp. salt
- ¼ cup finely chopped pecans, toasted
- 6 celery ribs, cut into 2-in. pieces

1. Finely chop the pickles and olives. In a small bowl, beat the cream cheese, Miracle Whip, juices and salt until blended. Stir in the pickles, olives and pecans.
2. Pipe or stuff filling into celery sticks. Store in the refrigerator.

1 PIECE 61 cal., 5g fat (2g sat. fat), 12mg chol., 228mg sod., 2g carb. (1g sugars, 0 fiber), 1g pro.

TEST KITCHEN TIP

Give limp celery a second chance to season entrees, soups and stews. Cut the ends from the limp celery stalks and place the stalks in a glass of cold water in the refrigerator for several hours or overnight. You'll be surprised how refreshed the celery will be.

CAPRESE SALAD KABOBS

Trade in the usual veggie party platter for these fun kabobs. I often make it for my family to snack on, and it's a great recipe for the kids to help with.
—Christine Mitchell, Glendora, CA

Takes: 10 min. • **Makes:** 12 kabobs

- 24 grape tomatoes
- 12 cherry-size fresh mozzarella cheese balls
- 24 fresh basil leaves
- 2 Tbsp. olive oil
- 2 tsp. balsamic vinegar

On each of 12 appetizer skewers, alternately thread 2 tomatoes, 1 cheese ball and 2 basil leaves. Whisk olive oil and vinegar; drizzle over kabobs.

1 KABOB 44 cal., 4g fat (1g sat. fat), 5mg chol., 10mg sod., 2g carb. (1g sugars, 0 fiber), 1g pro.

ICED RASPBERRY TEA

ICED RASPBERRY TEA

Frozen raspberries lend fruity flavor and lovely color to this pretty iced tea that's good throughout the year. The recipe calls for just a few common ingredients and offers make-ahead convenience.
—Lois McGrady, Hillsville, VA

Prep: 10 min. + chilling
Makes: 16 servings (4 qt.)

- 1½ cups sugar
- 4 qt. water
- 1 pkg. (12 oz.) frozen unsweetened raspberries
- 10 tea bags
- ¼ cup lemon juice
- Optional: Fresh raspberries and lemon slices

1. In a Dutch oven over high heat, bring sugar and water to a boil. Remove from heat; stir until sugar is dissolved. Add raspberries, tea bags and lemon juice. Steep, covered, for 3 minutes. Strain; discard berries and tea bags.
2. Transfer tea to a large container or pitcher. Refrigerate until chilled. Serve over ice. If desired, serve with raspberries and lemon slices.
1 CUP 87 cal., 0 fat (0 sat. fat), 0 chol., 8mg sod., 22g carb. (20g sugars, 0 fiber), 0 pro.
TOUCH-OF-MINT ICED TEA Bring 2 qt. of water to a boil. Steep 5 individual tea bags for 5 minutes and discard; cool for 15 minutes. Add 1⅓ cups packed fresh mint and steep for 5 minutes. Strain Tea and stir in 1 cup lemonade concentrate. Refrigerate until chilled. Serve over ice. Makes about 2 qt.

BUFFALO CHICKEN MEATBALLS

I like to make these game-day appetizer meatballs with blue cheese or ranch salad dressing for dipping. If I make them for a meal, I often skip the dressing and serve the meatballs with blue cheese polenta on the side. Yum!
—Amber Massey, Argyle, TX

Prep: 15 min. • **Bake:** 20 min.
Makes: 2 dozen

- ¾ cup panko bread crumbs
- ⅓ cup plus ½ cup Louisiana-style hot sauce, divided
- ¼ cup chopped celery
- 1 large egg white
- 1 lb. lean ground chicken
- Optional: Ranch or blue cheese salad dressing and chopped celery leaves

1. Preheat oven to 400°. In a large bowl, combine bread crumbs, ⅓ cup hot sauce, celery and egg white. Add chicken; mix lightly but thoroughly.
2. Shape into twenty-four 1-in. balls. Place on a greased rack in a shallow baking pan. Bake 20-25 minutes or until cooked through.
3. Toss meatballs with remaining hot sauce. If desired, drizzle with salad dressing and sprinkle with celery leaves.
1 MEATBALL 33 cal., 1g fat (0 sat. fat), 14mg chol., 338mg sod., 1g carb. (0 sugars, 0 fiber), 4g pro.

READER RAVES

"I made this tonight and two of us ate almost all of the meatballs. It was great. I only used 1/2 cup of panko. This is definitely a keeper."

—JOYCEMERRITT, TASTEOFHOME.COM

BUFFALO CHICKEN MEATBALLS

GARLIC GARBANZO BEAN SPREAD

My friends and family always ask me to make this. I guarantee you'll be asked for the recipe. You can serve it as an appetizer or a filling for sandwiches.
—Lisa Moore, North Syracuse, NY

Takes: 10 min. • **Makes:** 1½ cups

- 1 can (15 oz.) garbanzo beans or chickpeas, rinsed and drained
- ½ cup olive oil
- 2 Tbsp. minced fresh parsley
- 1 Tbsp. lemon juice
- 1 green onion, cut into 3 pieces
- 1 to 2 garlic cloves, peeled
- ¼ tsp. salt
- Assorted fresh vegetables and baked pita chips

In a food processor, combine the first 7 ingredients; cover and process until blended. Transfer to a bowl. Refrigerate until serving. Serve with vegetables and pita chips.

2 TBSP. 114 cal., 10g fat (1g sat. fat), 0 chol., 96mg sod., 6g carb. (1g sugars, 1g fiber), 1g pro.

GARLIC GARBANZO BEAN SPREAD

BLUE CHEESE POTATO CHIPS

Game day calls for something bold. I top potato chips with tomatoes, bacon and tangy blue cheese. I make two big pans, and they always disappear.
—Bonnie Hawkins, Elkhorn, WI

Takes: 15 min. • **Makes:** 10 servings

- 1 pkg. (8½ oz.) kettle-cooked potato chips
- 2 medium tomatoes, seeded and chopped
- 8 bacon strips, cooked and crumbled
- 6 green onions, chopped
- 1 cup crumbled blue cheese

1. Preheat broiler. In a 15x10x1-in. baking pan, arrange potato chips in an even layer. Top with remaining ingredients.
2. Broil 4-5 in. from heat until cheese begins to melt, 2-3 minutes. Serve immediately.

1 SERVING 215 cal., 14g fat (5g sat. fat), 17mg chol., 359mg sod., 16g carb. (2g sugars, 1g fiber), 6g pro.

SAUSAGE WONTON STARS

SAUSAGE WONTON STARS

These fancy-looking appetizers are ideal when entertaining. The cute crunchy cups are stuffed with a cheesy pork sausage filling that kids of all ages enjoy. We keep a few in the freezer so we can easily reheat them for late-night snacking.
—Mary Thomas, North Lewisburg, OH

Takes: 30 min. • **Makes:** 4 dozen

- 1 pkg. (12 oz.) wonton wrappers
- 1 lb. bulk pork sausage
- 2 cups shredded Colby cheese
- ½ medium green pepper, chopped
- ½ medium sweet red pepper, chopped
- 2 bunches green onions, sliced
- ½ cup ranch salad dressing

1. Preheat oven to 350°. Lightly press wonton wrappers onto the bottoms and up the sides of 48 greased miniature muffin cups. Bake until edges are browned, about 5 minutes.

2. In a large skillet, cook sausage over medium heat until no longer pink, breaking it into crumbles; drain. Stir in cheese, peppers, green onion and salad dressing. Spoon 1 rounded Tbsp. into each wonton cup. Bake until heated through, 6-7 minutes.

1 APPETIZER 69 cal., 5g fat (2g sat. fat), 10mg chol., 143mg sod., 4g carb. (0 sugars, 0 fiber), 3g pro.

READER RAVES

"I have made these for years and they are always a hit. You can vary the filling or make just as the recipe calls for!"

—RENA55, TASTEOFHOME.COM

MA

GOUGERES

I brought the recipe for these gougeres back from a trip to Nice, France. The original called for Gruyere cheese, but I found that Gouda is a more budget-friendly alternative. These puffs are a wonderful bite-sized treat. If you have leftovers, float a few of these gems on a bowl of soup in place of croutons.
—Lily Julow, Lawrenceville, GA

Prep: 40 min. • **Bake:** 20 min.
Makes: about 3 dozen

- 1 cup water
- 6 Tbsp. unsalted butter, cubed
- ½ tsp. sea salt
- ¼ tsp. pepper
- ¾ cup all-purpose flour
- 4 large eggs
- 1 cup (4 oz.) shredded regular or smoked Gouda cheese
- ⅓ cup minced fresh chives
- ⅛ tsp. ground nutmeg

TOPPING

- 1 large egg
- 1 tsp. water
- ⅓ cup shredded regular or smoked Gouda cheese

1. Preheat oven to 425°. In a large heavy saucepan, bring the first 4 ingredients to a rolling boil. Remove from heat; add all flour and beat until blended. Cook over medium-low heat, stirring vigorously until mixture pulls away from sides of pan and forms a ball, about 3 minutes.
2. Transfer to a large bowl; beat 1 minute to cool slightly. Add eggs, 1 at a time, beating well after each addition until smooth. Continue beating until shiny. Beat in cheese, chives and nutmeg. Drop dough by tablespoonfuls 2 in. apart onto parchment-lined baking sheets.
3. For topping, whisk together egg and water; brush lightly over tops. Sprinkle with cheese. Bake until puffed, firm and golden brown, 20-25 minutes. Serve warm.

FREEZE OPTION Freeze unbaked puffs on parchment-lined baking sheets until firm; transfer to resealable freezer containers and return to freezer. To use, place frozen puffs on parchment-lined baking sheets. Top and bake as directed, increasing time by 2-3 minutes.

1 APPETIZER 52 cal., 4g fat (2g sat. fat), 36mg chol., 71mg sod., 2g carb. (0 sugars, 0 fiber), 2g pro.

TEST KITCHEN TIP

Be patient when stirring in the flour. It will take a few minutes for the dough to come together and form a ball. The pastries will puff during baking then deflate slightly, which is normal. These bake up golden brown on the outside while the inside is tender and slightly moist.

CUCUMBER CANAPES

MA

CUCUMBER CANAPES

I always get requests for the recipe whenever I serve these delicate finger sandwiches with a creamy herb spread and festive red and green garnishes.
—Nadine Whittaker, South Plymouth, MA

Prep: 20 min. + chilling • **Makes:** 2 dozen

- 1 cup mayonnaise
- 3 oz. cream cheese, softened
- 1 Tbsp. grated onion
- 1 Tbsp. minced chives
- ½ tsp. cider vinegar
- ½ tsp. Worcestershire sauce
- 1 garlic clove, minced
- ¼ tsp. paprika
- ⅛ tsp. curry powder
- ⅛ tsp. each dried oregano, thyme, basil, parsley flakes and dill weed
- 1 loaf (1 lb.) white or rye bread
- 2 medium cucumbers, scored and thinly sliced
- Diced pimientos and additional dill weed

1. In a blender or food processor, combine the mayonnaise, cream cheese, onion, chives, vinegar, Worcestershire sauce, garlic and seasonings. Cover and process until blended. Cover and refrigerate for 24 hours.

2. Using a 2½-in. biscuit cutter, cut out circles from bread slices. Spread mayonnaise mixture over bread; top with cucumber slices. Garnish with pimientos and dill.

1 CANAPE 120 cal., 9g fat (2g sat. fat), 7mg chol., 134mg sod., 8g carb. (1g sugars, 1g fiber), 2g pro.

FIESTA PINWHEELS

FIESTA PINWHEELS

Whenever I serve this make-ahead pinwheel recipe, they disappear fast. When a friend at the office shared them with me, I knew in one bite I'd be taking her recipe home for the holidays.
—Diane Martin, Brown Deer, WI

Prep: 15 min. + chilling
Makes: about 5 dozen

- 1 pkg. (8 oz.) cream cheese, softened
- ½ cup sour cream
- ¼ cup picante sauce
- 2 Tbsp. taco seasoning
- Dash garlic powder
- 1 can (4½ oz.) chopped ripe olives, drained
- 1 can (4 oz.) chopped green chiles
- 1 cup finely shredded cheddar cheese
- ½ cup thinly sliced green onions
- 8 flour tortillas (10 in.), warmed
- Salsa

1. In a small bowl, beat cream cheese, sour cream, picante sauce, taco seasoning and garlic powder until smooth. Stir in olives, chiles, cheese and green onion. Spread about ½ cup on each tortilla.
2. Roll up jelly-roll style; cover and refrigerate for 2 hours or overnight. Slice into 1-in. pieces. Serve with salsa.
1 PIECE 59 cal., 3g fat (2g sat. fat), 6mg chol., 154mg sod., 6g carb. (1g sugars, 0 fiber), 2g pro.

TEST KITCHEN TIP

If the tortillas are cracking before rolling, try warming them. Warm tortillas are more flexible and less likely to crack during rolling. You can warm them in the microwave (wrapped in a damp towel), in a skillet or in the oven (wrapped in foil).

CHEESE & GRAPE APPETIZERS

CHEESE & GRAPE APPETIZERS

These small bites are well worth the time. Serve them as part of an antipasto or cheese platter alongside your favorite bottle of wine.
—Eleanor Grofvert, Kalamazoo, MI

Prep: 35 min. • **Bake:** 10 min. + cooling
Makes: about 5 dozen

- 4 oz. sliced almonds (about 1 cup)
- 1 pkg. (8 oz.) cream cheese, softened
- 2 oz. crumbled blue cheese, room temperature
- 2 Tbsp. minced fresh parsley
- 2 Tbsp. heavy whipping cream, room temperature
- Appetizer skewers or toothpicks
- 1 to 1¼ lbs. seedless red or green grapes, rinsed and patted dry

1. Preheat oven to 275°. Pulse almonds in a food processor until finely chopped (do not overprocess). Spread in a 15x10x1-in. pan; bake until golden brown, 6-9 minutes, stirring occasionally. Transfer to a shallow bowl; cool slightly.
2. In another bowl, mix cream cheese, blue cheese, parsley and cream until blended. Insert a skewer into each grape. Roll grapes in cheese mixture, then in almonds; place on waxed paper-lined baking sheets. Refrigerate, covered, until serving.
5 APPETIZERS 146 cal., 11g fat (6g sat. fat), 28mg chol., 124mg sod., 8g carb. (7g sugars, 1g fiber), 4g pro.

CURRIED CRAB SPREAD

At holiday time, I always have cream cheese and crabmeat on hand. In case of drop-ins, I just mix up an easy spread by adding mango chutney and spices.
—Jennifer Phillips, Goffstown, NH

Takes: 30 min. • **Makes:** 24 servings

- 1 pkg. (8 oz.) cream cheese, softened
- 1 tsp. grated lemon zest
- ¾ tsp. curry powder
- ¼ tsp. salt
- 1 to 2 tsp. Sriracha chili sauce, optional
- 1 can (6 oz.) lump crabmeat, drained
- 1 Tbsp. canola oil
- ½ cup panko bread crumbs
- ¾ cup mango chutney
- 1 Tbsp. minced fresh cilantro or chives
- Assorted crackers

1. In a small bowl, beat cream cheese, lemon zest, curry powder, salt and, if desired, chili sauce; gently fold in crab. Shape into a disk. Cover and refrigerate 15 minutes.
2. Meanwhile, in a large skillet, heat oil over medium heat. Add bread crumbs; cook and stir 2-3 minutes or until golden brown. Transfer bread crumbs to a shallow bowl.
3. Unwrap disk and press all sides into bread crumbs; place on a serving plate. Spoon chutney over top; sprinkle with cilantro. Serve with crackers.

1 SERVING 78 cal., 4g fat (2g sat. fat), 17mg chol., 188mg sod., 8g carb. (5g sugars, 0 fiber), 2g pro.

CURRIED CRAB SPREAD

FRUITY CHICKEN SALAD MINI SANDWICHES

Chicken salad ranks among the classics, and this version is great for parties of all kinds. Feel free to substitute green grapes for the red or toss in extra strawberries when they're in season. The filling also can be served on a bed of salad greens.
—Marcy Kamery, Blasdell, NY

Takes: 25 min. • **Makes:** 12 servings

- 6 cups chopped cooked chicken
- ¾ cup sliced fresh strawberries
- ½ cup halved seedless red grapes
- 2 celery ribs, finely chopped
- ⅓ cup chopped pecans, toasted
- ¾ cup sour cream
- ¾ cup mayonnaise
- ⅓ cup chopped fresh basil
- 2 tsp. lemon juice
- ¾ tsp. salt
- ¼ tsp. garlic powder
- ¼ tsp. pepper
- 24 potato dinner rolls or Hawaiian sweet rolls, split

1. Place first 5 ingredients in a large bowl. In a small bowl, mix sour cream, mayonnaise, basil, lemon juice and seasonings; stir into chicken mixture. Refrigerate, covered, until serving.
2. To serve, fill each roll with ⅓ cup chicken mixture.

NOTE To toast nuts, bake in a shallow pan in a 350° oven for 5-10 minutes or cook in a skillet over low heat until lightly browned, stirring occasionally.

2 SANDWICHES 524 cal., 23g fat (5g sat. fat), 67mg chol., 669mg sod., 49g carb. (8g sugars, 3g fiber), 29g pro.

EASY SMOKED SALMON

A magazine featured this recipe years ago, and it's still my favorite way to serve salmon. Just add crackers for a super simple yet elegant appetizer.
—Norma Fell, Boyne City, MI

Prep: 10 min. + marinating
Bake: 35 min. + chilling
Makes: 16 servings

- 1 salmon fillet (about 2 lbs.)
- 2 Tbsp. brown sugar
- 2 tsp. salt
- ½ tsp. pepper
- 1 to 2 Tbsp. liquid smoke
- Optional: Capers and lemon slices

1. Place salmon skin side down in an 11x7-in. baking pan coated with cooking spray. Sprinkle with brown sugar, salt and pepper. Drizzle with liquid smoke. Cover and refrigerate for 4-8 hours.
2. Drain salmon, discarding liquid. Bake, uncovered, at 350° until fish flakes easily with a fork, 35-45 minutes. Cool to room temperature. Cover and refrigerate for 8 hours or overnight. If desired, serve with capers and lemon slices.
1½ OZ. COOKED SALMON 95 cal., 5g fat (1g sat. fat), 28mg chol., 324mg sod., 2g carb. (2g sugars, 0 fiber), 10g pro.

SMOKING SALMON

To smoke the salmon another way you can use an outdoor smoker or a grill with soaked wood chips. These methods utilize hot smoking, cooking the salmon at temperatures between 250° to 350°. Salmon also can be cold smoked at lower temperatures, typically below 90°. Cold smoking will not cook the salmon, so it needs to be cured with salt so it's safe to eat.

EASY SMOKED SALMON

SPINACH TURNOVERS

The flaky cream cheese pastry adds sensational texture to these hot appetizers—and just wait until you taste the wonderful filling. I usually fix a double batch and freeze some to have on hand in case unexpected guests drop by.
—Jean von Bereghy, Oconomowoc, WI

Prep: 30 min. + chilling • **Bake:** 10 min.
Makes: about 4 dozen

- 2 pkg. (8 oz. each) cream cheese, softened
- ¾ cup butter, softened
- 2½ cups all-purpose flour
- ½ tsp. salt

FILLING

- 5 bacon strips, diced
- ¼ cup finely chopped onion
- 2 garlic cloves, minced
- 1 pkg. (10 oz.) frozen chopped spinach, thawed and well drained
- 1 cup 4% cottage cheese
- ¼ tsp. salt
- ¼ tsp. pepper
- ⅛ tsp. ground nutmeg
- 1 large egg, beaten
- Salsa, optional

1. In a bowl, beat cream cheese and butter until smooth. Combine flour and salt; gradually add to creamed mixture (dough will be stiff). Turn out onto a floured surface; gently knead 10 times. Cover and refrigerate at least 2 hours.
2. In a skillet, cook bacon until crisp. Remove bacon; reserve 1 Tbsp. drippings. Saute onion and garlic in drippings until tender. Remove from heat; stir in bacon, spinach, cottage cheese and seasonings. Cool.
3. On a lightly floured surface, roll out dough to ⅛-in. thickness. Cut into 3-in. circles; brush edges with egg. Place 1 heaping tsp. of filling on each circle. Fold over; seal edges. Prick tops with a fork. Brush with egg.
4. Bake at 400° for 10-12 minutes or until golden brown. Serve with salsa if desired.

1 TURNOVER 103 cal., 8g fat (4g sat. fat), 23mg chol., 129mg sod., 6g carb. (1g sugars, 0 fiber), 2g pro.

LAYERED HUMMUS DIP

My love for Greece inspired this fast, easy Mediterranean dip. It's fantastic for parties and a delicious way to include garden-fresh veggies on your menu.
—Cheryl Snavely, Hagerstown, MD

Takes: 15 min. • **Makes:** 12 servings

- 1 carton (10 oz.) hummus
- ¼ cup finely chopped red onion
- ½ cup Greek olives, chopped
- 2 medium tomatoes, seeded and chopped
- 1 large English cucumber, chopped
- 1 cup crumbled feta cheese
- Baked pita chips

Spread hummus in a shallow 10-in. round dish. Layer with onion, olives, tomatoes, cucumber and cheese. Refrigerate until serving. Serve with pita chips.

1 SERVING 88 cal., 5g fat (2g sat. fat), 5mg chol., 275mg sod., 6g carb. (1g sugars, 2g fiber), 4g pro.

BLT BITES

BLT BITES

These quick hors d'oeuvres may be mini, but their bacon and tomato flavor is full size. I serve them at parties, brunches and picnics, and they're always a hit ... even my kids love them.
—Kellie Remmen, Detroit Lakes, MN

Prep: 25 min. + chilling.
Makes: 20 appetizers

- 20 cherry tomatoes
- 1 lb. sliced bacon, cooked and crumbled
- ½ cup mayonnaise
- ⅓ cup chopped green onions
- 3 Tbsp. grated Parmesan cheese
- 2 Tbsp. snipped fresh parsley

1. Cut a thin slice off each tomato top. Scoop out and discard pulp. Invert tomatoes on a paper towel to drain.
2. In a small bowl, combine remaining ingredients. Spoon into tomatoes. Refrigerate for several hours.

1 STUFFED TOMATO 113 cal., 10g fat (3g sat. fat), 11mg chol., 206mg sod., 1g carb. (1g sugars, 0 fiber), 3g pro.

READER RAVES

"These are amazing! I made these for my in-laws' anniversary party and they were gone within minutes. I used precooked bacon pieces for convenience and a grapefruit spoon to hollow out the tomatoes."

—JMRUGREEN, TASTEOFHOME.COM

GARBANZO-STUFFED MINI PEPPERS

GARBANZO-STUFFED MINI PEPPERS

Mini peppers are the perfect size for a two-bite appetizer. They have the crunch of pita chips, without the extra calories.
—Christine Hanover, Lewiston, CA

Takes: 20 min. • **Makes:** 32 pieces

- 1 tsp. cumin seeds
- 1 can (15 oz.) garbanzo beans or chickpeas, rinsed and drained
- ¼ cup fresh cilantro leaves
- 3 Tbsp. water
- 3 Tbsp. cider vinegar
- ¼ tsp. salt
- 16 miniature sweet peppers, halved lengthwise
- Additional fresh cilantro leaves

1. In a dry small skillet, toast cumin seeds over medium heat until aromatic, 1-2 minutes, stirring frequently. Transfer to a food processor. Add garbanzo beans, cilantro, water, vinegar and salt; pulse until blended.
2. Spoon into pepper halves. Top with additional cilantro. Refrigerate peppers until serving.

1 PIECE 15 cal., 0 fat (0 sat. fat), 0 chol., 36mg sod., 3g carb. (1g sugars, 1g fiber), 1g pro.

SMOKED BLUEFISH SPREAD

While I was growing up, we spent summers on Block Island, Rhode Island, where we would surf-cast off the shores for bluefish. Its strong flavor makes it a terrific candidate for smoking. This is a snack that brings back memories of summer afternoons and cool ocean breezes while dining on this dip at seaside restaurants.
—Pamela Gelsomini, Miami, FL

Takes: 15 min. • **Makes:** 3 cups

- 1 lb. smoked bluefish fillets or flaked smoked trout
- 1 pkg. (8 oz.) cream cheese, softened
- ¾ cup finely chopped red onion
- ¼ cup snipped fresh dill
- ¼ cup lemon juice
- ¼ cup sour cream
- 3 Tbsp. capers, drained
- 2 Tbsp. prepared horseradish
- 2 Tbsp. grated lemon zest
- Assorted crackers, fresh vegetables and lemon wedges

1. Scrape skin from fish if needed. Place fish in a food processor; pulse until finely chopped. Combine cream cheese, red onion, dill, lemon juice, sour cream, capers, horseradish and zest; gently stir in fish. Refrigerate, covered, until serving.
2. Serve with crackers, vegetables and lemon wedges. If desired, top with additional red onion and dill.

2 TBSP. 64 cal., 5g fat (2g sat. fat), 14mg chol., 209mg sod., 2g carb. (1g sugars, 0 fiber), 4g pro.

READER RAVES

"This recipe is excellent. I added just a touch of cayenne pepper. Delicious!"

—DUBLINLAB, TASTEOFHOME.COM

SMOKED BLUEFISH SPREAD

MA

MINI MUFFULETTA

Mediterranean meets comfort food when French rolls are slathered with olive spread and stuffed with layers of salami and cheese. You can make these muffulettas the night before and cut them into appetizer-sized slices just before serving.

—Gareth Craner, Minden, NV

Prep: 25 min. + chilling • **Makes:** 3 dozen

- 1 cup pimiento-stuffed olives, drained and chopped
- 1 can (4¼ oz.) chopped ripe olives
- 1 Tbsp. balsamic vinegar
- 1½ tsp. red wine vinegar
- 1½ tsp. olive oil
- 1 garlic clove, minced
- ½ tsp. dried basil
- ½ tsp. dried oregano
- 6 French rolls, split
- ½ lb. sliced hard salami
- ¼ lb. sliced provolone cheese
- ½ lb. thinly sliced cotto salami
- ¼ lb. sliced part-skim mozzarella cheese

1. In a large bowl, combine the first 8 ingredients. Hollow out tops and bottoms of rolls, leaving ¾-in. shells (discard removed bread or save for another use).

2. Spread olive mixture over tops and bottoms of rolls. On roll bottoms, layer hard salami, provolone cheese, cotto salami and mozzarella cheese. Replace tops.

3. Wrap tightly. Refrigerate overnight. Cut each into 6 wedges; secure sandwiches with toothpicks.

1 WEDGE 119 cal., 8g fat (3g sat. fat), 16mg chol., 537mg sod., 7g carb. (0 sugars, 0 fiber), 6g pro.

MINI MUFFULETTA

QUICK & EASY
SWEDISH MEATBALLS

HOT CIDER PUNCH

My hot fruit punch has been a family fave since 1993—hard to believe that we've loved it for over 30 years! Adding clove-studded orange wedges makes it look especially festive.
—Anita Bell, Hermitage, TN

Prep: 5 min. • **Cook:** 30 min.
Makes: 12 servings (2¼ qt.)

- 3½ cups apple cider or juice
- 2 Tbsp. sugar
- 1 cinnamon stick (3 in.)
- ½ tsp. ground nutmeg
- 3 cups orange juice
- 3 cups unsweetened pineapple juice
- 1 tsp. whole cloves
- 1 medium orange, cut into wedges

1. Place cider, sugar, cinnamon stick and nutmeg in a large saucepan; bring to a boil. Reduce heat and simmer, covered, 20 minutes.
2. Stir in orange and pineapple juices. Insert cloves into orange wedges; add to cider mixture and heat through. Discard cinnamon stick. Serve warm.

¾ CUP 107 cal., 0 fat (0 sat. fat), 0 chol., 15mg sod., 26g carb. (21g sugars, 0 fiber), 0 pro.

QUICK & EASY SWEDISH MEATBALLS

Rich and creamy, this classic meatball sauce is a must in your recipe box.
—Taste of Home *Test Kitchen*

Takes: 30 min. • **Makes:** 20 servings

- 1 pkg. (22 oz.) frozen fully cooked Angus beef meatballs
- 2 Tbsp. butter
- 2 Tbsp. all-purpose flour
- 1 cup beef broth
- ⅓ cup heavy whipping cream
- ¼ tsp. dill weed
- ¼ cup minced fresh parsley, optional

1. Prepare meatballs according to package directions.
2. Meanwhile, in a large saucepan, melt butter. Stir in flour until smooth; gradually add broth. Bring to a boil; cook and stir until thickened, 1-2 minutes. Stir in cream and dill; simmer for 1 minute. Stir in meatballs; heat through. Garnish with parsley if desired.

1 MEATBALL 115 cal., 10g fat (5g sat. fat), 26mg chol., 253mg sod., 2g carb. (1g sugars, 0 fiber), 4g pro.

GRILLED CHICKEN WINGS

These simple grilled chicken wings are like a blank canvas ready to dress with your favorite sauce.
—Taste of Home *Test Kitchen*

Prep: 15 min. • **Grill:** 20 min.
Makes: 20 pieces

- 2 lbs. chicken wings
- 1 Tbsp. olive oil
- 2 Tbsp. cornstarch
- 1 tsp. salt
- ½ tsp. pepper

SAUCE

- ⅓ cup Louisiana-style hot sauce
- 1 Tbsp. white wine vinegar
- ⅛ tsp. garlic powder
- ¼ cup butter

1. Using a sharp knife, cut through the 2 wing joints; discard wing tips. Place remaining wing pieces in a large bowl. Add oil; toss to coat. Combine the cornstarch, salt and pepper. Sprinkle over wings; toss to coat.
2. Grill wings on an oiled grill rack, covered, over medium heat, or broil 4 in. from the heat until crisp and juices run clear, 20-25 minutes, turning occasionally.
3. Meanwhile, in a small saucepan over medium heat, combine hot sauce, vinegar and garlic powder. Whisk in butter until melted. Place chicken in a large bowl; add sauce and toss to coat. Remove to a serving plate with a slotted spoon.

1 PIECE 80 cal., 6g fat (2g sat. fat), 21mg chol., 302mg sod., 1g carb. (0 sugars, 0 fiber), 5g pro.

GRILLED CHICKEN WINGS

MA

MARINATED OLIVE & CHEESE RING

We love to make Italian meals into celebrations, and an antipasto always kicks off the party. This one is almost too pretty to eat, especially when sprinkled with pimientos, fresh basil and parsley.
—Patricia Harmon, Baden, PA

Prep: 25 min. + chilling
Makes: 16 servings

- 1 pkg. (8 oz.) cream cheese, cold
- 1 pkg. (10 oz.) sharp white cheddar cheese, cut into ¼-in. slices
- ⅓ cup pimiento-stuffed olives
- ⅓ cup pitted Greek olives
- ¼ cup balsamic vinegar
- ¼ cup olive oil
- 1 Tbsp. minced fresh parsley
- 1 Tbsp. minced fresh basil or 1 tsp. dried basil
- 2 garlic cloves, minced
- 1 jar (2 oz.) pimiento strips, drained and chopped
- Toasted French bread baguette slices

1. Cut cream cheese lengthwise in half; cut each half into ¼-in. slices. On a serving plate, arrange cheeses upright in a ring, alternating cheddar and cream cheese slices. Place olives in center.
2. In a small bowl, whisk vinegar, oil, parsley, basil and garlic until blended; drizzle over cheeses and olives. Sprinkle with pimientos. Refrigerate, covered, at least 8 hours or overnight. Serve with baguette slices.
1 SERVING 168 cal., 16g fat (7g sat. fat), 34mg chol., 260mg sod., 2g carb. (1g sugars, 0 fiber), 6g pro.

CHILES RELLENOS SQUARES

A friend gave me this recipe for a simple variation of chile rellenos, and now my family requests it often. It makes a tasty appetizer or complement to a Mexican-style meal.
—Fran Carll, Long Beach, CA

Prep: 10 min. • **Bake:** 25 min.
Makes: 16 servings

- 3 cups shredded Monterey Jack cheese
- 1½ cups shredded cheddar cheese
- 2 cans (4 oz. each) chopped green chiles, drained
- 2 large eggs, room temperature
- 2 Tbsp. 2% milk
- 1 Tbsp. all-purpose flour

1. Preheat oven to 375°. Sprinkle half of each cheese onto bottom of a greased 8-in. square baking dish. Layer with chiles and remaining cheeses.
2. Whisk together eggs, milk and flour; pour over the top. Bake, uncovered, until set, 25-30 minutes. Cool 15 minutes before cutting.
1 PIECE 130 cal., 10g fat (7g sat. fat), 57mg chol., 214mg sod., 1g carb. (0 sugars, 0 fiber), 8g pro.

GRANDMOTHER'S HOT DEVILED DUNGENESS CRAB DIP

GRANDMOTHER'S HOT DEVILED DUNGENESS CRAB DIP

Every December when Dungeness Crab season opened off the coast of Oregon, my grandmother always made this hot dip. I remember she had this old newspaper clipping with the recipe. My father then made it, and now every year I make it. It tastes the same and reminds me of the start of the holiday season.
—David Ross, Spokane Valley, WA

Takes: 15 min. • **Makes:** 2 cups

- 8 oz. cream cheese
- 2 Tbsp. 2% milk
- 1 cup fresh crabmeat
- 1 Tbsp. Worcestershire sauce
- 1 tsp. seafood seasoning
- 1 tsp. ground mustard
- ½ tsp. salt
- ½ tsp. pepper
- ¼ tsp. paprika
- ¼ tsp. cayenne pepper
- 3 Tbsp. chopped green onions
- 3 Tbsp. slivered almonds, toasted
- Assorted crackers and vegetables for dipping

In a small saucepan, heat cream cheese and milk until smooth. Stir in crab, Worcestershire, seafood seasoning, ground mustard, salt, pepper, paprika and cayenne pepper until well combined. Stir in green onion and almonds. Serve warm with crackers and vegetables of your choice.

¼ CUP 138 cal., 11g fat (6g sat. fat), 50mg chol., 427mg sod., 3g carb. (2g sugars, 1g fiber), 6g pro.

HERB-ROASTED OLIVES & TOMATOES

HERB-ROASTED OLIVES & TOMATOES

Eat these roasted veggies with a crunchy baguette or a couple of cheeses. You can also double or triple the amounts and have leftovers to toss with spaghetti the next day.
—Anndrea Bailey, Huntington Beach, CA

Takes: 25 min. • **Makes:** 4 cups

- 2 cups cherry tomatoes
- 1 cup garlic-stuffed olives
- 1 cup Greek olives
- 1 cup pitted ripe olives
- 8 garlic cloves, peeled
- 3 Tbsp. olive oil
- 1 Tbsp. herbes de Provence
- ¼ tsp. pepper

Preheat oven to 425°. Combine the first 5 ingredients on a greased 15x10x1-in. baking pan. Add oil and seasonings; toss to coat. Roast until tomatoes are softened, 15-20 minutes, stirring occasionally.

NOTE Look for herbes de Provence in the spice aisle.

¼ CUP 71 cal., 7g fat (1g sat. fat), 0 chol., 380mg sod., 3g carb. (1g sugars, 1g fiber), 0 pro.

PEPPER SHOOTERS

Pop one of these savory peppers into your mouth for a tantalizing array of flavors. It's like an antipasto platter all in one bite.
—Taste of Home *Test Kitchen*

Takes: 30 min. • **Makes:** 2 dozen

- 24 pickled sweet cherry peppers
- 4 oz. fresh mozzarella cheese, finely chopped
- 2¾ oz. thinly sliced hard salami, finely chopped
- 3 Tbsp. prepared pesto
- 2 Tbsp. olive oil

Cut tops off peppers and remove seeds. In a small bowl, combine the cheese, salami and pesto; spoon into peppers. Drizzle with oil. Chill until serving.

1 APPETIZER 55 cal., 4g fat (1g sat. fat), 7mg chol., 313mg sod., 2g carb. (1g sugars, 1g fiber), 3g pro.

PEPPER SHOOTER SWAPS

Beyond mozzarella and salami, pepper shooters can be filled with countless other options. Think shredded or diced provolone, olives, pepperoni, goat cheese, juicy tomatoes or even crunchy croutons.

PEPPER SHOOTERS

MARINATED SHRIMP

My husband's aunt shared this recipe with me ages ago. Not only is it a Christmas Eve tradition in my home but in the homes of our grown children as well.
—Delores Hill, Helena, MT

Prep: 10 min. + marinating • **Cook:** 10 min.
Makes: about 3 dozen

- 2 lbs. uncooked shrimp (16-20), peeled and deveined
- 1 cup olive oil
- 2 garlic cloves, minced
- 4 tsp. dried rosemary, crushed
- 2 tsp. dried oregano
- 2 bay leaves
- 1 cup chicken broth
- ¾ tsp. salt
- ⅛ tsp. pepper

1. In a bowl, combine the shrimp, oil, garlic, rosemary, oregano and bay leaves. Cover and refrigerate for 2-4 hours.
2. Pour shrimp and marinade into a large deep skillet. Add broth, salt and pepper. Cover and cook over medium-low heat for 10-15 minutes or until shrimp turn pink, stirring occasionally. Discard bay leaves. Transfer with a slotted spoon to a serving dish.

1 PIECE 40 cal., 2g fat (0 sat. fat), 31mg chol., 42mg sod., 0 carb. (0 sugars, 0 fiber), 4g pro.

SUMMERTIME TEA

You can't have a summer gathering around here without this sweet tea to cool you down. It's wonderful for sipping while basking by the pool.
—Angela Lively, Conroe, TX

Prep: 15 min. + chilling
Makes: 18 servings

- 14 cups water, divided
- 6 black tea bags
- 1½ cups sugar
- ¾ cup thawed orange juice concentrate
- ¾ cup thawed lemonade concentrate
- Optional: Fresh mint leaves and lemon, lime or orange slices

1. In a large saucepan, bring 4 cups water to a boil. Remove from the heat; add tea bags. Cover and steep for 3-5 minutes. Discard tea bags.
2. Stir in the sugar, concentrates and remaining 10 cups water. Refrigerate until chilled. Garnish with mint and lemon, lime or orange slices if desired.

¾ CUP 102 cal., 0 fat (0 sat. fat), 0 chol., 1mg sod., 26g carb. (26g sugars, 0 fiber), 0 pro.

BAKED ASPARAGUS DIP

BAKED ASPARAGUS DIP

Since I'm from Wisconsin, I thought it was only logical to put together a vegetable and a cheese—two of the foods my state produces in abundance. This cheesy asparagus dip fits the bill.
—Sandra Baratka, Phillips, WI

Takes: 30 min. • **Makes:** about 2 cups

- 1 lb. diced cooked fresh asparagus, drained
- 1 cup grated Parmesan cheese
- 1 cup mayonnaise
- Baked pita chips

In a large bowl, combine the asparagus, cheese and mayonnaise. Place in a 6-in. cast-iron skillet or 2-cup ovenproof bowl. Bake at 375° until heated through, about 20 minutes. Serve warm with pita chips.
2 TBSP. 120 cal., 11g fat (2g sat. fat), 5mg chol., 162mg sod., 2g carb. (1g sugars, 0 fiber), 2g pro.

FROTHY FESTIVE PUNCH

If you're looking for something special for those holiday celebrations, this is your punch! The mixture of ice cream and fruit makes a refreshing, delicious treat that the kids will love.
—Carol Gillespie, Chambersburg, PA

Prep: 10 min. + standing • **Makes:** 2½ qt.

- 1½ qt. vanilla ice cream, softened
- 4 cups cold whole milk
- 3 cups pineapple juice, chilled
- ½ cup orange juice, chilled
- 1 Tbsp. lemon juice
- 1 tsp. vanilla extract
- ¼ tsp. almond extract

Combine all ingredients; beat until frothy. Pour into a chilled punch bowl. Let stand for 15-20 minutes or until froth rises to the top.
1 CUP 271 cal., 12g fat (7g sat. fat), 45mg chol., 107mg sod., 34g carb. (30g sugars, 1g fiber), 6g pro.

SAVORY PARTY BREAD

SAVORY PARTY BREAD

It's impossible to stop nibbling on warm pieces of this cheesy, oniony loaf. The bread fans out for a fun presentation.
—Kay Daly, Raleigh, NC

Prep: 10 min. • **Bake:** 25 min.
Makes: 8 servings

- 1 unsliced round loaf sourdough bread (1 lb.)
- 1 lb. Monterey Jack cheese
- ½ cup butter, melted
- ½ cup chopped green onions
- 2 to 3 tsp. poppy seeds

1. Preheat oven to 350°. Cut bread widthwise into 1-in. slices to within ½ in. of bottom of loaf. Repeat cuts in opposite direction. Cut cheese into ¼-in. slices; cut slices into small pieces. Place cheese in cuts in bread.

2. In a small bowl, mix butter, green onion and poppy seeds. Drizzle over bread. Wrap in foil and place on a baking sheet. Bake for 15 minutes. Unwrap; bake until cheese is melted, about 10 minutes longer.
1 SERVING 481 cal., 31g fat (17g sat. fat), 91mg chol., 782mg sod., 32g carb. (1g sugars, 2g fiber), 17g pro.

TEST KITCHEN TIP

Make this bread your own by switching up the cheese (we love smoked Gouda and gooey Brie), customizing seasonings and adding meaty mix-ins. Bacon, diced salami or ham with sliced olives are all great choices.

MA

CRANBERRY BRIE PINWHEELS

People may wonder when you found the time to make these crisp, flaky pinwheels—but they're really quite easy to do. And the filling is bursting with savory goodness and a touch of sweetness.

—Marcia Kintz, South Bend, IN

Prep: 20 min. • **Bake:** 15 min.
Makes: 1 dozen

- 1 sheet frozen puff pastry, thawed
- 2 Tbsp. Dijon mustard
- 2 Tbsp. honey
- 1 cup finely chopped fresh spinach
- ½ cup finely chopped Brie cheese
- ½ cup finely chopped walnuts
- ¼ cup dried cranberries, finely chopped

1. Unfold pastry. Combine mustard and honey; spread over pastry. Layer with spinach, cheese, walnuts and cranberries. Roll up jelly-roll style; cut into 12 slices. Place cut side down on an ungreased baking sheet.

2. Bake at 400° until golden brown, 15-20 minutes.

FREEZE OPTION Freeze cooled appetizers in a freezer container. To use, reheat appetizers on a parchment-lined baking sheet in a preheated 400° oven until crisp and heated through.

1 SERVING 173 cal., 10g fat (3g sat. fat), 6mg chol., 167mg sod., 18g carb. (5g sugars, 2g fiber), 4g pro.

CRANBERRY BRIE PINWHEELS

CRISP CUCUMBER SALSA

CRISP CUCUMBER SALSA

Here's a fantastic way to use cucumbers. You'll love the creamy and crunchy texture and super fresh flavors.
—Charlene Skjerven, Hoople, ND

Takes: 20 min. • **Makes:** 2½ cups

- 2 cups finely chopped cucumber, peeled and seeded
- ½ cup finely chopped seeded tomato
- ¼ cup chopped red onion
- 2 Tbsp. minced fresh parsley
- 1 jalapeno pepper, seeded and chopped
- 4½ tsp. minced fresh cilantro
- 1 garlic clove, minced
- ¼ cup reduced-fat sour cream
- 1½ tsp. lemon juice
- 1½ tsp. lime juice
- ¼ tsp. ground cumin
- ¼ tsp. seasoned salt
- Baked tortilla chip scoops

In a small bowl, combine the first 7 ingredients. In another bowl, combine the sour cream, lemon juice, lime juice, cumin and seasoned salt. Pour over cucumber mixture and toss gently to coat. Serve immediately with chips.

NOTE You can roast your own peppers by broiling them close to the heat until blackened on all sides. Place in a bowl and cover tightly for 15 minutes or until skins are easy to remove. Seed peppers and slice as desired. Wear disposable gloves when cutting hot peppers; the oils can burn skin. Avoid touching your face.

¼ CUP 16 cal., 1g fat (0 sat. fat), 2mg chol., 44mg sod., 2g carb. (1g sugars, 0 fiber), 1g pro.

CINNAMON TOASTED ALMONDS

Crunchy cinnamon almonds are a spectacular treat to take to a party or gathering. They taste just like the cinnamon roasted almonds you get at the fair.
—Janice Thompson, Stacy, MN

Prep: 15 min. • **Bake:** 25 min. + cooling
Makes: about 4 cups

- 2 large egg whites
- 6 tsp. vanilla extract
- 4 cups unblanched almonds
- ⅓ cup sugar
- ⅓ cup packed brown sugar
- 1 tsp. salt
- ½ tsp. ground cinnamon

1. In a large bowl, beat egg whites until frothy; beat in vanilla. Add almonds; stir gently to coat. Combine the sugars, salt and cinnamon; add to nut mixture and stir gently to coat.

2. Spread evenly in 2 greased 15x10x1-in. baking pans. Bake at 300° for 25-30 minutes or until almonds are crisp, stirring once. Cool. Store in an airtight container.

¼ CUP 250 cal., 18g fat (1g sat. fat), 0 chol., 166mg sod., 16g carb. (10g sugars, 4g fiber), 8g pro.

PUMPKIN HUMMUS

Traditional hummus gets an update for autumn with the addition of canned pumpkin. Hot pepper sauce lends just the right amount of heat.
—Taste of Home *Test Kitchen*

Takes: 15 min. • **Makes:** 4 cups

- 2 cans (15 oz. each) garbanzo beans or chickpeas, rinsed and drained
- 1 can (15 oz.) pumpkin
- ½ cup olive oil
- ⅓ cup tahini
- 5 Tbsp. lemon juice
- 2 tsp. hot pepper sauce
- 2 garlic cloves, minced
- 1 tsp. salt
- Baked pita chips
- Assorted fresh vegetables, optional

Place the first 8 ingredients in a food processor; cover and process until blended. Serve with pita chips and, if desired, vegetables.

¼ CUP 173 cal., 13g fat (2g sat. fat), 0 chol., 243mg sod., 12g carb. (2g sugars, 4g fiber), 5g pro.

PUMPKIN HUMMUS

MA

BACON & SUN-DRIED TOMATO PHYLLO TARTS

Frozen mini phyllo tart shells are so convenient and easy to use. Just add a savory filling featuring sun-dried tomatoes and bacon, then pop them in the oven.

—Patricia Quinn, Omaha, NE

Prep: 40 min. • **Bake:** 10 min.
Makes: 45 tartlets

- 2 tsp. olive oil
- ¾ cup chopped onion (about 1 medium)
- ¾ cup chopped green pepper (about 1 small)
- ¾ cup chopped sweet red pepper (about 1 small)
- 1 garlic clove, minced
- Dash dried oregano
- 3 pkg. (1.9 oz. each) frozen miniature phyllo tart shells
- 1 pkg. (8 oz.) cream cheese, softened
- 1½ tsp. lemon juice
- ⅛ tsp. salt
- 1 large egg, lightly beaten
- ½ cup oil-packed sun-dried tomatoes, chopped and patted dry
- 2 bacon strips, cooked and crumbled
- 1 Tbsp. minced fresh basil or 1 tsp. dried basil
- ½ cup crushed butter-flavored crackers
- ½ cup shredded cheddar cheese

1. Preheat oven to 350°. In a large skillet, heat oil over medium-high heat. Add onion and peppers; cook and stir 6-8 minutes or until tender. Add garlic and oregano; cook 1 minute longer. Cool completely.

2. Place tart shells on ungreased baking sheets. In a large bowl, beat cream cheese, lemon juice and salt until smooth. Add egg; beat on low speed just until blended. Stir in tomatoes, bacon, basil and onion mixture.

3. Spoon 2 tsp. filling into each tart shell. Top each with ½ tsp. crushed crackers and ½ tsp. cheddar cheese.

4. Bake until set, 10-12 minutes. Serve warm.

FREEZE OPTION Freeze cooled baked pastries in freezer containers. To use, reheat pastries on a baking sheet in a preheated 350° oven 15-18 minutes or until heated through.

1 TARTLET 58 cal., 4g fat (1g sat. fat), 11mg chol., 59mg sod., 4g carb. (1g sugars, 0 fiber), 2g pro.

ORANGE ANISE SPARKLER

A spice infused simple syrup is the base for this orange juice beverage. If it has too adult a flavor for the kids, skip the simple syrup and just mix the orange juice with the club soda.

—Taste of Home *Test Kitchen*

Prep: 15 min. + standing • **Makes:** 2 qt.

- 1 cup sugar
- 1 cup water
- 4 whole star anise
- 1 cinnamon stick (3 in.)
- 3 cups orange juice, chilled
- 1 bottle (1 liter) club soda, chilled
- Orange slices and additional whole star anise

1. In a small saucepan, combine the sugar, water, star anise and cinnamon. Bring to a boil over medium heat. Cook and stir for 1 minute. Remove from the heat; cover and let stand for 1 hour. Strain mixture, discarding spices. Refrigerate until chilled.

2. In a large pitcher, combine the orange juice and soda; stir in sugar syrup. Serve in cocktail glasses; garnish with orange slices and star anise.

1 CUP 138 cal., 0 fat (0 sat. fat), 0 chol., 26mg sod., 35g carb. (33g sugars, 0 fiber), 0 pro.

CHERRY LIMEADE

My guests enjoy this refreshing cherry-topped drink. It's just right on a hot southern summer afternoon, and it's pretty, too.
—Awynne Thurstenson, Siloam Springs, AR

Takes: 10 min. • **Makes:** 8 servings

- ¾ cup lime juice
- 1 cup sugar
- ½ cup maraschino cherry juice
- 2 liters lime carbonated water, chilled
- Ice cubes
- 8 maraschino cherries with stems
- 8 lime slices

In a large pitcher, combine lime juice and sugar. Cover and refrigerate. Just before serving, stir cherry juice, carbonated water and some ice cubes into lime juice mixture. Garnish with maraschino cherries and lime slices.

1 CUP 142 cal., 0 fat (0 sat. fat), 0 chol., 2mg sod., 39g carb. (31g sugars, 2g fiber), 0 pro.

TZATZIKI SHRIMP CUCUMBER ROUNDS

I created this recipe with what I had on hand one night, and now it's one of my husband's favorites! The bacon-wrapped shrimp, garlicky sauce and burst of cool cuke flavor make these irresistible.
—Shannon Trelease, East Hampton, NY

Prep: 25 min. • **Cook:** 10 min./batch
Makes: 2 dozen

- ¼ cup reduced-fat plain yogurt
- 2 Tbsp. finely chopped peeled cucumber
- ⅛ tsp. garlic salt
- ⅛ tsp. dill weed
- 6 bacon strips
- 24 uncooked shrimp (31-40 per lb.), peeled and deveined
- 1 to 2 Tbsp. canola oil
- 2 medium cucumbers, cut into ¼-in. slices

1. In a small bowl, combine the yogurt, chopped cucumber, garlic salt and dill.
2. Cut each bacon strip in half widthwise and then lengthwise. Wrap a piece of bacon around each shrimp. Secure with toothpicks.
3. In a large nonstick skillet, heat oil over medium heat; cook shrimp in batches for 3-4 minutes on each side or until bacon is crisp.
4. Spoon a rounded ½ tsp. yogurt sauce onto each cucumber slice; top with shrimp.

1 APPETIZER 30 cal., 2g fat (0 sat. fat), 18mg chol., 64mg sod., 1g carb. (0 sugars, 0 fiber), 3g pro.

READER RAVES

"So simple, delicious and elegant. I brought these to a function and everyone loved them!"

—CINDIAK, TASTEOFHOME.COM

TZATZIKI SHRIMP CUCUMBER ROUNDS

COPYCAT APPLEBEE'S SPINACH ARTICHOKE DIP

COPYCAT APPLEBEE'S SPINACH ARTICHOKE DIP

My husband and I love going out to eat and ordering spinach and artichoke dip, but now that we have our own recipe it's become a favorite at home. I use this for important game days, and it's always a hit at school for treat day!
—Hollie Gabriel, Topeka, KS

Prep: 20 min. • **Bake:** 20 min.
Makes: 3½ cups

- 1 jar (15 oz.) Alfredo sauce
- 4 oz. cream cheese, softened
- ½ cup grated Parmesan and Romano cheese blend
- ½ cup shredded mozzarella cheese, divided
- 1 garlic clove, minced
- 1 can (14 oz.) water-packed artichoke hearts, drained and chopped
- 1 pkg. (10 oz.) frozen chopped spinach, thawed and squeezed dry
- Tortilla chips

1. Preheat oven to 350°. In a large bowl, combine Alfredo sauce, cream cheese, Parmesan cheese, Romano cheese, ¼ cup mozzarella cheese and garlic; mix well. Stir in artichokes and spinach. Transfer to a greased 4- or 5-cup broiler-safe baking dish. Sprinkle with remaining ¼ cup mozzarella cheese.
2. Bake, uncovered, until bubbly, 20-25 minutes. Preheat broiler. Place baking dish on a baking sheet. Broil 4-6 in. from heat until top is golden brown, 1-2 minutes. Serve with tortilla chips.
¼ CUP 118 cal., 8g fat (5g sat. fat), 24mg chol., 330mg sod., 6g carb. (0 sugars, 1g fiber), 6g pro.

CILANTRO TOMATO BRUSCHETTA

CILANTRO TOMATO BRUSCHETTA

This is an easy, tasty appetizer that all of my family and friends love. The ingredients meld together for a great-tasting hors d'oeuvre that goes well with many different main dishes.
—Lisa Kane, Milwaukee, WI

Takes: 25 min. • **Makes:** about 2 dozen

- 1 loaf (1 lb.) French bread, cut into 1-in. slices
- ½ cup olive oil, divided
- 1 Tbsp. balsamic vinegar
- 3 small tomatoes, seeded and chopped
- ¼ cup finely chopped onion
- ¼ cup fresh cilantro leaves, coarsely chopped
- ¼ tsp. salt
- ¼ tsp. pepper
- ¼ cup shredded part-skim mozzarella cheese

1. Preheat oven to 325°. Place bread slices on ungreased baking sheets; brush with ¼ cup oil. Bake until golden brown, 10-12 minutes.
2. In a small bowl, whisk together vinegar and remaining ¼ cup oil. Stir in tomatoes, onion, cilantro, salt and pepper.
3. To serve, spoon scant 1 Tbsp. tomato mixture onto each slice of bread. Top with cheese.
1 PIECE 98 cal., 5g fat (1g sat. fat), 1mg chol., 147mg sod., 11g carb. (1g sugars, 1g fiber), 2g pro.

SPICY CHICKEN WINGS WITH BLUE CHEESE DIP

These fall-off-the-bone tender wings have just the right amount of heat, and the cool blue cheese dressing makes the perfect dip.

—Kevalyn Henderson, Hayward, WI

Prep: 25 min. + marinating • **Bake:** 2 hours
Makes: 2 dozen (1¾ cups dip)

- 1 cup reduced-sodium soy sauce
- ⅔ cup sugar
- 2 tsp. salt
- 2 tsp. grated orange zest
- 2 garlic cloves, minced
- ½ tsp. pepper
- 3 lbs. chicken wingettes and drumettes
- 3 tsp. chili powder
- ¾ tsp. cayenne pepper
- ¾ tsp. hot pepper sauce

BLUE CHEESE DIP

- 1 cup mayonnaise
- ½ cup blue cheese salad dressing
- ⅓ cup buttermilk
- 2 tsp. Italian salad dressing mix

1. In a small bowl, combine soy sauce, sugar, salt, orange zest, garlic and pepper. Pour half the marinade into a large shallow dish. Add chicken; turn to coat. Cover and refrigerate for 1 hour. Cover and refrigerate the remaining marinade.
2. Drain chicken, discarding marinade. Transfer chicken to a greased 13x9-in. baking dish. Cover and bake at 325° for 1½ hours or until chicken juices run clear.
3. Using tongs, transfer chicken to a greased 15x10x1-in. baking pan. In a small bowl, combine chili powder, cayenne, pepper sauce and reserved marinade. Drizzle over chicken.
4. Bake, uncovered, for 30 minutes, turning once. In another small bowl, whisk together dip ingredients. Serve with wings.

1 SERVING 237 cal., 19g fat (4g sat. fat), 47mg chol., 588mg sod., 4g carb. (3g sugars, 0 fiber), 11g pro.

SPICY CHICKEN WINGS WITH BLUE CHEESE DIP

TACO MEATBALL RING

TACO MEATBALL RING

While it looks complicated, this attractive meatball-filled ring is really very easy to assemble. My family loves tacos, and we find that the crescent roll dough is a nice change from the usual tortilla shells or chips.
—Brenda Johnson, Davison, MI

Prep: 30 min. • **Bake:** 15 min.
Makes: 16 servings

- 2 cups shredded cheddar cheese, divided
- 2 Tbsp. water
- 2 to 4 Tbsp. taco seasoning
- ½ lb. ground beef
- 2 tubes (8 oz. each) refrigerated crescent rolls
- ½ medium head iceberg lettuce, shredded
- 1 medium tomato, chopped
- 4 green onions, sliced
- ½ cup sliced ripe olives
- 2 jalapeno peppers, sliced
- Optional: Sour cream and salsa

1. In a large bowl, combine 1 cup cheese, water and taco seasoning. Crumble beef over mixture and mix lightly but thoroughly. Shape into 16 balls.
2. Place meatballs on a greased rack in a shallow baking pan. Bake, uncovered, at 400° until meat is no longer pink, about 12 minutes. Drain meatballs on paper towels. Reduce heat to 375°.
3. Arrange crescent rolls on a greased 15-in. pizza pan, forming a ring with pointed ends facing the outer edge of the pan and wide ends overlapping.
4. Place a meatball on each roll; fold pointed end over meatball and tuck under wide end of roll (meatball will be visible). Repeat. Bake until rolls are golden brown, 15-20 minutes.
5. Transfer to a serving platter. Fill the center of the ring with lettuce, tomato, onions, olives, jalapenos, remaining 1 cup cheese and, if desired, sour cream and salsa.

NOTE Wear disposable gloves when cutting hot peppers; the oils can burn skin. Avoid touching your face.

1 PIECE 203 cal., 12g fat (5g sat. fat), 24mg chol., 457mg sod., 14g carb. (3g sugars, 1g fiber), 8g pro.

TEST KITCHEN TIP

Lining your pizza pan with parchment or nonstick foil (and leaving a little extra hanging over the sides) will help ensure a seamless transfer from pan to platter.

EASY SHRIMP COCKTAIL

Tender, well-cooked shrimp is paired with a flavorful sauce of sweet ketchup, tart lemon juice, sharp horseradish and savory Worcestershire sauce for an easy and delicious dish. The best part—it takes only 30 minutes to make!
—Taste of Home *Test Kitchen*

Takes: 30 min. • **Makes:** 32 servings

- 1 cup ketchup
- 2 Tbsp. lemon juice
- 2 Tbsp. prepared horseradish
- 2 tsp. Worcestershire sauce
- Dash hot pepper sauce, optional
- 3 qt. water
- 1 small onion, sliced
- ½ medium lemon, sliced
- 2 sprigs fresh parsley
- 2 tsp. salt
- 5 whole peppercorns
- 1 bay leaf
- ¼ tsp. dried thyme
- 2 lbs. uncooked shell-on shrimp (26-30 per lb.)

1. In a small bowl, combine ketchup, lemon juice, horseradish, Worcestershire sauce and, if desired, hot pepper sauce.
2. In a large saucepan, combine water, onion, lemon, parsley, salt, peppercorns, bay leaf and thyme; bring to a boil. Add shrimp. Cook just until shrimp turn pink, 1-2 minutes. Drain; immediately drop shrimp into a bowl of ice water. Discard onion, lemon, parsley, peppercorns and bay leaf. Drain shrimp. Peel shrimp, leaving tails on. Devein if needed. Serve shrimp with sauce.
1 OZ. COOKED SHRIMP WITH ABOUT 2 TSP. SAUCE 42 cal., 1g fat (0 sat. fat), 44mg chol., 193mg sod., 3g carb. (3g sugars, 0 fiber), 6g pro.

DIJON-BACON DIP FOR PRETZELS

With just a few ingredients you probably already have in your pantry, this quick appetizer comes together in a snap. If you like the zip of horseradish, start with 1 or 2 teaspoons and add more to your taste.
—Isabelle Rooney, Summerville, SC

Takes: 5 min. • **Makes:** 1½ cups

- 1 cup mayonnaise
- ½ cup Dijon mustard
- ¼ cup bacon bits or crumbled cooked bacon
- 1 to 3 tsp. prepared horseradish
- Pretzels or pretzel crisps

In a small bowl, combine the mayonnaise, mustard, bacon and horseradish. Cover and chill until serving. Serve with pretzels.
2 TBSP. 154 cal., 16g fat (2g sat. fat), 8mg chol., 428mg sod., 1g carb. (0 sugars, 0 fiber), 2g pro.

READER RAVES

"This is my go-to recipe for any family or church gathering! It is amazing and so easy to make. I have family members who have to eat gluten free, and they love this dip with corn tortilla chips, too."

—DECKERROAD, TASTEOFHOME.COM

DIJON-BACON DIP
FOR PRETZELS

SOUTHERN DEVILED EGGS

There is nothing simpler or tastier than these eggs. I make them for every BBQ, tailgate or picnic, and they're always a hit.
—Ellen Riley, Murfreesboro, TN

Takes: 20 min. • **Makes:** 1 dozen

- 6 hard-boiled large eggs
- 2 Tbsp. mayonnaise
- 2 Tbsp. sweet pickle relish, drained
- ½ tsp. prepared mustard
- ¼ tsp. salt
- ⅛ tsp. pepper
- Optional: Paprika and fresh dill

1. Slice eggs in half lengthwise. Remove yolks; set whites aside. In a small bowl, mash yolks. Stir in the mayonnaise, relish, mustard, salt and pepper.
2. Pipe or spoon mixture into egg whites. Refrigerate until serving. If desired, sprinkle with paprika and dill before serving.

1 STUFFED EGG HALF 57 cal., 4g fat (1g sat. fat), 94mg chol., 114mg sod., 1g carb. (1g sugars, 0 fiber), 3g pro.

SOUTHERN DEVILED EGGS TIP

You can make deviled eggs up to 2 days in advance. To optimize their freshness, wait to add the yolk filling to the egg whites until you're just about ready to serve. Simply store the egg whites in an airtight container, and keep the egg yolk filling in a resealable bag, making sure to press out all the air. When it's time to serve, simply snip off a corner of the bag, and the filling is conveniently ready to be piped into the egg whites.

SOUTHERN DEVILED EGGS

TOMATO-WALNUT PESTO SPREAD

Whenever I bring this popular spread to parties, I know to bring copies of the recipe. Once people taste it, they always ask how I make it. The red, green and white layers make it especially festive for Christmastime.
—Marsha Dawson, Appleton, WI

Prep: 15 min. + chilling • **Makes:** 2⅓ cups

3 Tbsp. chopped oil-packed sun-dried tomatoes, patted dry
1 pkg. (8 oz.) cream cheese, softened
½ cup grated Parmesan cheese
¼ cup sour cream
2 Tbsp. butter, softened
½ cup finely chopped walnuts
½ cup prepared pesto
Assorted crackers

1. Line a 4-cup mold with plastic wrap; coat with cooking spray. Place tomatoes in bottom of mold.
2. In a large bowl, beat the cheeses, sour cream and butter until blended. In another bowl, combine walnuts and pesto. Spread cheese mixture over tomatoes in prepared mold; top with walnut mixture.
3. Bring edges of plastic wrap together over pesto; press down gently to seal. Refrigerate for at least 4 hours or until firm. Open plastic wrap; invert mold onto a serving plate. Serve with crackers.
2 TBSP. 129 cal., 12g fat (5g sat. fat), 24mg chol., 137mg sod., 2g carb. (0 sugars, 0 fiber), 4g pro.

KIDS' FAVORITE PUMPKIN SEEDS

My kids love these pumpkin seeds and want them every fall. A little bit of pulp in the mix really adds to the flavor, so don't rinse the seeds.
—Gwyn Reiber, Spokane, WA

Prep: 5 min. • **Bake:** 45 min. + cooling
Makes: 2 cups

2 cups fresh pumpkin seeds
¼ cup butter, melted
½ tsp. garlic salt
¼ tsp. cayenne pepper
¼ tsp. Worcestershire sauce

1. In a small bowl, combine all the ingredients; transfer to an ungreased 15x10x1-in. baking pan.
2. Bake at 250° for 45-50 minutes or until lightly browned and dry, stirring occasionally. Cool completely. Store in an airtight container.
¼ CUP 122 cal., 9g fat (4g sat. fat), 15mg chol., 150mg sod., 9g carb. (0 sugars, 1g fiber), 3g pro.

TERRIFIC TOMATO TART

TERRIFIC TOMATO TART

Fresh, colorful tomatoes, feta cheese and prepared pesto perfectly complement the appetizer's crispy phyllo dough crust.
—Diane Halferty, Corpus Christi, TX

Prep: 15 min. • **Bake:** 20 min.
Makes: 8 servings

- 12 sheets phyllo dough (14x9 in.)
- 2 Tbsp. olive oil
- 2 Tbsp. dry bread crumbs
- 2 Tbsp. prepared pesto
- ¾ cup crumbled feta cheese
- 1 medium tomato, cut into ¼-in. slices
- 1 large yellow tomato, cut into ¼-in. slices
- ¼ tsp. pepper
- 5 to 6 fresh basil leaves, thinly sliced

1. Preheat oven to 400°. Place 1 sheet of phyllo dough on a baking sheet lined with parchment. (Keep remaining phyllo covered with a damp towel to prevent it from drying out.) Brush with ½ tsp. oil and sprinkle with ½ tsp. bread crumbs. Repeat layers, being careful to brush oil all the way to edges.
2. Fold each side ¾ in. toward center to form a rim. Spread with pesto and sprinkle with half the feta cheese. Alternately arrange the red and yellow tomato slices over cheese. Sprinkle with pepper and remaining feta.
3. Bake until crust is golden brown and crispy, 20-25 minutes. Cool on a wire rack for 5 minutes. Remove parchment before cutting. Garnish with basil.
1 PIECE 135 cal., 7g fat (2g sat. fat), 7mg chol., 221mg sod., 13g carb. (1g sugars, 1g fiber), 5g pro.

CIDER CHEESE FONDUE

CIDER CHEESE FONDUE

Cheese lovers are sure to enjoy dipping into this creamy, quick-to-fix fondue that has just a hint of apple. You can also serve the appetizer with pear wedges.
—Kenny Van Rheenen, Mendota, IL

Takes: 15 min. • **Makes:** 2⅔ cups

- ¾ cup apple cider or apple juice
- 2 cups shredded cheddar cheese
- 1 cup shredded Swiss cheese
- 1 Tbsp. cornstarch
- ⅛ tsp. pepper
- Cubed French bread and sliced apples and green peppers

1. In a large saucepan, bring cider to a boil. Reduce heat to medium-low. Toss the cheeses with cornstarch and pepper; stir into cider. Cook and stir until cheese is melted, 3-4 minutes.
2. Transfer to a small fondue pot or 1½-qt. slow cooker; keep warm. Serve with bread cubes and sliced apples and green peppers.

¼ CUP 111 cal., 8g fat (6g sat. fat), 28mg chol., 138mg sod., 3g carb. (2g sugars, 0 fiber), 7g pro.

TEST KITCHEN TIP

Cornstarch needs just a few minutes of boiling to thicken a sauce, gravy or dessert filling. If it cooks too long, the cornstarch will begin to lose its thickening power. Carefully follow the recipe for the best results.

CHIPOTLE MEXICAN STREET CORN DIP WITH GOAT CHEESE

I was craving Mexican street corn that I had during a recent trip to Puerto Vallarta, so I came up with this fabulous dip. It blends the traditional profile of the popular street food with updated flavors for a tasty twist.

—Joseph Sciascia, San Mateo, CA

Prep: 30 min. • **Bake:** 35 min.
Makes: 3 cups

- 3 medium ears sweet corn
- 1 Tbsp. olive oil
- 1 cup crumbled goat cheese
- ¾ cup mayonnaise
- 1 can (4 oz.) chopped green chiles
- 1 jar (4 oz.) diced pimientos, drained
- 2 green onions, chopped
- 2 Tbsp. finely chopped chipotle peppers in adobo sauce
- 1 Tbsp. minced fresh cilantro
- 1 to 2 Tbsp. lime juice
- 1½ tsp. grated lime zest
- 1 tsp. ground cumin
- 1 tsp. chili powder
- Tortilla chips

1. Brush corn with oil. Grill corn, covered, over medium heat until lightly browned and tender, 10-12 minutes, turning occasionally. Cool slightly.

2. Preheat oven to 350°. Cut corn from cobs; transfer to a large bowl. Stir in goat cheese, mayonnaise, green chiles, pimientos, green onion, chipotle pepper, cilantro, lime juice, zest, cumin and chili powder. Transfer to a greased 1½-qt. baking dish. Bake until bubbly and golden brown, 35-40 minutes. Serve with tortilla chips.

¼ CUP 157 cal., 14g fat (3g sat. fat), 13mg chol., 182mg sod., 7g carb. (2g sugars, 1g fiber), 3g pro.

CHIPOTLE MEXICAN STREET CORN DIP WITH GOAT CHEESE

FRUIT & CHEESE KABOBS

MA

FRUIT & CHEESE KABOBS

This fresh and fruity snack is easy to make ahead and carry to the ballpark, beach or playing field. The cinnamon-spiced yogurt dip adds that special touch everyone loves!
—Taste of Home *Test Kitchen*

Takes: 20 min.
Makes: 12 kabobs (1½ cups dip)

- 1 cup vanilla yogurt
- ½ cup sour cream
- 2 Tbsp. honey
- ½ tsp. ground cinnamon
- 2 cups fresh strawberries, halved
- 1½ cups green grapes
- 8 oz. cubed cheddar or Monterey Jack cheese, or a combination of cheeses

For dip, mix first 4 ingredients. On 12 wooden skewers, alternately thread strawberries, grapes and cheese cubes. Serve immediately or refrigerate.

1 KABOB WITH 2 TBSP. DIP 147 cal., 9g fat (5g sat. fat), 22mg chol., 143mg sod., 12g carb. (11g sugars, 1g fiber), 6g pro.

ONION BRIE APPETIZERS

Guests will think you spent hours preparing these cute appetizers, but they're really easy to assemble, using purchased puff pastry. And the tasty combination of Brie, caramelized onions and caraway is terrific.
—Carole Resnick, Cleveland, OH

Prep: 25 min. + chilling • **Bake:** 15 min.
Makes: 1½ dozen

- 2 medium onions, thinly sliced
- 3 Tbsp. butter
- 2 Tbsp. brown sugar
- ½ tsp. white wine vinegar
- 1 sheet frozen puff pastry, thawed
- 4 oz. Brie cheese, rind removed, softened
- 1 to 2 tsp. caraway seeds
- 1 large egg
- 2 tsp. water

1. In a large skillet, cook the onions, butter, brown sugar and vinegar over medium-low heat until onions are golden brown, stirring frequently. Remove with a slotted spoon; cool onions to room temperature.
2. On a lightly floured surface, roll out puff pastry into an 11x8-in. rectangle. Cut Brie into thin slices; distribute evenly over pastry. Cover with the onions and sprinkle with caraway seeds.
3. Roll up 1 long side to the middle of the dough; roll up the other side so the 2 rolls meet in the center. Using a serrated knife, cut into ½-in. slices. Place on parchment-lined baking sheets; flatten to ¼-in. thickness. Refrigerate for 15 minutes. Preheat oven to 375°.
4. In a small bowl, whisk egg and water; brush over slices. Bake until puffed and golden brown, 12-14 minutes. Serve appetizers warm.

1 APPETIZER 121 cal., 8g fat (3g sat. fat), 23mg chol., 109mg sod., 11g carb. (3g sugars, 1g fiber), 3g pro.

BREAKFAST FOR A BUNCH

P. 77

P. 52

P. 61

APPLE-CRANBERRY GRAINS

MINI HAM QUICHES

These adorable quiches are delightful for an after-church brunch when you don't want to fuss. Replace the ham with bacon, sausage, chicken or shrimp, or substitute chopped onion, red pepper or zucchini for the olives if you'd like.
—Marilou Robinson, Portland, OR

Prep: 15 min. • **Bake:** 20 min.
Makes: 1 dozen

- ¾ cup diced fully cooked ham
- ½ cup shredded sharp cheddar cheese
- ½ cup chopped ripe olives
- 3 large eggs, lightly beaten
- 1 cup half-and-half cream
- ¼ cup butter, melted
- 3 drops hot pepper sauce
- ½ cup biscuit/baking mix
- 2 Tbsp. grated Parmesan cheese
- ½ tsp. ground mustard

1. In a large bowl, combine the ham, cheddar cheese and olives; divide among 12 greased muffin cups. In another bowl, combine the remaining ingredients just until blended.
2. Pour egg mixture over ham mixture. Bake at 375° until a knife inserted in the center comes out clean, 20-25 minutes. Let stand for 5 minutes before serving.

1 MINI QUICHE 141 cal., 11g fat (6g sat. fat), 84mg chol., 332mg sod., 5g carb. (1g sugars, 0 fiber), 6g pro.

APPLE-CRANBERRY GRAINS

I made some changes to my diet in order to lose weight. My kids are skeptical when it comes to healthy food, but they adore these wholesome grains.
—Sherisse Dawe, Black Diamond, AB

Prep: 10 min. • **Cook:** 4 hours
Makes: 16 servings (3 qt.)

- 2 medium apples, peeled and chopped
- 1 cup sugar
- 1 cup fresh cranberries
- ½ cup wheat berries
- ½ cup quinoa, rinsed
- ½ cup oat bran
- ½ cup medium pearl barley
- ½ cup chopped walnuts
- ½ cup packed brown sugar
- 1½ to 2 tsp. ground cinnamon
- 6 cups water
- Optional toppings: Milk, sliced apples, dried cranberries and chopped walnuts

In a 4- or 5-qt. slow cooker, combine the first 11 ingredients. Cook, covered, on low until grains are tender, 4-5 hours. Serve with toppings as desired.

¾ CUP 180 cal., 3g fat (0 sat. fat), 0 chol., 3mg sod., 37g carb. (22g sugars, 4g fiber), 3g pro.

GLAZED CHOCOLATE DOUGHNUTS

GLAZED CHOCOLATE DOUGHNUTS

This recipe will give you the best baked doughnuts—perfectly soft, chocolaty, and not overly sweet. You can store frosted donuts in an airtight container at room temperature or in the refrigerator for up to 2 days and in the freezer for up to 2 months. Thaw in the refrigerator overnight.
—Jennifer Sobjack, Clarksville, TN

Takes: 30 min. • **Makes:** 1½ dozen

- 1 cup all-purpose flour
- ½ cup baking cocoa
- ½ cup packed light brown sugar
- 1 tsp. baking powder
- ½ tsp. baking soda
- ¼ tsp. salt
- 2 large eggs, room temperature
- ¾ cup buttermilk
- ¼ cup unsalted butter, melted

GLAZE
- 1 cup confectioners' sugar
- ¼ tsp. vanilla extract
- 4 to 5 Tbsp. heavy whipping cream

1. Preheat oven to 350°. In a large bowl, whisk the first 6 ingredients. In another bowl, whisk eggs, buttermilk and butter until blended. Add to dry ingredients; stir until blended (batter will be thick).
2. Transfer batter to a pastry bag fitted with a round tip. Pipe into three 6-cavity doughnut pans coated with cooking spray, filling cavities two-thirds full.
3. Bake until doughnuts spring back when touched, 10-12 minutes. Cool for 5 minutes before removing from pans to wire racks to cool completely.
4. For glaze, in a small bowl, combine confectioners' sugar, vanilla and enough heavy cream to reach desired consistency. Dip each doughnut halfway, allowing excess to drip off. Place on wire rack; let stand until set.

1 DOUGHNUT 118 cal., 4g fat (2g sat. fat), 31mg chol., 125mg sod., 18g carb. (11g sugars, 1g fiber), 2g pro.

CROISSANT BREAKFAST CASSEROLE

Turning croissants and marmalade into a classic overnight casserole makes a wonderful treat for family and guests the next morning.
—Joan Hallford, North Richland Hills, TX

Prep: 15 min. + chilling • **Bake:** 25 min.
Makes: 10 servings

- 1 jar (18 oz.) orange marmalade
- ½ cup apricot preserves
- ⅓ cup orange juice
- 3 tsp. grated orange zest
- 10 croissants, split
- 5 large eggs
- 1 cup half-and-half cream
- 1 tsp. almond or vanilla extract
- Optional: Quartered fresh strawberries and whipped cream

1. In a small bowl, mix marmalade, preserves, orange juice and zest. Spread croissant bottoms with marmalade mixture; replace tops. Cut croissants in half; arrange in a greased 13x9-in. baking dish.
2. In another bowl, whisk eggs, half-and-half and extract; pour over croissants. Refrigerate, covered, overnight.
3. Preheat oven to 350°. Remove casserole from refrigerator while oven heats. Bake, uncovered, 25-30 minutes or until a knife inserted in the center comes out clean. Let stand 5 minutes before serving. Serve with strawberries and whipped cream as desired.

1 SERVING 376 cal., 12g fat (6g sat. fat), 128mg chol., 242mg sod., 62g carb. (43g sugars, 1g fiber), 7g pro.

CROISSANT
BREAKFAST CASSEROLE

EVERYTHING BAGEL & LOX BRUNCH PIZZA

I took my favorite brunch flavors and put them all on this pizza! It's a good way to feed a crowd.

—Pamela Gelsomini, Miami, FL

Prep: 20 min. + rising • **Bake:** 15 min.
Makes: 8 servings

- 2 Tbsp. cornmeal
- 1 frozen pizza dough, thawed (1 lb.)
- 1 pkg. (5.2 oz.) Boursin garlic and fine herbs cheese
- ¾ cup shredded mozzarella cheese
- 1 large egg, room temperature, beaten
- 1 Tbsp. everything seasoning blend
- ¼ cup sour cream
- 1 Tbsp. heavy whipping cream
- 1 cup fresh arugula
- 2 tsp. olive oil
- 2 tsp. lemon juice
- 2 smoked salmon fillets (2 oz. each)
- ½ cup thinly sliced cucumber
- ½ cup pickled red onions
- 1 Tbsp. capers, drained
- 4 lemon slices, optional

1. Preheat oven to 425°. Grease a 14-in. pizza pan; sprinkle with cornmeal. Punch down dough; roll to fit pan, pinch edge to form a rim. Cover; let rest 10 minutes.
2. Spread with Boursin cheese; top with mozzarella. Brush edges of dough with egg; sprinkle with everything seasoning. Bake on a lower oven rack until crust and cheese are lightly browned, 10-12 minutes.
3. Meanwhile, in a small bowl, whisk sour cream and heavy whipping cream. In a separate bowl, toss arugula, olive oil and lemon juice. Remove pizza from oven; top with salmon, cucumbers, red onion and capers. Drizzle with cream sauce; top with arugula mixture. If desired, garnish with lemon slices.

1 PIECE 328 cal., 17g fat (8g sat. fat), 61mg chol., 642mg sod., 30g carb. (3g sugars, 1g fiber), 13g pro.

EVERYTHING BAGEL & LOX BRUNCH PIZZA

SAUSAGE BRUNCH BRAID

I needed something stunning for a party and this crescent braid did the trick. It's an edible centerpiece for a breakfast or appetizer buffet.
—Amelia Meaux, Crowley, LA

Prep: 30 min. • **Bake:** 20 min.
Makes: 8 servings

- ¾ lb. bulk pork sausage
- 1 small onion, chopped
- ¼ cup chopped celery
- ¼ cup chopped green pepper
- 1 garlic clove, minced
- 3 oz. cream cheese, cubed
- 1 green onion, chopped
- 2 Tbsp. minced fresh parsley
- 1 tube (8 oz.) refrigerated crescent rolls
- 1 large egg, lightly beaten

1. Preheat oven to 350°. In a large skillet, cook the first 5 ingredients over medium heat, breaking up sausage into crumbles, until sausage is no longer pink and vegetables are tender, 6-8 minutes; drain. Add cream cheese, green onion and parsley; cook and stir over low heat until cheese is melted.
2. Unroll crescent dough onto a greased baking sheet. Roll into a 12x10-in. rectangle, pressing perforations to seal. Spoon sausage mixture lengthwise down center third of rectangle. On each long side, cut ¾-in.-wide strips 3 in. into center. Starting at 1 end, fold alternating strips at an angle across filling; seal ends. Brush with egg.
3. Bake until golden brown, 20-25 minutes. Refrigerate leftovers.

1 PIECE 249 cal., 18g fat (7g sat. fat), 50mg chol., 449mg sod., 14g carb. (4g sugars, 0 fiber), 7g pro.

MA

MAPLE FRENCH TOAST BAKE

This yummy French toast casserole is a breeze to whip up the night before a busy morning. My family loves the richness it gets from cream cheese and maple syrup.
—Cindy Steffen, Cedarburg, WI

Prep: 15 min. + chilling • **Bake:** 50 min.
Makes: 8 servings

- 12 slices bread, cubed
- 1 pkg. (8 oz.) cream cheese, cubed
- 8 large eggs
- 1 cup 2% milk
- ½ cup maple syrup
- Additional maple syrup

1. Arrange half of the bread cubes in a greased shallow 2-qt. baking dish. Top with cream cheese and remaining bread. In a large bowl, whisk the eggs, milk and syrup; pour over bread. Cover and refrigerate overnight. Remove from the refrigerator 30 minutes before baking.
2. Cover and bake at 350° for 30 minutes. Uncover; bake 20-25 minutes longer or until golden brown. Serve with additional syrup.

1 SERVING 372 cal., 17g fat (9g sat. fat), 318mg chol., 464mg sod., 42g carb. (17g sugars, 1g fiber), 14g pro.

RASPBERRY-CINNAMON FRENCH TOAST

We came up with this moist French toast bake that's a snap to assemble at night and bake the next morning. While it's pleasantly sweet as is, let guests drizzle raspberry syrup over the top for a finishing touch.
—Taste of Home *Test Kitchen*

Prep: 10 min. + chilling • **Bake:** 35 min.
Makes: 8 servings

- 12 slices cinnamon bread, cubed
- 5 large eggs, beaten
- 1¾ cups 2% milk
- 1 cup packed brown sugar, divided
- ¼ tsp. ground cinnamon
- ¼ tsp. ground nutmeg
- ½ cup slivered almonds
- ¼ cup butter, melted
- 2 cups fresh raspberries
- Optional: Confectioners' sugar and maple syrup

1. Place bread cubes in a greased 13x9-in. baking dish. In a bowl, whisk eggs, milk, ¾ cup brown sugar, cinnamon and nutmeg; pour over bread. Cover and refrigerate 8 hours or overnight.
2. Remove from the refrigerator 30 minutes before baking. Preheat oven to 400°. Sprinkle almonds over egg mixture. Combine melted butter and remaining ¼ cup brown sugar; drizzle over the top.
3. Bake, uncovered, for 25 minutes. Sprinkle with raspberries. Bake until a knife inserted in center comes out clean, about 10 minutes longer. If desired, sprinkle with confectioners' sugar and serve with syrup.

1 PIECE 421 cal., 18g fat (7g sat. fat), 153mg chol., 289mg sod., 56g carb. (37g sugars, 6g fiber), 12g pro.

RASPBERRY-CINNAMON FRENCH TOAST

MA

APPLE-SAGE SAUSAGE PATTIES

Apple and sausage naturally go together. Add sage, and you've got a standout patty. They're freezer-friendly, so I make them ahead and grab when needed.
—Scarlett Elrod, Newnan, GA

Prep: 35 min. + chilling
Cook: 10 min./batch • **Makes:** 16 servings

- 1 large apple
- 1 large egg, lightly beaten
- ½ cup chopped fresh parsley
- 3 to 4 Tbsp. minced fresh sage
- 2 garlic cloves, minced
- 1¼ tsp. salt
- ½ tsp. pepper
- ½ tsp. crushed red pepper flakes
- 1¼ lbs. lean ground turkey
- 6 tsp. olive oil, divided

1. Peel and coarsely shred apple; place apple in a colander over a plate. Let stand 15 minutes. Squeeze and blot dry with paper towels.
2. In a large bowl, combine egg, parsley, sage, garlic, seasonings and apple. Add turkey; mix lightly but thoroughly. Shape into sixteen 2-in. patties. Place patties on waxed-paper-lined baking sheets. Refrigerate, covered, 8 hours or overnight.
3. In a large nonstick skillet, heat 2 tsp. oil over medium heat. In batches, cook patties 3-4 minutes on each side or until golden brown and a thermometer reads 165°, adding more oil as needed.

FREEZE OPTION Place uncooked patties on waxed paper-lined baking sheets; wrap and freeze until firm. Remove from pans and transfer to a freezer container; return to freezer. To use, cook frozen patties as directed, increasing time to 4-5 minutes on each side.

1 PATTY 79 cal., 5g fat (1g sat. fat), 36mg chol., 211mg sod., 2g carb. (1g sugars, 0 fiber), 8g pro.

FRESH FRUIT BOWL

The glorious colors of the fruit make this a festive salad. Slightly sweet and chilled, it makes a nice accompaniment to almost any entree.
—Marion Kirst, Troy, MI

Prep: 15 min. + chilling
Makes: 16 servings

- 8 cups fresh melon cubes
- 1 to 2 Tbsp. corn syrup
- 1 pint fresh strawberries, halved
- 2 cups fresh pineapple chunks
- 2 oranges, sectioned
- Fresh mint leaves, optional

In a large bowl, combine melon cubes and corn syrup. Cover and refrigerate overnight. Just before serving, stir in remaining fruit. Garnish with fresh mint leaves if desired.

¾ CUP 56 cal., 0 fat (0 sat. fat), 0 chol., 14mg sod., 14g carb. (11g sugars, 2g fiber), 1g pro.

MAPLE & BACON BARS

MAPLE & BACON BARS

This bacon maple bar recipe is the perfect treat when you're craving both salty and sweet. The aroma will tantalize you while the bars are baking.
—Taste of Home *Test Kitchen*

Prep: 15 min. • **Bake:** 20 min. + cooling
Makes: 9 servings

- ½ cup butter, softened
- ¾ cup packed brown sugar
- 2 large eggs, room temperature
- 1 Tbsp. 2% milk
- 1 tsp. vanilla extract
- ¾ cup all-purpose flour
- ¾ cup quick-cooking oats
- ½ tsp. baking powder
- ¼ tsp. salt
- 4 bacon strips, cooked and crumbled
- ⅓ cup chopped pecans, toasted

MAPLE GLAZE

- 1 cup confectioners' sugar
- 2 Tbsp. maple syrup
- ½ to 1 tsp. maple flavoring, optional

1. Preheat oven to 350°. In a large bowl, cream butter and brown sugar until light and fluffy, 5-7 minutes. Beat in eggs, milk and vanilla. Combine flour, oats, baking powder and salt; gradually add to creamed mixture. Fold in bacon and pecans.
2. Spread into a greased 9-in. square baking pan. Bake until a toothpick inserted in center comes out clean, 20-25 minutes. Cool on a wire rack. For glaze, in a small bowl, mix confectioners' sugar, syrup and, if desired, maple flavoring. Drizzle over bars; let stand until set.

1 BAR 351 cal., 16g fat (8g sat. fat), 72mg chol., 261mg sod., 48g carb. (34g sugars, 1g fiber), 5g pro.

MA

APPLE & SAUSAGE SHEET-PAN PANCAKES

After my daughter told me about sheet-pan pancakes, I thought it sounded like something I needed to try! Using my homegrown sweet potatoes for inspiration, I created this tasty breakfast dish. My husband and I thought it was delicious, and I liked the fact that it was easier to make than traditional pancakes!I like to line the sheet pan with foil for easier cleanup.
—*Sue Gronholz, Beaver Dam, WI*

Prep: 25 min. • **Bake:** 15 min.
Makes: 8 servings

- 1 pkg. (7 oz.) frozen fully cooked breakfast sausage links
- 1½ cups all-purpose flour
- 2 Tbsp. brown sugar
- 2 tsp. baking powder
- 1½ tsp. pumpkin pie spice
- ½ tsp. baking soda
- ½ tsp. salt
- 1½ cups buttermilk
- ½ cup mashed sweet potato
- 2 large eggs, room temperature
- 2 Tbsp. butter, melted
- 1 tsp. vanilla extract
- ¾ cup shredded peeled apple
- Maple syrup and butter

1. Preheat oven to 425°. Spray a 15x10x1-in. baking pan with cooking spray. Arrange sausages in pan and bake until heated through, about 10 minutes. Cool sausages slightly. Remove to a cutting board; cut into ½-in. slices. Wipe any excess oil from pan with a paper towel.
2. Meanwhile, in a large bowl, whisk together flour, brown sugar, baking powder, pie spice, baking soda and salt. In a separate bowl, whisk together buttermilk, sweet potato, eggs, butter and vanilla; stir in shredded apple.
3. Pour buttermilk mixture into flour mixture and stir until just combined. Stir in half the sliced sausages. Spread batter into same baking pan; top with remaining sausages. Bake until pancake is set, 12-15 minutes. Cut into 8 pieces and serve with maple syrup and butter.

1 PIECE 285 cal., 14g fat (6g sat. fat), 71mg chol., 718mg sod., 30g carb. ([illegible]g sugars, 2g fiber), 9g pro.

BLUEBERRY KUCHEN

In the summer, we can get beautiful, plump blueberries, which I use in this easy-to-make dessert. I like to freeze extra blueberries so I have them available any time I want this treat.
—Anne Krueger, Richmond, BC

Prep: 10 min. • **Bake:** 40 min.
Makes: 12 servings

- 1½ cups all-purpose flour
- ¾ cup sugar
- 2 tsp. baking powder
- 1½ tsp. grated lemon zest
- ½ tsp. ground nutmeg
- ¼ tsp. salt
- ⅔ cup 2% milk
- ¼ cup butter, melted
- 1 large egg, room temperature, beaten
- 1 tsp. vanilla extract
- 2 cups fresh or frozen blueberries

TOPPING

- ¾ cup sugar
- ½ cup all-purpose flour
- ¼ cup butter, melted

1. In a bowl, combine first 6 ingredients. Add milk, butter, egg and vanilla. Beat for 2 minutes or until well blended.
2. Pour into a greased 13x9-in. baking dish. Sprinkle with blueberries. In another bowl, combine sugar and flour; add butter. Toss with a fork until crumbly; sprinkle over blueberries. Bake at 350° for 40 minutes or until lightly browned.

NOTE If using frozen blueberries, use without thawing to avoid discoloring the batter.

1 PIECE 271 cal., 9g fat (5g sat. fat), 37mg chol., 189mg sod., 45g carb. (28g sugars, 1g fiber), 3g pro.

BLUEBERRY KUCHEN

BACON & EGG LASAGNA

My sister-in-law served this special dish for Easter breakfast one year, and our whole family loved the mix of bacon, eggs, noodles and cheese. Now I sometimes assemble it the night before and bake it in the morning for a terrific hassle-free brunch entree.
—Dianne Meyer, Graniteville, VT

Prep: 45 min. • **Bake:** 35 min. + standing
Makes: 12 servings

- 1 lb. bacon strips, diced
- 1 large onion, chopped
- ⅓ cup all-purpose flour
- ½ to 1 tsp. salt
- ¼ tsp. pepper
- 4 cups 2% milk
- 12 lasagna noodles, cooked and drained
- 12 hard-boiled large eggs, sliced
- 2 cups shredded Swiss cheese
- ⅓ cup grated Parmesan cheese
- 2 Tbsp. minced fresh parsley, optional

1. Preheat oven to 350°. In a large skillet, cook bacon until crisp. Remove with a slotted spoon to paper towels. Drain, reserving ⅓ cup drippings. In the drippings, saute onion until tender. Stir in the flour, salt and pepper until blended. Gradually stir in milk. Bring to a boil; cook and stir for 2 minutes or until thickened. Remove from the heat.
2. Spread ½ cup sauce in a greased 13x9-in. baking dish. Layer with 4 noodles and a third each of the eggs, bacon, Swiss cheese and remaining sauce. Repeat layers twice. Sprinkle with Parmesan cheese.
3. Bake, uncovered, until bubbly, 35-40 minutes. If desired, sprinkle with parsley. Let stand for 15 minutes before cutting.

1 PIECE 386 cal., 20g fat (9g sat. fat), 252mg chol., 489mg sod., 28g carb. (7g sugars, 1g fiber), 23g pro.

DEEP SOUTH JALAPENO CHEESE GRITS

DEEP SOUTH JALAPENO CHEESE GRITS

Grits are a true Deep South staple that warms the soul. I've made these spicy, cheesy baked grits for family, friends and church potlucks for many years. They're always a hit!
—Tamera Hazen, Daphne, AL

Prep: 25 min. • **Bake:** 40 min.
Makes: 8 servings

- 4 cups water
- 1 tsp. salt
- 1 cup quick-cooking grits
- ½ tsp. onion powder
- ½ tsp. garlic powder
- 2 large eggs
- 3 cups shredded sharp cheddar cheese, divided
- 2 jalapeno peppers, seeded and finely chopped
- 3 Tbsp. unsalted butter
- 1 tsp. Cajun seasoning
- 1 tsp. Worcestershire sauce
- ½ tsp. coarsely ground pepper
- Dash hot pepper sauce

1. Preheat oven to 350°. In a large saucepan, bring water and salt to a boil. Slowly stir in grits and onion and garlic powders. Reduce heat to medium-low; cook, covered, until thickened, about 5 minutes, stirring occasionally.
2. In a large bowl, whisk a small amount of hot grits into eggs; return all to pan, whisking constantly. Stir in 2 cups cheddar, jalapenos, butter, Cajun seasoning, Worcestershire sauce, pepper and hot sauce. Pour into a greased 2-qt. baking dish. Sprinkle with remaining 1 cup cheddar.
3. Bake grits until cheese is browned, 40-45 minutes. Garnish with additional jalapenos.

NOTE Wear disposable gloves when cutting hot peppers; the oils can burn skin. Avoid touching your face.

¾ CUP 295 cal., 20g fat (11g sat. fat), 100mg chol., 648mg sod., 17g carb. (1g sugars, 1g fiber), 13g pro.

MA

MAKE-AHEAD EGGS BENEDICT TOAST CUPS

When I was growing up, we had a family tradition of having eggs Benedict with champagne and orange juice for our Christmas breakfast. But now that I'm cooking, a fussy breakfast isn't my style. I wanted to come up with a dish I could make ahead that would mimic the flavors of traditional eggs Benedict and would also freeze well.

—Lyndsay Wells, Ladysmith, BC

Prep: 30 min. • **Bake:** 10 min.
Makes: 1 dozen

- 6 English muffins, split
- 1 envelope hollandaise sauce mix
- 12 slices Canadian bacon, quartered
- 1 tsp. pepper
- 1 Tbsp. olive oil
- 6 large eggs
- 1 Tbsp. butter

1. Preheat oven to 375°. Flatten muffin halves with a rolling pin; press into 12 greased muffin cups. Bake until lightly browned, about 10 minutes.
2. Meanwhile, prepare hollandaise sauce according to package directions; cool slightly. Sprinkle bacon with pepper. In a large skillet, cook bacon in oil over medium heat until partially cooked but not crisp. Remove to paper towels to drain. Divide bacon among muffin cups. Wipe skillet clean.
3. Whisk eggs and ½ cup cooled hollandaise sauce until blended. In same skillet, heat butter over medium heat. Pour in egg mixture; cook and stir until eggs are thickened and no liquid egg remains. Divide egg mixture among muffin cups; top with remaining hollandaise sauce.
4. Bake until heated through, 8-10 minutes. Serve warm.

OVERNIGHT OPTION Refrigerate unbaked cups, covered, overnight. Bake until golden brown, 10-12 minutes.

FREEZE OPTION Cover and freeze unbaked cups in muffin cups until firm. Transfer to an airtight container; return to freezer. To use, bake cups in muffin tin as directed, increasing time to 25-30 minutes. Cover loosely with foil if needed to prevent overbrowning.

1 TOAST CUP 199 cal., 11g fat (5g sat. fat), 114mg chol., 495mg sod., 15g carb. (2g sugars, 1g fiber), 9g pro.

READER RAVES

"We love this recipe! So yummy and easy to make. The English muffins are a little tricky to roll out and press in, but it is worth the extra effort."

—KYMBERLYFLEWELLING, TASTEOFHOME.COM

EVERYTHING BREAKFAST SLIDERS

EVERYTHING BREAKFAST SLIDERS

These breakfast sliders combine all your favorite morning foods—like eggs, bacon and bagels—into one tasty package.
—Rashanda Cobbins, Aurora, CO

Prep: 30 min. • **Bake:** 15 min.
Makes: 8 servings

- 8 large eggs
- ¼ cup 2% milk
- 2 green onions, thinly sliced
- ¼ tsp. pepper
- 8 Tbsp. spreadable chive and onion cream cheese
- 8 Hawaiian sweet rolls or miniature bagels, split
- 8 slices cheddar cheese, halved
- 8 slices Canadian bacon
- 8 cooked bacon strips, halved

GLAZE

- 2 Tbsp. butter, melted
- 1½ tsp. maple syrup
- ⅛ tsp. garlic powder
- 2 Tbsp. everything seasoning blend

1. Preheat oven to 375°. Heat a large nonstick skillet over medium heat. In a large bowl, whisk eggs, milk, green onions and pepper until blended; pour into skillet. Cook and stir until eggs are thickened and no liquid egg remains; remove from heat.
2. Spread cream cheese over roll bottoms; place in a greased 13x9-in. baking dish. Layer each with 1 piece of cheese and 1 slice of Canadian bacon. Spoon scrambled eggs over top. Layer with remaining cheese pieces and cooked bacon. Replace roll tops. For glaze, stir together butter, maple syrup and garlic powder; brush over roll tops. Sprinkle with everything seasoning blend.
3. Bake until tops are golden brown and cheese is melted, 12-15 minutes.

1 SLIDER 417 cal., 26g fat (14g sat. fat), 250mg chol., 1072mg sod., 18g carb. (4g sugars, 1g fiber), 24g pro.

HEARTY BREAKFAST EGG BAKE

HEARTY BREAKFAST EGG BAKE

I always fix this casserole ahead of time when overnight guests are visiting so I have more time to spend with them. I simply add some toast or biscuits and fresh fruit for a complete meal that everyone loves.
—Pamela Norris, Fenton, MO

Prep: 15 min. + chilling
Bake: 45 min. + standing
Makes: 8 servings

- 1½ lbs. bulk pork sausage
- 3 cups frozen shredded hash brown potatoes, thawed
- 2 cups shredded cheddar cheese
- 8 large eggs, lightly beaten
- 1 can (10¾ oz.) condensed cream of mushroom soup, undiluted
- ¾ cup evaporated milk

1. Crumble sausage into a large skillet. Cook over medium heat until no longer pink; drain. Transfer to a greased 13x9-in. baking dish. Sprinkle with hash browns and cheese.
2. In a large bowl, whisk the remaining ingredients; pour over the top. Cover and refrigerate overnight.
3. Remove from refrigerator 30 minutes before baking. Bake, uncovered, at 350° for 45-50 minutes or until a knife inserted in center comes out clean. Let stand for 10 minutes before cutting.

1 PIECE 427 cal., 32g fat (15g sat. fat), 281mg chol., 887mg sod., 12g carb. (4g sugars, 1g fiber), 21g pro.

RICHARD'S BREAKFAST BARS

RICHARD'S BREAKFAST BARS

My chewy fiber bars with a complex taste are extremely addictive. For clean slices, spray a pizza cutter with cooking spray before cutting.
—Richard Cole, Richmond, TX

Prep: 10 min. • **Bake:** 25 min. + cooling
Makes: 2 dozen

- 1 can (14 oz.) sweetened condensed milk
- 2 large eggs, beaten
- 2 cups Fiber One bran cereal
- 2 cups quick-cooking oats
- 1½ cups chopped pecans
- 1 cup miniature semisweet chocolate chips
- 1 cup golden raisins
- 1 cup sweetened shredded coconut
- 1 can (8 oz.) unsweetened crushed pineapple, undrained

1. Preheat oven to 350°. Whisk together condensed milk and eggs; mix in remaining ingredients. Firmly press mixture evenly into a greased 13x9-in. baking dish.
2. Bake, uncovered, until edges are golden brown, 25-30 minutes. Cool completely in dish on a wire rack. Chill 1 hour; cut into bars. Store refrigerated in an airtight container.

1 BAR [illegible] cal., 11g fat (4g sat. fat), 21mg chol., 57mg sod., 31g carb. (20g sugars, 5g fiber), 4g pro.

HAM & EGG SANDWICH

Whenever the whole family gets together for a holiday or long weekend, they request this big breakfast sandwich. I can feed everyone by stacking our favorite breakfast fixings inside a loaf of French bread. Then I simply pop it in the oven to warm up.
—DeeDee Newton, Toronto, ON

Prep: 30 min. • **Bake:** 15 min.
Makes: 8 servings

- 1 unsliced loaf (1 lb.) French bread
- 4 Tbsp. butter, softened, divided
- 2 Tbsp. mayonnaise
- 8 thin slices deli ham
- 1 large tomato, sliced
- 1 small onion, thinly sliced
- 8 eggs, lightly beaten
- 8 slices cheddar cheese

1. Preheat oven to 375°. Cut bread in half lengthwise; carefully hollow out top and bottom, leaving ½-in. shells (discard removed bread or save for another use). Spread 3 Tbsp. butter and all of the mayonnaise inside bread shells. Line bottom bread shell with ham; top with tomato and onion.
2. In a large skillet, melt the remaining 1 Tbsp. butter; add eggs. Cook over medium heat, stirring occasionally until edges are almost set.
3. Spoon into bottom bread shell; top with cheese. Cover with bread top. Wrap in greased foil. Bake 15-20 minutes or until heated through. Cut into serving-size pieces.

1 SERVING 543 cal., 31g fat (14g sat. fat), 298mg chol., 1644mg sod., 33g carb. (3g sugars, 2g fiber), 32g pro.

SAUSAGE & HASH BROWN BREAKFAST PIZZA

Pizza for breakfast? Kids will love making—and eating—this hearty morning meal that's made with crescent roll dough and frozen hash browns.
—Rae Truax, Mattawa, WA

Prep: 10 min. • **Bake:** 30 min. + standing
Makes: 8 servings

- 1 tube (8 oz.) refrigerated crescent rolls
- 1 lb. bulk pork sausage
- 1 cup frozen shredded hash brown potatoes, thawed
- 1 cup shredded cheddar cheese
- 3 large eggs
- ¼ cup whole milk
- ¼ tsp. pepper
- ¼ cup grated Parmesan cheese

1. Unroll crescent dough and place on a greased 12-in. pizza pan; press seams together and press up sides of pan to form a crust.
2. In a large skillet, brown sausage over medium heat; drain and cool slightly. Sprinkle the sausage, hash browns and cheddar cheese over crust.
3. In a small bowl, whisk the eggs, milk and pepper; pour over pizza. Sprinkle with Parmesan cheese. Bake at 375° for 28-30 minutes or until a knife inserted in the center comes out clean. Let stand for 10 minutes before cutting.

1 PIECE 346 cal., 25g fat (10g sat. fat), 117mg chol., 727mg sod., 16g carb. (4g sugars, 0 fiber), 15g pro.

SAUSAGE & HASH BROWN BREAKFAST PIZZA

PISTACHIO GRANOLA

After a search for the perfect granola, I found this recipe and tweaked it just a little for my taste. Enjoy it as a crunchy topping on your yogurt or give it away as a thoughtful homemade gift.
—Candy Summerhill, Alexander, AR

Prep: 10 min. • **Cook:** 15 min. + cooling
Makes: 6 cups

- 2 cups old-fashioned oats
- ⅔ cup packed brown sugar
- ¼ cup apple cider or unsweetened apple juice
- ½ tsp. ground cinnamon
- ¼ tsp. salt
- ⅔ cup Cheerios
- ⅔ cup pistachios, chopped
- ⅔ cup dried cherries
- ½ cup dried apples, chopped
- ½ cup dried blueberries
- ½ cup sunflower kernels

1. In a large cast-iron or other heavy skillet, toast oats over medium heat until golden brown. Remove and set aside. In the same skillet, cook and stir brown sugar and apple cider over medium-low heat until brown sugar is dissolved, 1-2 minutes. Add cinnamon and salt; stir to combine.
2. Stir in the cereal, pistachios, fruits, sunflower kernels and toasted oats until coated. Cool. Store in an airtight container.

½ CUP 233 cal., 7g fat (1g sat. fat), 0 chol., 122mg sod., 39g carb. (22g sugars, 4g fiber), 5g pro.

PISTACHIO GRANOLA

HAM & CHEESE QUICHE

MA

HAM & CHEESE QUICHE

When I was expecting our daughter, I made and froze these cheesy quiches as well as several other dishes. After her birth, it was nice to have dinner waiting in the freezer when my husband and I were too tired to cook.
—Christena Palmer, Green River, WY

Prep: 20 min. • **Bake:** 35 min.
Makes: 2 quiches (6 servings each)

- 2 sheets refrigerated pie crust
- 2 cups diced fully cooked ham
- 2 cups shredded sharp cheddar cheese
- 2 tsp. dried minced onion
- 4 large eggs
- 2 cups half-and-half cream
- ½ tsp. salt
- ¼ tsp. pepper

1. Preheat oven to 400°. Unroll pie crusts into two 9-in. pie plates; flute edges. Line unpricked pie crusts with a double thickness of heavy-duty foil. Fill with pie weights, dried beans or uncooked rice. Bake until light golden brown, 10-12 minutes. Remove foil and weights; bake until bottom is golden brown, 3-5 minutes longer. Cool on wire racks.
2. Divide ham, cheese and onion between crusts. In a large bowl, whisk eggs, cream, salt and pepper until blended. Pour into crusts. Cover edges loosely with foil. Bake until a knife inserted in the center comes out clean, 35-40 minutes. Let stand 5-10 minutes before cutting.

FREEZE OPTION Cover and freeze the unbaked quiche. To use, remove from freezer 30 minutes before baking (do not thaw). Preheat oven to 350°. Place quiche on a baking sheet; cover edge loosely with foil. Bake as directed, increasing time as necessary, until knife inserted in the center comes out clean.

NOTE Let pie weights cool before storing. Beans and rice may be reused for pie weights, but not for cooking.

1 PIECE 349 cal., 23g fat (12g sat. fat), 132mg chol., 596mg sod., 20g carb. (3g sugars, 0 fiber), 13g pro.

SHEET-PAN BACON & EGGS BREAKFAST

I re-created this recipe from inspiration I found on social media and it was a huge hit! Use any cheeses and spices you like; you can even try seasoned potatoes.
—Bonnie Hawkins, Elkhorn, WI

Prep: 20 min. • **Bake:** 40 min.
Makes: 8 servings

- 10 bacon strips
- 1 pkg. (30 oz.) frozen shredded hash brown potatoes, thawed
- 1 tsp. garlic powder
- 1 tsp. dried basil
- 1 tsp. dried oregano
- ½ tsp. salt
- ½ tsp. crushed red pepper flakes
- 1½ cups shredded pepper jack cheese
- 1 cup shredded cheddar cheese
- 8 large eggs
- ¼ tsp. pepper
- ¼ cup chopped green onions

1. Preheat oven to 400°. Place bacon in a single layer in a 15x10x1-in. baking sheet. Bake until partially cooked but not crisp, about 10 minutes. Remove to paper towels to drain. When cool enough to handle, chop bacon.
2. In a large bowl, combine potatoes and seasonings; spread evenly into drippings in pan. Bake until golden brown, 25-30 minutes.
3. Sprinkle with cheeses. With the back of a spoon, make 8 wells in the potato mixture. Break 1 egg in each well; sprinkle with pepper and bacon. Bake until egg whites are completely set and yolks begin to thicken but are not hard, 12-14 minutes. Sprinkle with green onion.

1 SERVING 446 cal., 30g fat (13g sat. fat), 246mg chol., 695mg sod., 22g carb. (2g sugars, 1g fiber), 22g pro.

MA

CHAI BUTTERNUT SQUASH PANCAKES

Hot or cold, chai tea is my absolute favorite drink. I wanted to enjoy the spicy chai flavor in a different way, and that's when the idea for these pancakes was born. Serve with your choice of syrup; I enjoy them with some added roasted walnuts.

—Corinna Nguyen, Hutto, TX

Prep: 40 min. + cooling
Cook: 5 min./batch • **Makes:** 8 servings

- ¾ tsp. ground cinnamon
- ½ tsp. ground cardamom
- ¼ tsp. ground ginger
- ¼ tsp. ground cloves
- ⅛ tsp. ground nutmeg
- ⅛ tsp. ground allspice
- Dash pepper
- 2 Tbsp. butter
- 3 cups cubed peeled butternut squash
- 3 Tbsp. brown sugar
- 1 Tbsp. minced fresh gingerroot

BATTER

- 2 cups all-purpose flour
- ¼ cup packed brown sugar
- 2 tsp. baking powder
- ½ tsp. salt
- ¼ tsp. baking soda
- ¾ cup 2% milk
- ¾ cup chai tea latte concentrate
- 2 large eggs, room temperature, separated
- 2 Tbsp. butter, melted
- 1 tsp. vanilla extract
- Optional: maple syrup, butter and chopped walnuts

1. In a small bowl, combine the first 7 ingredients. In a large skillet, heat butter over medium-high heat. Add squash, brown sugar and fresh ginger. Cook, covered, until tender, 15-20 minutes, stirring occasionally. Remove from the heat; cool.
2. Preheat griddle over medium heat. For batter, in a large bowl, combine flour, brown sugar, baking powder, salt, baking soda and reserved cinnamon mixture. In a blender, combine milk, chai concentrate, egg yolks, melted butter, vanilla and cooled squash mixture. Cover and process until pureed. Stir into dry ingredients just until combined. In a small bowl, beat egg whites until stiff peaks form; fold into batter.
3. Lightly grease griddle. Pour batter by ¼ cupfuls onto griddle; cook until bubbles on top begin to pop and bottoms are golden brown. Turn; cook until second side is golden brown. If desired, serve with maple syrup and chopped walnuts.

FREEZE OPTION Freeze cooled pancakes between layers of waxed paper in a freezer container. To use, place pancakes on an ungreased baking sheet, cover with foil and reheat in a preheated 375° oven until heated through, 5-10 minutes. Or, place 2 pancakes on a microwave-safe plate and microwave on high until heated through, 45-90 seconds.

2 PANCAKES 289 cal., 8g fat (4g sat. fat), 64mg chol., 394mg sod., 49g carb. (18g sugars, 2g fiber), 6g pro.

MIXED BERRY FRENCH TOAST BAKE

MIXED BERRY FRENCH TOAST BAKE

I just love this recipe! It's perfect for fuss-free holiday breakfasts or laid-back company. It's scrumptious and so easy to put together the night before.
—Amy Berry, Poland, ME

Prep: 20 min. + chilling • **Bake:** 45 min.
Makes: 8 servings

- 6 large eggs
- 1¾ cups fat-free milk
- 1 tsp. sugar
- 1 tsp. ground cinnamon
- 1 tsp. vanilla extract
- ¼ tsp. salt
- 1 loaf (1 lb.) French bread, cubed
- 1 pkg. (12 oz.) frozen unsweetened mixed berries
- 2 Tbsp. cold butter
- ⅓ cup packed brown sugar
- Optional: Confectioners' sugar and maple syrup

1. Whisk together first 6 ingredients. Place bread cubes in a 13x9-in. or 3-qt. baking dish coated with cooking spray. Pour egg mixture over top. Refrigerate, covered, 8 hours or overnight.
2. Preheat oven to 350°. Remove berries from freezer and French toast mixture from refrigerator and let stand while oven heats. Bake French toast mixture, covered, 30 minutes.
3. In a small bowl, cut butter into brown sugar until crumbly. Top French toast mixture with berries; sprinkle with brown sugar mixture. Bake, uncovered, until a knife inserted in the center comes out clean, 15-20 minutes. If desired, dust with confectioners' sugar and serve with syrup.

1 SERVING 310 cal., 8g fat (3g sat. fat), 148mg chol., 517mg sod., 46g carb. (17g sugars, 3g fiber), 13g pro.

BACON QUICHE TARTS

MA

BACON QUICHE TARTS

Here's a fun way to make single-serving quiches that people of all ages are sure to enjoy. Flavored with bacon, cheese and veggies, these little bites are just the thing for your next brunch spread.
—Kendra Schertz, Nappanee, IN

Prep: 15 min. • **Bake:** 20 min.
Makes: 8 servings

- 6 oz. cream cheese, softened
- 5 tsp. 2% milk
- 2 large eggs
- ½ cup shredded Colby cheese
- 2 Tbsp. chopped green pepper
- 1 Tbsp. finely chopped onion
- 1 tube (8 oz.) refrigerated crescent rolls
- 5 bacon strips, cooked and crumbled
- Thinly sliced green onions, optional

1. Preheat oven to 375°. In a small bowl, beat cream cheese and milk until smooth. Add the eggs, cheese, green pepper and onion.
2. Separate the crescent dough into 8 triangles; press onto the bottom and up the side of 8 greased muffin cups. Sprinkle half of the bacon into cups. Pour egg mixture over bacon; top with remaining bacon.
3. Bake, uncovered, for 18-22 minutes or until a knife inserted in the center comes out clean. Serve warm. If desired, top with green onions.

FREEZE OPTION Freeze cooled baked tarts in a freezer container. To use, reheat tarts on a baking sheet in a preheated 375° oven until heated through.

1 TART 258 cal., 19g fat (9g sat. fat), 87mg chol., 409mg sod., 12g carb. (3g sugars, 0 fiber), 8g pro.

BLUEBERRY SOUR CREAM COFFEE CAKE

BLUEBERRY SOUR CREAM COFFEE CAKE

At our house, special breakfasts would not be the same without this delicious coffee cake. Folks rave about the treat when I bring it to special occasions.
—Susan Walschlager, Anderson, IN

Prep: 25 min. • **Bake:** 55 min. + cooling
Makes: 12 servings

- ¾ cup butter, softened
- 1½ cups sugar
- 4 large eggs, room temperature
- 1 tsp. vanilla extract
- 3 cups all-purpose flour
- 1½ tsp. baking powder
- ¾ tsp. baking soda
- ¼ tsp. salt
- 1 cup sour cream

FILLING

- ¼ cup packed brown sugar
- 1 Tbsp. all-purpose flour
- ½ tsp. ground cinnamon
- 2 cups fresh or frozen blueberries

GLAZE

- 1 cup confectioners' sugar
- 2 to 3 Tbsp. 2% milk

1. Preheat oven to 350°. In a large bowl, cream butter and sugar until light and fluffy, 5-7 minutes. Add eggs, 1 at a time, beating well after each addition. Beat in the vanilla. Combine the flour, baking powder, baking soda and salt; add to creamed mixture alternately with sour cream, beating well after each addition.
2. Spoon a third of the batter into a greased and floured 10-in. fluted tube pan. Combine brown sugar, flour and cinnamon; sprinkle half over batter. Top with half of the berries. Repeat layers. Top with remaining batter.
3. Bake 55-65 minutes or until a toothpick inserted in the center comes out clean. Cool 10 minutes before removing from pan to a wire rack to cool completely. Combine glaze ingredients; drizzle over coffee cake.

NOTE If using frozen blueberries, use without thawing to avoid discoloring the batter.

1 PIECE 448 cal., 17g fat (10g sat. fat), 114mg chol., 328mg sod., 68g carb. (42g sugars, 1g fiber), 6g pro.

HAM & CHEESE BREAKFAST SLIDERS

I turned one of my favorite sliders into a breakfast sandwich, then exchanged the regular mustard for spicy brown to give it more zip. I added the same mustard to the eggs, and the recipe is now a mainstay. When we host overnight guests, I make these sandwiches the night before and finish them in the morning before popping them into the oven to bake.
—Jill Landis, Shinnston, WV

Takes: 30 min. • **Makes:** 1 dozen

- ½ cup butter, cubed, plus 1 Tbsp. butter, divided
- 2 Tbsp. brown sugar
- 2 Tbsp. spicy brown mustard, divided
- 1 tsp. Worcestershire sauce
- 12 dinner rolls, split
- 6 slices deli ham, halved
- 6 large eggs
- 2 Tbsp. 2% milk
- 6 slices cheddar cheese, halved

1. Preheat oven to 350°. In a small saucepan, combine ½ cup butter, the brown sugar, 1 Tbsp. mustard and the Worcestershire sauce; bring to a boil. Cook and stir until sugar is dissolved, 1-2 minutes. Remove from the heat.
2. Place roll bottoms, cut side up, in an ungreased 13x9-in. baking dish. Top each with 1 piece of ham.
3. In a large bowl, whisk eggs, milk and remaining 1 Tbsp. mustard until blended. In a large nonstick skillet, heat remaining 1 Tbsp. butter over medium heat. Pour in egg mixture; cook and stir until eggs are thickened and no liquid egg remains. Spoon scrambled eggs evenly over ham. Top with cheese. Replace roll tops. Brush butter mixture over roll tops. Bake, uncovered, until cheese is melted, 10-15 minutes.

1 SLIDER 299 cal., 18g fat (10g sat. fat), 154mg chol., 524mg sod., 22g carb. (4g sugars, 1g fiber), 12g pro.

HAM & CHEESE BREAKFAST SLIDERS

ICED COFFEE LATTE

This amazing alternative to regular hot coffee is much more economical than store-bought coffee drinks. Sweetened condensed milk and a hint of chocolate lend a special touch.
—Heather Nandell, Johnston, IA

Takes: 10 min. • **Makes:** 8 servings

- ½ cup instant coffee granules
- ½ cup boiling water
- 4 cups chocolate milk
- 2 cups cold water
- 1 can (14 oz.) sweetened condensed milk
- Ice cubes

In a large bowl, dissolve coffee in boiling water. Stir in the chocolate milk, cold water and condensed milk. Serve over ice.

1 CUP 270 cal., 9g fat (5g sat. fat), 32mg chol., 139mg sod., 41g carb. (39g sugars, 1g fiber), 8g pro.

BRUNCH LASAGNA

BRUNCH LASAGNA

Everyone can appreciate make-ahead dishes like this one. Pop it into the oven before guests arrive—add fresh fruit and muffins—and you have an instant brunch. You can serve it as a hearty supper, too, drizzled with a little salsa.
—Judy Munger, Warren, MN

Prep: 25 min. • **Bake:** 45 min. + standing
Makes: 9 servings

- 6 lasagna noodles
- 8 large eggs, beaten
- ½ cup whole milk
- 1 Tbsp. butter
- 2 jars (16 oz. each) Alfredo sauce
- 3 cups diced fully cooked ham
- ½ cup chopped green pepper
- ¼ cup chopped green onions
- 1 cup shredded cheddar cheese
- ¼ cup grated Parmesan cheese
- Thinly sliced green onions, optional

1. Cook noodles according to package directions. Meanwhile, in a large bowl, beat eggs and milk. In a large nonstick skillet, melt butter over medium heat; cook eggs until set but moist. Remove from heat. Drain noodles.
2. Spread ½ cup Alfredo sauce in a greased 10-in. square baking dish or 13x9-in. baking dish. Layer with 3 lasagna noodles (trim noodles if necessary to fit dish), ham, green pepper and onions.
3. Top with half of the remaining Alfredo sauce and the remaining noodles. Layer with scrambled eggs, remaining Alfredo sauce and cheddar cheese. Sprinkle with Parmesan cheese.
4. Bake, uncovered, at 375° for 45-50 minutes or until bubbly. Let stand for 10 minutes before cutting. If desired, top with sliced green onions.

1 SERVING 408 cal., 24g fat (13g sat. fat), 257mg chol., 1175mg sod., 24g carb. (2g sugars, 2g fiber), 26g pro.

GOOEY LEMON ROLLS

My mother made these hard-to-resist rolls when I was young. I always warm up after having one, and so will your family.
—*Cora Patterson, Lewiston, ID*

Prep: 25 min. + rising • **Bake:** 20 min.
Makes: 1 dozen

- 1 Tbsp. active dry yeast
- ½ cup warm water (110° to 115°)
- ½ cup warm 2% milk (110° to 115°)
- ¼ cup butter, melted
- 1 large egg, room temperature
- ½ cup sugar
- 1 tsp. salt
- 3 to 3½ cups all-purpose flour

FILLING

- ½ cup sugar
- 2 tsp. grated lemon zest
- ½ tsp. ground cinnamon
- 1 Tbsp. poppy seeds, optional
- ¼ cup butter, melted
- 1 cup slivered almonds, toasted

GLAZE

- ½ cup sugar
- 1 can (12 oz.) frozen lemonade concentrate, thawed
- 1 Tbsp. butter
- 2 tsp. grated lemon zest

1. In a small bowl, dissolve yeast in warm water. In a large bowl, combine milk, butter, egg, sugar, salt, yeast mixture and 2 cups flour; beat on medium speed until smooth. Stir in enough remaining flour to form a soft dough (dough will be sticky).
2. Turn out dough onto a floured surface; knead until smooth and elastic, 6-8 minutes. Place in a greased bowl, turning once to grease the top. Cover and let rise in a warm place until doubled, about 1 hour.
3. For filling, in a small bowl, mix sugar, lemon zest, cinnamon and, if desired, poppy seeds. Punch down dough; roll out into an 18x12-in. rectangle. Brush with melted butter to within ¼ in. of edges; sprinkle with sugar mixture and almonds. Roll up jelly-roll style, starting with a long side; pinch seam to seal. Cut into 12 slices.
4. Place in a greased 13x9-in. baking pan, cut side down. Cover with a kitchen towel; let rise in a warm place until almost doubled, about 45 minutes.
5. Preheat oven to 400°. Bake rolls for 15 minutes. Meanwhile, for glaze, in a small saucepan, combine sugar and lemonade concentrate. Cook and stir over medium-low heat until sugar is dissolved. Stir in butter and lemon zest; simmer, uncovered, until slightly thickened, 10-12 minutes. Remove rolls from oven; pour glaze over rolls. Bake until golden brown, 5-10 minutes longer. Cool in pan for 5 minutes. Run a knife around sides of pan before inverting onto a serving plate. Serve warm.

1 ROLL 430 cal., 15g fat (6g sat. fat), 39mg chol., 280mg sod., 71g carb. (42g sugars, 3g fiber), 7g pro.

BREAKFAST PIGS IN A BLANKET

BREAKFAST PIGS IN A BLANKET

Hard-boiled eggs and sausages wrapped in crescent dough make for the breakfast version of the classic pigs in a blanket. They're perfect for those days when you want to stay curled up in your blanket.
—James Schend, Pleasant Prairie, WI

Takes: 30 min. • **Makes:** 2 dozen

- 4 hard-boiled large eggs
- 1 tube (8 oz.) refrigerated crescent rolls
- 12 uncooked breakfast sausage links, cut in half widthwise
- 12 cherry tomatoes, halved
- 1 large egg, beaten
- 1 Tbsp. poppy seeds

1. Preheat oven to 325°. Cut each egg into 6 wedges. Unroll crescent dough and separate into 8 triangles; cut each triangle lengthwise into 3 thin triangles.
2. Place 1 sausage piece on wide end of each smaller triangle; top with an egg wedge and a cherry tomato half. Roll up tightly and place point-side down on a parchment-lined baking sheet.
3. Brush with beaten egg; sprinkle with poppy seeds. Bake until sausage is no longer pink and crescent rolls are golden brown on the bottom, 14-16 minutes.

1 PIECE 83 cal., 5g fat (1g sat. fat), 45mg chol., 195mg sod., 5g carb. (1g sugars, 0 fiber), 4g pro.

GLUTEN-FREE BANANA BREAD

GLUTEN-FREE BANANA BREAD

Tired of gluten-free baked goods that are dry and crumbly? This banana bread tastes like the real thing and goes over well with everyone.
—Gladys Arnold, Pittsburgh, PA

Prep: 20 min. • **Bake:** 45 min. + cooling
Makes: 2 loaves (12 pieces each)

- 2 cups gluten-free all-purpose baking flour (without xanthan gum)
- 1 tsp. baking soda
- ¼ tsp. salt
- 4 large eggs, room temperature
- 2 cups mashed ripe bananas (4-5 medium)
- 1 cup sugar
- ½ cup unsweetened applesauce
- ⅓ cup canola oil
- 1 tsp. vanilla extract
- ½ cup chopped walnuts

1. Preheat oven to 350°. In a large bowl, combine flour, baking soda and salt. In a small bowl, whisk eggs, bananas, sugar, applesauce, oil and vanilla. Stir into dry ingredients just until moistened.
2. Transfer to 2 greased 8x4-in. loaf pans. Sprinkle with walnuts. Bake until a toothpick inserted in the center comes out clean, 45-55 minutes. Cool bread 10 minutes before removing from pans to wire racks.

NOTE Read all ingredient labels for possible gluten content prior to use. Ingredient formulas can change, and production facilities vary among brands. If you're concerned that your brand may contain gluten, contact the company.

1 PIECE 147 cal., 6g fat (1g sat. fat), 31mg chol., 89mg sod., 22g carb. (11g sugars, 1g fiber), 3g pro.

POTATO CRUST QUICHE

POTATO CRUST QUICHE

My husband and I have lived in four different states, and we've grown potatoes in every one of them. I mostly make this dish for family, but company loves it too. It's almost a meal in itself—all you need to add is a salad.
—Nancy Smith, Scottsdale, AZ

Prep: 50 min. • **Bake:** 35 min.
Makes: 8 servings

CRUST

- 5 to 6 medium potatoes, peeled
- 1 cup all-purpose flour
- ½ cup chopped onion
- 1 large egg, lightly beaten
- ½ tsp. salt

FILLING

- 1½ cups shredded Colby cheese, divided
- ½ cup chopped onion
- 1½ cups cubed fully cooked ham
- 1½ cups fresh broccoli florets
- 3 large eggs, lightly beaten
- 1 cup half-and-half cream
- ½ tsp. salt
- Dash ground nutmeg
- Paprika
- Minced fresh parsley, optional

1. Preheat oven to 400°. Shred potatoes into a large bowl to measure 4 cups. Immediately cover potatoes with water to prevent browning. Drain shredded potatoes in a colander, pressing to remove water. Transfer to a clean kitchen towel. Squeeze out as much liquid as possible. In a large bowl, combine potatoes, flour, onion, egg and salt; press into a well-greased 10-in. deep-dish pie plate. Bake until edge is lightly browned, 35-40 minutes.
2. Remove from oven; reduce heat to 350°. Add 1 cup cheese, onion, ham and broccoli to crust. Whisk eggs, cream, salt and nutmeg; pour over broccoli. Sprinkle with paprika.
3. Bake until a knife inserted in the center comes out clean, 35-40 minutes. Sprinkle with remaining ½ cup cheese. Let stand for 5 minutes before serving. If desired, sprinkle with parsley.

1 PIECE 338 cal., 14g fat (7g sat. fat), 144mg chol., 798mg sod., 34g carb. (4g sugars, 2g fiber), 19g pro.

OVERNIGHT CHERRY DANISH

MA

OVERNIGHT CHERRY DANISH

These rolls with their cherry-filled centers melt in your mouth and store well, unfrosted, in the freezer.
—Leann Sauder, Tremont, IL

Prep: 1½ hours + chilling • **Bake:** 15 min.
Makes: 3 dozen

- 2 pkg. (¼ oz. each) active dry yeast
- ½ cup warm 2% milk (110° to 115°)
- 6 cups all-purpose flour
- ⅓ cup sugar
- 2 tsp. salt
- 1 cup cold butter, cubed
- 1½ cups warm half-and-half cream (70° to 80°)
- 6 large egg yolks, room temperature
- 1 can (21 oz.) cherry pie filling

ICING

- 3 cups confectioners' sugar
- 2 Tbsp. butter, softened
- ¼ tsp. vanilla extract
- Dash salt
- 4 to 5 Tbsp. half-and-half cream

1. In a small bowl, dissolve yeast in warm milk. In a large bowl, combine flour, sugar and salt. Cut in butter until crumbly. Add yeast mixture, cream and egg yolks; stir until mixture forms a soft dough (dough will be sticky). Refrigerate, covered, overnight.
2. Punch down dough. Turn onto a lightly floured surface; divide into 4 portions. Roll out each portion into an 18x4-in. rectangle; cut into 4x1-in. strips.
3. Place 2 strips side by side; twist together. Shape into a ring and pinch ends together. Place 2 in. apart on greased baking sheets. Repeat with remaining strips. Cover with kitchen towels; let rise in a warm place until doubled, about 45 minutes.
4. Preheat oven to 350°. Using the end of a wooden spoon handle, make a ½-in.-deep indentation in the center of each Danish. Fill each with about 1 Tbsp. pie filling. Bake 14-16 minutes or until lightly browned. Remove from pans to wire racks to cool.
5. For icing, in a bowl, beat confectioners' sugar, butter, vanilla, salt and enough cream to reach desired consistency. Drizzle over Danishes.

1 PASTRY 218 cal., 8g fat (5g sat. fat), 55mg chol., 188mg sod., 33g carb. (16g sugars, 1g fiber), 3g pro.

MINI HAM & CHEESE FRITTATAS

I found this recipe a few years ago and made some little changes to it. I'm diabetic, and it fits into my low-carb and low-fat diet. Every time I serve a brunch, the frittatas are the first to disappear, and nobody knows they are low in fat!
—Susan Watt, Basking Ridge, NJ

Prep: 15 min. • **Bake:** 25 min.
Makes: 8 servings

- 6 large eggs
- 4 large egg whites
- 2 Tbsp. fat-free milk
- ¼ tsp. salt
- ¼ tsp. pepper
- 3 Tbsp. minced fresh chives
- ¾ cup cubed fully cooked ham (about 4 oz.)
- 1 cup shredded fat-free cheddar cheese

1. Preheat oven to 375°. In a bowl, whisk the first 5 ingredients until blended; stir in chives. Divide ham and cheese among 8 muffin cups coated with cooking spray. Top with egg mixture, filling each cup three-fourths full.
2. Bake until a knife inserted in the center comes out clean, 22-25 minutes. Carefully run a knife around sides to loosen.

1 MINI FRITTATA 106 cal., 4g fat (1g sat. fat), 167mg chol., 428mg sod., 2g carb. (1g sugars, 0 fiber), 14g pro.

MINI HAM & CHEESE FRITTATAS

MA

AIR-FRYER SAUSAGE BACON BITES

Try surprising your family one Sunday morning by pulling these out of the air fryer as they head to breakfast, and get ready for oohs and aahs. They're equally delicious as a party appetizer.
—Pat Waymire, Yellow Springs, OH

Prep: 20 min. + chilling
Cook: 15 min./batch
Makes: about 3½ dozen

- ¾ lb. bacon strips
- 2 pkg. (8 oz. each) frozen fully cooked breakfast sausage links, thawed
- ½ cup plus 2 Tbsp. packed brown sugar, divided

1. Cut bacon strips widthwise in half; cut sausage links in half. Wrap 1 piece of bacon around each sausage. Place ½ cup brown sugar in a shallow bowl; roll sausages in sugar. Secure each with a toothpick. Place in a large bowl. Cover and refrigerate 4 hours or overnight.
2. Preheat air fryer to 325°. Sprinkle wrapped sausages with 1 Tbsp. brown sugar. In batches, arrange sausages in a single layer on a greased tray in air-fryer basket. Cook until bacon is crisp, 15-20 minutes, turning once. Sprinkle with remaining 1 Tbsp. brown sugar.

NOTE Cook times vary dramatically among brands of air fryers. Refer to your air fryer manual for general cook times and adjust if necessary.

1 PIECE 74 cal., 6g fat (2g sat. fat), 9mg chol., 154mg sod., 4g carb. (4g sugars, 0 fiber), 2g pro.

AIR-FRYER SAUSAGE BACON BITES

MA

BRIE & SAUSAGE BRUNCH BAKE

I've made this brunch bake for holidays as well as for a weekend at a friend's cabin and I always get requests for the recipe. It's make-ahead convenient, reheats well and even tastes great the next day.
—Becky Hicks, Forest Lake, MN

Prep: 30 min. + chilling
Bake: 50 min. + standing
Makes: 12 servings

- 1 lb. bulk Italian sausage
- 1 small onion, chopped
- 8 cups cubed day-old sourdough bread
- ½ cup chopped roasted sweet red peppers
- ½ lb. Brie cheese, rind removed, cubed
- ⅔ cup grated Parmesan cheese
- 2 Tbsp. minced fresh basil or 2 tsp. dried basil
- 8 large eggs
- 2 cups heavy whipping cream
- 1 Tbsp. Dijon mustard
- 1 tsp. pepper
- ½ tsp. salt
- ¾ cup shredded part-skim mozzarella cheese
- 3 green onions, sliced

1. In a large skillet, cook and stir sausage and onion over medium heat, crumbling sausage, until meat is no longer pink, 5-7 minutes; drain.
2. Place bread cubes in a greased 13x9-in. baking dish. Layer with the sausage mixture, red peppers, Brie and Parmesan cheeses and basil. In a large bowl, whisk eggs, cream, mustard, pepper and salt; pour over top. Cover and refrigerate overnight.
3. Remove from refrigerator 30 minutes before baking. Preheat oven to 350°. Bake, uncovered, until a knife inserted in the center comes out clean, 45-50 minutes.
4. Sprinkle with mozzarella cheese. Bake until cheese is melted, 4-6 minutes longer. Let stand 10 minutes before cutting. Sprinkle with green onions.

1 SERVING 451 cal., 34g fat (18g sat. fat), 217mg chol., 843mg sod., 16g carb. (3g sugars, 1g fiber), 19g pro.

AMISH BREAKFAST CASSEROLE

We enjoyed hearty breakfast casseroles during a visit to an Amish inn. When I asked for a recipe, one of the women told me the ingredients right off the top of her head. I modified it a bit to create this version, which my family loves. Try breakfast sausage in place of bacon.
—Beth Notaro, Kokomo, IN

Prep: 15 min. • **Bake:** 35 min. + standing
Makes: 12 servings

- 1 lb. sliced bacon, diced
- 1 medium sweet onion, chopped
- 6 large eggs, lightly beaten
- 4 cups frozen shredded hash brown potatoes, thawed
- 2 cups shredded cheddar cheese
- 1½ cups 4% cottage cheese
- 1¼ cups shredded Swiss cheese

1. Preheat oven to 350°. In a large skillet, cook bacon and onion over medium heat until bacon is crisp; drain. In a large bowl, combine remaining ingredients; stir in bacon mixture. Transfer to a greased 13x9-in. baking dish.
2. Bake, uncovered, until a knife inserted in the center comes out clean, 35-40 minutes. Let stand 10 minutes before cutting.

1 SERVING 273 cal., 18g fat (10g sat. fat), 153mg chol., 477mg sod., 8g carb. (3g sugars, 1g fiber), 18g pro.

TEST KITCHEN TIP

Create a pretty burst of color and fresh flavor by adding a pinch of minced herbs to the egg mixture. Thyme and parsley are perfect candidates; try 1 tsp. fresh or ¼ tsp. dried thyme.

SALMON QUICHE

Cooking is something that I've always liked doing. I pore over cookbooks the way other people read novels. This recipe came to me from my mother—it's the kind of recipe you request after just one bite. And unlike some quiches, it's very hearty!

—Deanna Baldwin, Bermuda Dunes, CA

Prep: 15 min. • **Bake:** 45 minutes
Makes: 8 servings

- 1 sheet refrigerated pie crust
- 1 medium onion, chopped
- 1 Tbsp. butter
- 2 cups shredded Swiss cheese
- 1 can (14¾ oz.) salmon, drained, flaked and bones removed
- 5 large eggs
- 2 cups half-and-half cream
- ¼ tsp. salt
- Minced fresh parsley, optional

1. Unroll the crust into a 9-in. pie plate. Line unpricked pie crust with a double thickness of heavy-duty foil. Bake at 450° for 8 minutes. Remove foil; bake 5 minutes longer. Cool on a wire rack.
2. In a small skillet, saute onion in butter until tender. Sprinkle cheese in the crust; top with salmon and sauteed onion.
3. In a small bowl, whisk the eggs, half-and-half and salt; pour over salmon mixture. Bake at 350° for 45-50 minutes or until a knife inserted in the center comes out clean. Sprinkle with parsley if desired. Let stand 5 minutes before cutting.

1 PIECE 456 cal., 30g fat (15g sat. fat), 221mg chol., 524mg sod., 17g carb. (4g sugars, 0 fiber), 27g pro.

SALMON QUICHE

APPLE BUTTER BISCUIT BREAKFAST BAKE

My grandmother created this recipe to use up the leftovers from Christmas Eve dinner. By combining the leftover ham and biscuits with her homemade apple butter, milk and eggs, she could serve us all a warm, delicious breakfast and still have enough time to spend with the grandchildren.
—Mary M. Leverette, Columbia, SC

Prep: 30 min. + chilling
Bake: 50 min. + standing
Makes: 12 servings

- 10 leftover biscuits (3-in. diameter)
- ¾ cup apple butter
- 2 cups shredded sharp cheddar cheese
- 1½ cups cubed fully cooked ham
- ¼ cup minced fresh parsley
- 6 large eggs
- 2½ cups 2% milk
- 1 tsp. salt
- ½ tsp. pepper
- ¼ tsp. ground mustard

1. Cut biscuits crosswise in half. Spread apple butter over cut sides of biscuits. Replace tops. Cut each biscuit into quarters; arrange in a single layer in a greased 13x9-in. baking dish. Top with cheese, ham and parsley.
2. In a large bowl, whisk eggs, milk, salt, pepper and mustard. Pour over biscuits. Cover and refrigerate overnight.
3. Preheat oven to 325°. Remove strata from refrigerator while oven heats. Bake, uncovered, until puffed and edges are golden brown, 50-60 minutes. Let stand 10 minutes before cutting.

1 PIECE 331 cal., 15g fat (7g sat. fat), 126mg chol., 976mg sod., 31g carb. (12g sugars, 1g fiber), 16g pro.

HOMEMADE CRANBERRY JUICE

This refreshing and sweet cranberry juice has a mild tartness level. Its jewel red color looks very attractive served in glassware.
—Carol Domes, Whitehorse, YT

Prep: 35 min. + chilling
Makes: 8 servings (2 qt.)

- 2 qt. water
- 8 cups fresh or frozen cranberries
- 1½ cups sugar
- ½ cup lemon juice
- ½ cup orange juice

1. In a Dutch oven or large saucepan, bring water and cranberries to a boil. Reduce heat; cover and simmer until berries begin to pop, 20 minutes.
2. Strain through a fine strainer, pressing mixture with a spoon; discard berries. Return cranberry juice to the pan. Stir in the sugar, lemon juice and orange juice. Bring to a boil; cook and stir until sugar is dissolved.
3. Remove from the heat. Cool. Transfer to a pitcher; cover and refrigerate until chilled.

1 CUP 227 cal., 0 fat (0 sat. fat), 0 chol., 31mg sod., 58g carb. (48g sugars, 0 fiber), 0 pro.

PRETTY PUMPKIN CINNAMON BUNS

I make sticky buns and cinnamon rolls quite often because my husband loves them. One day, I had some fresh pumpkin on hand and decided to try pumpkin cinnamon buns. We loved the results!
—Glenda Joseph, Chambersburg, PA

Prep: 45 min. + rising • **Bake:** 25 min.
Makes: 2 dozen

- 2 Tbsp. active dry yeast
- ½ cup warm water (110° to 115°)
- 4 large eggs, room temperature
- 1 cup shortening
- 1 cup canned pumpkin
- 1 cup warm whole milk (110° to 115°)
- ½ cup sugar
- ½ cup packed brown sugar
- ⅓ cup instant vanilla pudding mix
- ⅓ cup instant butterscotch pudding mix
- 1 tsp. salt
- 8 to 9 cups all-purpose flour

FILLING

- ¼ cup butter, melted
- 1 cup packed brown sugar
- 2 tsp. ground cinnamon

ICING

- 3 Tbsp. water
- 2 Tbsp. butter, softened
- 1 tsp. ground cinnamon
- 2 cups confectioners' sugar
- 1½ tsp. vanilla extract

1. In a large bowl, dissolve yeast in warm water. Add the eggs, shortening, pumpkin, milk, sugars, pudding mixes, salt and 6 cups flour. Beat until smooth. Stir in enough remaining flour to form a soft dough (dough will be sticky).
2. Turn out onto a floured surface; knead until smooth and elastic, 6-8 minutes. Place in a greased bowl, turning once to grease top. Cover and let rise in a warm place until doubled, about 1 hour.
3. Punch dough down; divide in half. Roll each portion into a 12x8-in. rectangle; brush with butter. Combine brown sugar and cinnamon; sprinkle over dough to within ½ in. of edges.
4. Roll up jelly-roll style, starting with a long side; pinch seams to seal. Cut each into 12 slices. Place cut side down in 2 greased 13x9-in. pans. Cover and let rise until doubled, about 30 minutes.
5. Bake at 350° until golden brown, 22-28 minutes. In a small bowl, combine the water, butter and cinnamon. Add the confectioners' sugar and vanilla; beat until smooth. Spread over buns. Serve warm.

1 BUN 399 cal., 13g fat (4g sat. fat), 40mg chol., 188mg sod., 65g carb. (31g sugars, 2g fiber), 6g pro.

PRETTY PUMPKIN CINNAMON BUNS

EGGNOG FRENCH TOAST

This recipe is a favorite of our family not only at Christmas but at any time of the year. We especially like to prepare it when we go camping. It makes a hearty breakfast.
—Robert Northrup, Las Cruces, NM

Prep: 10 min. • **Cook:** 30 min.
Makes: 8 servings

- 8 large eggs
- 2 cups eggnog
- ¼ cup sugar
- ½ tsp. vanilla or imitation rum extract
- 24 slices English muffin bread
- Confectioners' sugar, optional
- Maple syrup

In a bowl, beat eggs, eggnog, sugar and extract; soak bread for 2 minutes per side. Cook on a greased hot griddle until golden brown on both sides and cooked through. Dust with confectioners' sugar if desired. Serve with syrup.

3 PIECES 541 cal., 10g fat (4g sat. fat), 223mg chol., 832mg sod., 87g carb. (18g sugars, 6g fiber), 24g pro.

EGGS BENEDICT CASSEROLE

Here's a casserole that delivers all the flavor of eggs Benedict without the hassle. Simply assemble the ingredients ahead and bake it the next morning.
—Sandie Heindel, Liberty, MO

Prep: 25 min. + chilling • **Bake:** 45 min.
Makes: 12 servings (1⅔ cups sauce)

- 12 oz. Canadian bacon, chopped
- 6 English muffins, split and cut into 1-in. pieces
- 8 large eggs
- 2 cups 2% milk
- 1 tsp. onion powder
- ¼ tsp. paprika

HOLLANDAISE SAUCE

- 4 large egg yolks, room temperature
- ½ cup heavy whipping cream
- 2 Tbsp. lemon juice
- 1 tsp. Dijon mustard
- ½ cup butter, melted
- Minced chives, optional

1. Place half the bacon in a greased 3-qt. or 13x9-in. baking dish; top with English muffin pieces and remaining bacon. In a large bowl, whisk eggs, milk and onion powder; pour over the top. Refrigerate, covered, overnight.
2. Preheat oven to 375°. Remove the casserole from refrigerator while oven heats. Sprinkle top with paprika. Bake, covered, 35 minutes. Uncover; bake 10-15 minutes longer or until a knife inserted in the center comes out clean.
3. For sauce, in top of a double boiler or a metal bowl over simmering water, whisk egg yolks, heavy cream, lemon juice and mustard until blended; cook until mixture is just thick enough to coat a metal spoon and temperature reaches 160°, whisking constantly. Reduce heat to very low. Slowly drizzle in melted butter, whisking constantly. Serve immediately with casserole. If desired, sprinkle with chives.

1 PIECE WITH ABOUT 2 TBSP. SAUCE 286 cal., 19g fat (10g sat. fat), 256mg chol., 535mg sod., 16g carb. (4g sugars, 1g fiber), 14g pro.

BLUEBERRY PAN-CAKE WITH MAPLE FROSTING

Here's your excuse to have cake for breakfast. The batter is made with pancake mix!
—Matthew Hass, Ellison Bay, WI

Prep: 10 min. • **Bake:** 15 min. + cooling
Makes: 12 servings

- 3 cups complete buttermilk pancake mix
- 1¾ cups water
- 1 cup fresh blueberries
- 2 tsp. all-purpose flour

FROSTING

- 2 cups confectioners' sugar
- ⅓ cup maple syrup
- ¼ cup butter, softened

1. Preheat oven to 350°. Stir pancake mix and water just until moistened. In another bowl, toss blueberries with flour. Fold into batter.
2. Transfer to a greased 13x9-in. baking pan. Bake until a toothpick inserted in center comes out clean, 15-18 minutes. Cool completely in pan on a wire rack.
3. Beat frosting ingredients until smooth; spread over cooled cake.

1 PIECE 257 cal., 5g fat (2g sat. fat), 10mg chol., 449mg sod., 51g carb. (30g sugars, 1g fiber), 3g pro.

COASTAL CAROLINA
MUFFIN-TIN FRITTATAS

COASTAL CAROLINA MUFFIN-TIN FRITTATAS

Incorporating the flavors of a Lowcountry South Carolina crab boil, these tasty frittatas are easy to make and fun to eat. If you have leftover cooked potatoes (roasted or boiled), try dicing them and substituting them for the refrigerated shredded potatoes in this recipe.
—Shannon Kohn, Murrells Inlet, SC

Prep: 15 min. • **Bake:** 30 min.
Makes: 1 dozen

- ½ cup mayonnaise
- 1 Tbsp. lemon juice
- 2 tsp. sugar
- 1 tsp. seafood seasoning
- 1⅓ cups refrigerated shredded hash brown potatoes
- 1 cup smoked sausage, chopped
- 1 can (8 oz.) jumbo lump crabmeat, drained
- ¼ cup chopped roasted sweet red peppers
- 6 large eggs
- ½ cup heavy whipping cream
- 2 tsp. Louisiana-style hot sauce
- ½ tsp. salt
- 6 bacon strips, cooked and crumbled
- ¼ cup thinly sliced green onions

1. Preheat oven to 350°. In a small bowl, combine mayonnaise, lemon juice, sugar and seafood seasoning. Refrigerate until serving.
2. Meanwhile, in a large bowl, combine potatoes, sausage, crabmeat and red peppers. Divide among 12 greased muffin cups. In another large bowl, whisk the eggs, cream, hot sauce and salt. Pour over potato mixture. Top with the bacon.
3. Bake until a knife inserted in center comes out clean, 30-35 minutes. Serve with sauce and green onion.

1 FRITTATA 223 cal., 18g fat (6g sat. fat), 135mg chol., 604mg sod., 5g carb. (2g sugars, 0 fiber), 10g pro.

CHEESE & CRAB BRUNCH BAKE

CHEESE & CRAB BRUNCH BAKE

Who doesn't love an easy, cheesy seafood casserole that can be pulled together in thirty minutes, refrigerated overnight and baked up the next morning?
—Joyce Conway, Westerville, OH

Prep: 30 min. + chilling • **Bake:** 50 min.
Makes: 12 servings

- 2 Tbsp. Dijon mustard
- 6 English muffins, split
- 8 oz. lump crabmeat, drained
- 2 Tbsp. lemon juice
- 2 tsp. grated lemon zest
- 2 cups shredded white cheddar cheese
- 12 large eggs
- 1 cup half-and-half cream
- 1 cup 2% milk
- ½ cup mayonnaise
- 1 tsp. salt
- ½ tsp. cayenne pepper
- ½ tsp. pepper
- 2 cups shredded Swiss cheese
- 1 cup grated Parmesan cheese
- 4 green onions, chopped
- ¼ cup finely chopped sweet red pepper
- ¼ cup finely chopped sweet yellow pepper

1. Spread mustard over bottom half of muffins. Place in a greased 13x9-in. baking dish. Top with crab, lemon juice and zest. Sprinkle with cheddar cheese. Top with muffin tops.
2. In a large bowl, whisk eggs, cream, milk, mayonnaise, salt, cayenne and pepper. Pour over muffins; sprinkle with Swiss cheese, Parmesan cheese, onions and sweet peppers. Cover and refrigerate overnight.
3. Remove from refrigerator 30 minutes before baking. Preheat oven to 375°. Cover and bake 30 minutes. Uncover; bake until set, 20-25 minutes longer. Let stand 5 minutes before serving. If desired, top with additional chopped green onions.

1 SERVING 428 cal., 28g fat (13g sat. fat), 286mg chol., 844mg sod., 18g carb. (4g sugars, 1g fiber), 26g pro.

ITALIAN BRUNCH TORTE

We always pair this impressive layered breakfast bake with a salad of mixed greens and tomato wedges. Served warm or cold, it's one of our most-requested dishes.

—Danny Diamond, Farmington Hills, MI

Prep: 50 min. • **Bake:** 1 hour + standing
Makes: 10 servings

- 2 tubes (8 oz. each) refrigerated crescent rolls, divided
- 1 tsp. olive oil
- 1 pkg. (6 oz.) fresh baby spinach
- 1 cup sliced fresh mushrooms
- 7 large eggs, divided use
- 1 cup grated Parmesan cheese
- 2 tsp. Italian seasoning
- ⅛ tsp. pepper
- ½ lb. thinly sliced deli ham
- ½ lb. thinly sliced hard salami
- ½ lb. sliced provolone cheese
- 2 jars (12 oz. each) roasted sweet red peppers, drained, sliced and patted dry

1. Preheat oven to 350°. Place a greased 9-in. springform pan on a double thickness of heavy-duty foil (about 18 in. square). Securely wrap foil around pan. Unroll 1 tube of crescent dough and separate into triangles. Press onto bottom of prepared pan to form a crust, sealing seams well. Bake until set, 10-15 minutes.
2. Meanwhile, in a large skillet, heat oil over medium-high heat. Add spinach and mushrooms; cook and stir until the mushrooms are tender. Drain on several layers of paper towels, blotting well. In a large bowl, whisk 6 eggs, Parmesan cheese, Italian seasoning and pepper.
3. Layer crust with half each of the following: ham, salami, provolone cheese, red peppers and spinach mixture. Pour half the egg mixture over the top. Repeat layers; top with remaining egg mixture.
4. On a work surface, unroll and separate remaining crescent dough into triangles. Press together to form a circle and seal seams; place over filling. Whisk the remaining egg; brush over the top.
5. Bake, uncovered, until a thermometer reads 160°, 1-1¼ hours, covering loosely with foil if needed to prevent overbrowning. Carefully loosen side from pan with a knife; remove rim from pan. Let stand 20 minutes.

1 PIECE 480 cal., 29g fat (13g sat. fat), 191mg chol., 1674mg sod., 25g carb. (8g sugars, 0 fiber), 26g pro.

BREAKFAST ENCHILADAS

Draped in gooey cheese and a savory sauce, these enchiladas are a popular option at any holiday brunch. Chorizo gives a southwestern kick to the hearty filling.

—Tahnia Fox, Trenton, MI

Prep: 25 min. • **Bake:** 25 min.
Makes: 8 servings

- ½ lb. uncooked chorizo or spicy pork sausage
- 1 small onion, finely chopped
- ½ medium green pepper, finely chopped
- 2 tsp. butter
- 6 large eggs, beaten
- ¾ cup shredded cheddar cheese, divided
- ¾ cup shredded pepper jack cheese, divided
- 1 can (10 oz.) enchilada sauce
- 8 flour tortillas (6 in.), warmed
- 1 green onion, finely chopped

1. Crumble chorizo into a large skillet; add onion and green pepper. Cook over medium heat for 6-8 minutes or until sausage is fully cooked; drain.
2. In another skillet, heat butter over medium heat. Add eggs; cook and stir until almost set. Remove from heat; stir in the chorizo mixture and ⅓ cup each cheddar and pepper jack.
3. Spread ½ cup enchilada sauce into a greased 11x7-in. baking dish. Spoon 3 Tbsp. egg mixture down the center of each tortilla. Roll up and place seam side down in prepared baking dish.
4. Pour remaining enchilada sauce over the top; sprinkle with remaining cheeses.
5. Bake, uncovered, at 350° until heated through, 25-30 minutes. Sprinkle with green onion.

1 ENCHILADA 369 cal., 23g fat (10g sat. fat), 189mg chol., 1028mg sod., 20g carb. (2g sugars, 1g fiber), 20g pro.

BREAKFAST ENCHILADAS

MAIN DISHES

P. 117

P. 120

P. 103

HAM & SWISS CASSEROLE

When I prepare this noodle casserole for church gatherings, it's always a hit. It can easily be doubled or tripled for a crowd.
—Doris Barb, El Dorado, KS

Prep: 15 min. • **Bake:** 40 min.
Makes: 8 servings

- 1 pkg. (8 oz.) egg noodles, cooked and drained
- 2 cups cubed fully cooked ham
- 2 cups shredded Swiss cheese
- 1 can (10¾ oz.) condensed cream of celery soup, undiluted
- 1 cup sour cream
- ½ cup chopped green pepper
- ½ cup chopped onion

1. In a greased 13x9-in. baking dish, layer half each of the noodles, ham and cheese.
2. In a large bowl, combine the soup, sour cream, green pepper and onion; spread half over the top. Repeat layers. Bake, uncovered, at 350° for 40-45 minutes or until heated through.

1 SERVING 360 cal., 18g fat (10g sat. fat), 92mg chol., 815mg sod., 27g carb. (4g sugars, 1g fiber), 20g pro.

MA

GRILLED HULI HULI CHICKEN

When I lived in Hawaii, a friend shared this recipe for chicken marinated in a ginger-soy sauce. Huli means turn in Hawaiian and refers to turning the meat on the grill.
—Sharon Boling, San Diego, CA

Prep: 15 min. + marinating • **Grill:** 15 min.
Makes: 12 servings

- 1 cup packed brown sugar
- ¾ cup ketchup
- ¾ cup reduced-sodium soy sauce
- ⅓ cup chicken broth
- 2½ tsp. minced fresh gingerroot
- 1½ tsp. minced garlic
- 24 boneless skinless chicken thighs (about 6 lbs.)

1. In a small bowl, combine the first 6 ingredients. Reserve 1⅓ cups for basting; cover and refrigerate. Divide remaining marinade between 2 large shallow dishes. Add 12 chicken thighs to each; turn to coat. Refrigerate, covered, for 8 hours or overnight.
2. Drain chicken, discarding marinade.
3. Grill chicken, covered, on an oiled rack over medium heat for 6-8 minutes on each side or until a thermometer inserted into chicken reads 170°; baste occasionally with reserved marinade during last 5 minutes.

2 CHICKEN THIGHS 391 cal., 16g fat (5g sat. fat), 151mg chol., 651mg sod., 15g carb. (14g sugars, 0 fiber), 43g pro.

READER RAVES

"Amazing recipe. So easy to prepare and wonderful flavor. My family loved it and I can't wait to make it again."

—J-JAN, TASTEOFHOME.COM

STUFFED PASTA SHELLS

STUFFED PASTA SHELLS

These savory shells never fail to make a big impression, even though the recipe is easy. One or two of the shells makes a perfect individual serving at a potluck, so a single batch goes a long way.

—Jena Coffey, St. Louis, MO

Prep: 15 min. • **Bake:** 30 min.
Makes: 12 servings

- 4 cups shredded mozzarella cheese
- 1 carton (15 oz.) ricotta cheese
- 1 pkg. (10 oz.) frozen chopped spinach, thawed and squeezed dry
- ½ tsp. dried basil
- ½ tsp. dried oregano
- ½ tsp. salt
- ¼ tsp. pepper
- ¼ tsp. crushed red pepper flakes, optional
- 1 pkg. (12 oz.) jumbo pasta shells, cooked and drained
- 3½ cups spaghetti sauce
- Optional: grated Parmesan cheese

Preheat oven to 350°. In a large bowl, combine mozzarella, ricotta, spinach, basil, oregano, salt, pepper and, if desired, crushed red pepper flakes; stuff into shells. Arrange in a greased 13x9-in. baking dish. Pour spaghetti sauce over the shells. Cover and bake until heated through, 30-45 minutes. If desired, sprinkle with Parmesan cheese just before serving.

1 SERVING 314 cal., 13g fat (7g sat. fat), 44mg chol., 576mg sod., 32g carb. (9g sugars, 3g fiber), 18g pro.

ROAST PORK WITH APPLES & ONIONS

The sweetness of the apples and onions nicely complements the roast pork. With its crisp exterior and melt-in-your-mouth flavor, this is my family's favorite weekend dinner.

—Lily Julow, Lawrenceville, GA

Prep: 30 min. • **Bake:** 45 min. + standing
Makes: 8 servings

- 1 boneless pork loin roast (2 lbs.)
- ¼ tsp. salt
- ¼ tsp. pepper
- 1 Tbsp. olive oil
- 3 large Golden Delicious apples, cut into 1-in. wedges
- 2 large onions, cut into ¾-in. wedges
- 5 garlic cloves, peeled
- 1 Tbsp. minced fresh rosemary or 1 tsp. dried rosemary, crushed

1. Preheat oven to 350°. Sprinkle roast with salt and pepper. In a large nonstick skillet, heat oil over medium heat; brown roast on all sides. Transfer to a roasting pan coated with cooking spray. Place apples, onions and garlic around roast; sprinkle with rosemary.
2. Roast until a thermometer inserted in pork reads 145°, 45-55 minutes, turning apples, onion and garlic once. Remove from oven; tent with foil. Let stand 10 minutes before slicing roast. Serve with apple mixture.

1 SERVING 210 cal., 7g fat (2g sat. fat), 57mg chol., 109mg sod., 14g carb. (9g sugars, 2g fiber), 23g pro.

READER RAVES

"This was fabulous. Pork was tender and juicy, and apples and onions were just right. I'll make this again."

—EUROTAHNY, TASTEOFHOME.COM

ROAST PORK WITH APPLES & ONIONS

SICILIAN PIZZA (SFINCIONE)

My favorite pizza from childhood is still my favorite today. The crunchy bread-crumb topping sets it apart from its American counterpart. I like to top this pie with torn fresh basil.

—Susan Falk, Sterling Heights, MI

Prep: 20 min. • **Bake:** 20 min.
Makes: 12 servings

- 2 loaves (1 lb. each) fresh or frozen pizza dough, thawed
- 3 Tbsp. olive oil, divided
- 1 can (28 oz.) whole tomatoes, drained and crushed
- 1 medium onion, finely chopped
- 1 can (2 oz.) anchovy fillets, drained and broken into ¼-in. pieces
- 1 cup shredded mozzarella cheese
- ½ cup soft bread crumbs
- Fresh torn basil leaves

1. Preheat oven to 425°. Grease a 15x10x1-in. baking pan. Press dough to fit bottom and ½ in. up sides of pan. Brush with 2 Tbsp. oil; top with tomatoes, onion and anchovies. Sprinkle with mozzarella. Combine bread crumbs and remaining 1 Tbsp. oil; sprinkle over pizza.
2. Bake on a lower oven rack until edges are golden brown and cheese is melted, 20-25 minutes. Sprinkle with basil before serving.

1 PIECE 277 cal., 9g fat (2g sat. fat), 11mg chol., 527mg sod., 38g carb. (4g sugars, 3g fiber), 11g pro.

SICILIAN PIZZA (SFINCIONE)

GRILLED CHICKEN RAMEN SALAD

GRILLED CHICKEN RAMEN SALAD

This is one of those recipes that I love because it's pretty much a complete meal in one bowl, and when it goes on the table, everyone says, "Yeah!"
—Karen Carlson, San Luis Obispo, CA

Takes: 30 min. • **Makes:** 8 servings

- 2 Tbsp. canola oil
- 2 pkg. (3 oz. each) ramen noodles, crumbled
- ⅔ cup canola oil
- 2 tsp. sesame oil
- ⅓ cup seasoned rice vinegar
- 1 Tbsp. sugar
- 2 Tbsp. reduced-sodium soy sauce
- 1½ lbs. boneless skinless chicken breast halves
- ½ tsp. pepper
- ¼ tsp. salt
- 1 pkg. (14 oz.) coleslaw mix
- ½ cup minced fresh cilantro
- 3 cups fresh snow peas, thinly sliced lengthwise
- 2 cups shredded carrots
- 4 cups torn mixed salad greens
- 3 thinly sliced green onions
- ⅓ cup crumbled cooked bacon, optional

1. In a large saucepan, heat oil over medium-low heat. Add ramen noodles; cook and stir until toasted, 5-8 minutes. Remove from pan.
2. In a small bowl, whisk oils, vinegar, sugar and soy sauce until blended.
3. Sprinkle chicken with pepper and salt. Place chicken on a lightly oiled grill rack. Grill, covered, over medium heat, or broil 4-5 in. from heat until a thermometer reads 165°, 8-10 minutes on each side. Cool slightly and chop into ½-in. pieces.
4. In a large bowl, combine coleslaw mix and cilantro. Layer coleslaw mixture, peas, chicken, carrots, salad greens, noodles and green onions in an 8- to 10-qt. dish. Sprinkle with bacon; serve with vinaigrette.

1 SERVING 458 cal., 29g fat (4g sat. fat), 47mg chol., 738mg sod., 28g carb. (10g sugars, 4g fiber), 22g pro.

SWEET HORSERADISH GLAZED RIBS

If you like to prep ahead of camping, roast these ribs, wrap them and finish with a sweet, savory sauce at your campfire or grill.
—Ralph Jones, San Diego, CA

Prep: 10 min. + chilling • **Cook:** 2¼ hours
Makes: 8 servings

- 3 racks pork baby back ribs (about 8 lbs.)
- 1½ tsp. salt, divided
- 1½ tsp. coarsely ground pepper, divided
- 3 cups unsweetened apple juice
- 1 jar (12 oz.) apricot preserves
- ¼ cup prepared horseradish, drained
- 2 Tbsp. honey or maple syrup
- 1 tsp. liquid smoke, optional

1. Preheat oven to 325°. If necessary, remove thin membrane from ribs and discard. Sprinkle 1 tsp. each salt and pepper over ribs. Transfer to a large shallow roasting pan, bone side down; add juice. Bake, covered, until tender, 2-3 hours.
2. Meanwhile, puree the preserves, horseradish, honey, remaining ½ tsp. salt and ½ tsp. pepper and, if desired, liquid smoke in a blender.
3. Drain ribs. Place 1 rib rack on a large piece of aluminum foil. Brush with apricot-horseradish mixture; wrap tightly. Repeat with remaining ribs. Refrigerate up to 2 days.
4. Prepare campfire or grill for medium heat. Remove ribs from foil; grill until browned, 10-15 minutes, turning occasionally.

1 SERVING 690 cal., 42g fat (15g sat. fat), 163mg chol., 674mg sod., 33g carb. (23g sugars, 0 fiber), 45g pro.

KENTUCKY HOT BROWN SLIDERS

I transformed the Hot Brown sandwich, traditionally open-faced, into a party-ready slider. Just cover and refrigerate the assembled sandwiches so you can pop them in the oven when company arrives.

—Blair Lonergan, Rochelle, VA

Prep: 20 min. • **Bake:** 30 min.
Makes: 12 servings

- 1 pkg. (12 oz.) Hawaiian sweet rolls
- 3 Tbsp. mayonnaise
- 12 slices deli turkey, folded into quarters
- 12 slices cooked bacon strips, halved widthwise
- 1 jar (4 oz.) diced pimientos, drained, or 2 plum tomatoes, cut into 12 slices
- 6 slices Gruyere cheese, halved
- ¼ cup grated Parmesan cheese
- ½ cup butter, cubed
- 2 Tbsp. finely chopped onion
- 2 Tbsp. brown sugar
- 1½ tsp. Worcestershire sauce
- ¼ tsp. garlic powder

1. Preheat oven to 350°. Without separating rolls, cut in half horizontally; arrange bottom halves in a greased 11x7-in. baking pan. Spread mayonnaise evenly across the bottom halves. Top each with turkey, bacon, pimientos, Gruyere and Parmesan cheese. Replace top halves of rolls.
2. In a small skillet, melt butter over medium heat. Add onion; cook and stir until tender, 1-2 minutes. Whisk in brown sugar, Worcestershire sauce and garlic powder. Cook and stir until sugar is dissolved; drizzle over sandwiches.
3. Cover and bake 25 minutes. Uncover and bake until golden brown, 5-10 minutes longer.

1 SLIDER 327 cal., 21g fat (10g sat. fat), 67mg chol., 652mg sod., 20g carb. (9g sugars, 1g fiber), 16g pro.

KENTUCKY HOT BROWN SLIDERS

GRILLED RIBEYES WITH BLUE CHEESE BUTTER

Fire up the grill for steaks that practically melt in your mouth. They're garlic-infused, and the grilled flavor is off the charts. With this recipe on hand, any menu is sure to sizzle!
—Mona Engelbrecht, Wichita, KS

Takes: 25 min. • **Makes:** 8 servings

- 8 beef ribeye steaks (10 oz. each)
- 12 garlic cloves, sliced
- ¼ cup olive oil
- 1 tsp. salt
- ¾ tsp. cayenne pepper
- ½ tsp. pepper
- ½ cup crumbled blue cheese
- ¼ cup butter, softened

1. Cut slits into each steak; insert garlic slices. Brush with oil and sprinkle with salt, cayenne and pepper.
2. Grill, covered, over medium heat or broil 4 in. from the heat for 4-6 minutes on each side or until meat reaches desired doneness (for medium-rare, a thermometer should read 135°; medium, 140°; medium-well, 145°).
3. Combine blue cheese and butter. Serve with steaks.

1 STEAK WITH 1 TBSP. BUTTER MIXTURE
766 cal., 60g fat (24g sat. fat), 189mg chol., 567mg sod., 2g carb. (0 sugars, 0 fiber), 52g pro.

DIJON-RUBBED PORK WITH RHUBARB SAUCE

This moist and tender pork loin roast is served with a rhubarb sauce that's just delicious! It's great for company and makes an extra-special weeknight meal.
—Marilyn Rodriguez, Sparks, NV

Prep: 15 min. • **Bake:** 1 hour + standing
Makes: 12 servings (1½ cups sauce)

- 1 boneless pork loin roast (3 lbs.)
- ¼ cup Dijon mustard
- 6 garlic cloves, minced
- 1 Tbsp. minced fresh rosemary or 1 tsp. dried rosemary, crushed
- ¾ tsp. salt
- ½ tsp. pepper

SAUCE

- 3 cups sliced fresh or frozen rhubarb
- ⅓ cup orange juice
- ⅓ cup sugar
- 1 Tbsp. cider vinegar

1. Score the surface of the pork, making diamond shapes ¼ in. deep. In a small bowl, combine the mustard, garlic, rosemary, salt and pepper; rub mixture over pork.
2. Coat a roasting pan and rack with cooking spray; place pork on rack in pan. Bake, uncovered, at 350° for 1 hour or until a thermometer reads 145°. Let stand for 10 minutes before slicing.
3. Meanwhile, in a small saucepan, bring the sauce ingredients to a boil. Reduce heat; cover and simmer for 8-12 minutes or until rhubarb is tender. Serve warm, with pork.

NOTE If using frozen rhubarb, measure rhubarb while still frozen, then thaw completely. Drain in a colander, but do not press liquid out.

3 OZ. COOKED PORK WITH 2 TBSP. SAUCE
181 cal., 6g fat (2g sat. fat), 56mg chol., 308mg sod., 9g carb. (7g sugars, 1g fiber), 23g pro.

SPAGHETTI MEATBALL BAKE

SPAGHETTI MEATBALL BAKE

On some nights, we're in the mood for pasta—and it seems nothing else will do!
—Kimberly Forni, Laconia, NH

Prep: 45 min. • **Bake:** 30 min.
Makes: 10 servings

- 1½ cups dry bread crumbs, divided
- 3 large eggs, lightly beaten
- 1½ cups cooked spaghetti (3 oz. uncooked), coarsely chopped
- 2 garlic cloves, minced
- 2 tsp. dried basil
- ¾ tsp. salt
- 1 tsp. dried oregano
- 1 tsp. pepper
- 2 lbs. ground beef

SAUCE

- 2 jars (24 oz. each) meatless pasta sauce
- 1 small onion, finely chopped
- 2 garlic cloves, minced
- 2 tsp. dried basil
- 1 tsp. dried oregano
- 2 cups shredded part-skim mozzarella cheese
- Optional: Additional hot cooked spaghetti for serving

1. Preheat oven to 375°. Place 1 cup bread crumbs in a shallow bowl. In a large bowl, combine eggs, chopped spaghetti, garlic, seasonings and remaining bread crumbs. Add beef; mix lightly but thoroughly. Shape into 1½-in. balls.
2. Roll meatballs in bread crumbs; place in a greased 13x9-in. baking dish. Bake 15-20 minutes or until cooked through.
3. In a large saucepan, combine pasta sauce, onion, garlic and seasonings; bring to a boil over medium heat, stirring occasionally. Pour over meatballs; sprinkle with cheese. Bake 15-20 minutes longer or until cheese is lightly browned.

4 MEATBALLS WITH ½ CUP SAUCE 390 cal., 17g fat (7g sat. fat), 124mg chol., 1074mg sod., 29g carb. (10g sugars, 3g fiber), 29g pro.

POMEGRANATE, CHICKEN & FARRO SALAD

This salad recipe is special—simple, yet sophisticated—and never fails to win rave reviews. I use quick-cooking farro, which takes only 10 minutes on the stovetop. Many stores now carry packaged pomegranate seeds in the refrigerated section year-round.
—David Dahlman, Chatsworth, CA

Prep: 15 min. • **Cook:** 25 min. + cooling
Makes: 8 servings

- 1½ cups uncooked farro, rinsed, or wheat berries
- 2 medium ripe avocados, peeled, pitted and chopped
- 3 cups shredded rotisserie chicken
- ¾ cup chopped dried apricots
- ½ cup thinly sliced green onions
- ½ cup chopped walnuts, toasted
- 1 Tbsp. chopped seeded jalapeno pepper, optional
- ¾ cup pomegranate seeds
- ⅓ cup olive oil
- ¼ cup orange juice
- 3 Tbsp. white wine vinegar
- 1 Tbsp. Dijon mustard
- ½ tsp. salt
- ½ tsp. pepper

1. Place farro in a large saucepan; add water to cover. Bring to a boil. Reduce heat; cook, covered, until tender, 25-30 minutes. Drain and cool.
2. Arrange farro, avocados, chicken, apricots, green onions, walnuts and, if desired, jalapeno on a platter. Sprinkle with pomegranate seeds. For dressing, in a small bowl, whisk the remaining ingredients until blended. Serve dressing with salad.

NOTE Wear disposable gloves when cutting hot peppers; the oils can burn skin. Avoid touching your face.

1 SERVING 482 cal., 24g fat (3g sat. fat), 47mg chol., 251mg sod., 44g carb. (9g sugars, 9g fiber), 23g pro.

POMEGRANATE, CHICKEN & FARRO SALAD

COMPANY MAC & CHEESE

I'm not usually a fan of homemade macaroni and cheese, but when a friend served this, I had to have the recipe. This is by far the creamiest, tastiest and most special macaroni and cheese I have ever tried. Simple to make and well received, it's a terrific potluck dish.

—Catherine Ogden, Middlegrove, NY

Takes: 30 min. • **Makes:** 8 servings

- 1¾ cups uncooked elbow macaroni
- 6 Tbsp. butter, divided
- 3 Tbsp. all-purpose flour
- 2 cups whole milk
- 1 pkg. (8 oz.) cream cheese, cubed
- 2 cups shredded cheddar cheese
- 2 tsp. spicy brown mustard
- ½ tsp. salt
- ¼ tsp. pepper
- ¾ cup dry bread crumbs
- 2 Tbsp. minced fresh parsley

1. Preheat oven to 400°. Cook macaroni according to package directions. Meanwhile, melt 4 Tbsp. butter in a large saucepan. Stir in flour until smooth. Gradually add milk. Bring to a boil; cook and stir for 2 minutes.

2. Reduce heat; add cheeses, mustard, salt and pepper. Stir until cheese is melted and sauce is smooth. Drain macaroni; add to cheese sauce and stir to coat.

3. Transfer to a greased shallow 3-qt. or 13x9-in. baking dish. Melt remaining 2 Tbsp. butter; toss with bread crumbs and parsley. Sprinkle over macaroni. Bake, uncovered, until golden brown, 15-20 minutes.

1 CUP 468 cal., 31g fat (18g sat. fat), 86mg chol., 604mg sod., 33g carb. (6g sugars, 1g fiber), 15g pro.

COMPANY MAC & CHEESE

BUFFALO CHICKEN LASAGNA

BUFFALO CHICKEN LASAGNA

This lasagna recipe was inspired by my daughter's favorite food—Buffalo wings! It tastes just as though it came from a restaurant.
—Melissa Millwood, Lyman, SC

Prep: 1½ hours • **Bake:** 40 min. + standing
Makes: 12 servings

- 1 Tbsp. canola oil
- 1½ lbs. ground chicken
- 1 small onion, chopped
- 1 celery rib, finely chopped
- 1 large carrot, grated
- 2 garlic cloves, minced
- 1 can (14½ oz.) diced tomatoes, drained
- 1 bottle (12 oz.) Buffalo wing sauce
- ½ cup water
- 1½ tsp. Italian seasoning
- ½ tsp. salt
- ¼ tsp. pepper
- 9 lasagna noodles
- 1 carton (15 oz.) ricotta cheese
- 1¾ cups crumbled blue cheese, divided
- ½ cup minced Italian flat-leaf parsley
- 1 large egg, lightly beaten
- 3 cups shredded part-skim mozzarella cheese
- 2 cups shredded white cheddar cheese

1. In a Dutch oven, heat oil over medium heat. Add chicken, onion, celery and carrot; cook and stir until meat is no longer pink and vegetables are tender. Add garlic; cook 2 minutes longer. Stir in tomatoes, wing sauce, water, Italian seasoning, salt and pepper; bring to a boil. Reduce heat; cover and simmer 1 hour.
2. Meanwhile, cook noodles according to package directions; drain. In a small bowl, mix the ricotta cheese, ¾ cup blue cheese, parsley and egg. Preheat oven to 350°.
3. Spread 1½ cups sauce in a greased 13x9-in. baking dish. Layer with 3 noodles, 1½ cups sauce, ⅔ cup ricotta mixture, 1 cup mozzarella cheese, ⅔ cup cheddar cheese and ⅓ cup blue cheese. Repeat layers twice.
4. Bake, covered, 20 minutes. Uncover; bake until bubbly and cheese is melted, 20-25 minutes. Let stand 10 minutes before serving.

1 PIECE 466 cal., 28g fat (15g sat. fat), 124mg chol., 1680mg sod., 22g carb. (6g sugars, 2g fiber), 33g pro.

TEST KITCHEN TIP

If you're looking to tone down the heat, reduce the Buffalo wing sauce to 4 oz. (about half a cup) and add an 8-oz. can of tomato sauce.

MOUSSAKA

Moussaka is traditionally made with lamb, but I often use ground beef instead. The recipe looks a bit daunting, but if you prepare one step while working on another, it will save time.
—Kim Powell, Knoxville, TN

Prep: 45 min. • **Bake:** 30 min. + standing
Makes: 8 servings

- 3 medium potatoes, peeled and cut into ¼-in. slices
- 1 medium eggplant, cut into ½-in. slices
- 1½ lbs. ground lamb or ground beef
- 1 small onion, chopped
- 2 garlic cloves, minced
- 2 plum tomatoes, chopped
- 1¼ cups hot water
- 1 can (6 oz.) tomato paste
- 1¼ tsp. salt, divided
- ½ tsp. dried oregano
- ½ tsp. paprika
- ½ tsp. ground cinnamon
- ½ tsp. ground nutmeg, divided
- 3 Tbsp. butter
- ¼ cup all-purpose flour
- 4 cups 2% milk
- 2 cups shredded mozzarella cheese

1. Preheat oven to 450°. Arrange potato slices in a greased 15x10x1-in. baking pan, overlapping as needed. Arrange eggplant slices similarly in another greased 15x10x1-in. baking pan. Bake both until parcooked, about 20 minutes; set aside. Reduce oven setting to 400°.
2. In a large skillet, cook lamb, onion and garlic over medium heat until meat is no longer pink, 7-9 minutes, breaking into crumbles; drain. Stir in tomatoes, water, tomato paste, ¼ tsp. salt, oregano, paprika, cinnamon and ¼ tsp. nutmeg. Bring to a boil. Reduce heat; simmer, uncovered, 5 minutes.
3. In a large saucepan, melt butter over medium heat. Stir in flour until smooth; gradually whisk in milk. Bring to a boil, stirring constantly; cook and stir until thickened, 2-3 minutes. Stir in remaining 1 tsp. salt and ¼ tsp. nutmeg.
4. Arrange parcooked potato slices in a greased 13x9-in. baking dish, overlapping as needed. Top with lamb mixture. Arrange eggplant over top, overlapping as needed.
5. Top with bechamel sauce. Sprinkle with mozzarella cheese. Bake, uncovered, until bubbly and golden brown, about 30 minutes. Let stand 20 minutes before serving.

1 SERVING 453 cal., 25g fat (13g sat. fat), 99mg chol., 700mg sod., 30g carb. (12g sugars, 4g fiber), 28g pro.

CUT IT RIGHT

For this moussaka recipe, we recommend cutting eggplant lengthwise into ½-in. pieces.

BIG JOHN'S CHILI-RUBBED RIBS

BIG JOHN'S CHILI-RUBBED RIBS

When my family thinks of summer grilling, it's ribs all the way. Our Asian-inspired recipe is a welcome change from the usual barbecue-sauce versions.
—Ginger Sullivan, Cutler Bay, FL

Prep: 20 min. + chilling • **Grill:** 1½ hours
Makes: 10 servings

- 3 Tbsp. packed brown sugar
- 2 Tbsp. paprika
- 2 Tbsp. chili powder
- 3 tsp. ground cumin
- 2 tsp. garlic powder
- 1 tsp. salt
- 6 lbs. pork baby back ribs

GLAZE

- 1 cup reduced-sodium soy sauce
- 1 cup packed brown sugar
- ⅔ cup ketchup
- ⅓ cup lemon juice
- 1½ tsp. minced fresh gingerroot
- Chopped fresh parsley, optional

1. Mix the first 6 ingredients; rub over ribs. Refrigerate, covered, 30 minutes.
2. Wrap rib racks in large pieces of heavy-duty foil; seal tightly. Grill, covered, over indirect medium heat until tender, 1 to 1½ hours.
3. In a large saucepan, combine glaze ingredients; cook, uncovered, over medium heat until heated through and sugar is dissolved, 6-8 minutes, stirring occasionally.
4. Carefully remove ribs from foil. Place ribs over direct heat; brush with some of the glaze. Grill, covered, over medium heat until browned, 25-30 minutes, turning and brushing ribs occasionally with remaining glaze. If desired, sprinkle with parsley just before serving.

1 SERVING 406 cal., 26g fat (9g sat. fat), 98mg chol., 1543mg sod., 34g carb. (30g sugars, 1g fiber), 29g pro.

SAVORY RUBBED ROAST CHICKEN

SAVORY RUBBED ROAST CHICKEN

A blend of paprika, onion powder, garlic and cayenne creates a delicious, slightly spicy roast chicken. The aroma of this dish while it's cooking drives my family nuts!
—Margaret Cole, Imperial, MO

Prep: 20 min. • **Bake:** 2 hours + standing
Makes: 12 servings

- 2 tsp. paprika
- 1 tsp. salt
- 1 tsp. onion powder
- 1 tsp. white pepper
- 1 tsp. cayenne pepper
- 1 tsp. dried thyme
- ¾ tsp. garlic powder
- ½ tsp. pepper
- 1 roasting chicken (6 to 7 lbs.)
- 1 large onion, cut into wedges

1. Preheat oven to 350°. In a small bowl, mix the first 8 ingredients.
2. Pat chicken dry and place on a rack in a roasting pan, breast side up. Rub seasoning mixture over the outside and inside of chicken. Place onion inside cavity. Tuck wings under chicken; tie drumsticks together.
3. Roast 2 to 2½ hours or until a thermometer inserted in thickest part of thigh reads 170°-175°. (Cover loosely with foil if chicken browns too quickly.) Remove chicken from oven; tent with foil. Let stand 15 minutes before carving.

4 OZ. COOKED CHICKEN 272 cal., 16g fat (4g sat. fat), 90mg chol., 284mg sod., 2g carb. (1g sugars, 1g fiber), 29g pro.

BACON CHEESEBURGER SLOPPY JOES

My family doesn't even like sloppy joes. But we are big fans of this recipe. Win!
—Janine Smith, Columbia, SC

Takes: 25 min. • **Makes:** 8 servings

- 1½ lbs. ground turkey
- 1 large red onion, finely chopped
- 12 bacon strips, cooked and crumbled
- 2 medium tomatoes, chopped
- ¾ cup ketchup
- ½ cup chopped dill pickles
- 2 Tbsp. yellow mustard
- 1½ cups shredded cheddar cheese
- 8 hamburger buns, split

1. In a large skillet, cook turkey with onion over medium heat until turkey is no longer pink, 6-8 minutes, crumbling meat. Stir in bacon, tomatoes, ketchup, pickles and mustard; heat through.
2. Stir in cheese until melted. Spoon meat mixture onto bun bottoms. Replace tops.

1 SANDWICH 431 cal., 20g fat (8g sat. fat), 90mg chol., 1022mg sod., 32g carb. (11g sugars, 2g fiber), 31g pro.

SLOW COOKER SWITCH

It's easy to make cheeseburger sloppy joes in the slow cooker as well! Simply follow step 1 of the recipe, stir in the cheese, then transfer the mixture to a 3-qt. slow cooker. Cover and cook on low for 4 to 5 hours, or until the flavors are blended. Spoon onto buns and enjoy!

BACON CHEESEBURGER SLOPPY JOES

MA

MEATY PASTA CASSEROLES

I love this recipe because it makes not one but two hearty casseroles. I add a little something different every time I make it, such as extra garlic, to give it an added boost of flavor.
—Debra Butcher, Decatur, IN

Prep: 45 min. • **Bake:** 35 min.
Makes: 2 casseroles (6 servings each)

- 1 pkg. (16 oz.) penne pasta
- 1 lb. ground beef
- 1 lb. bulk Italian pork sausage
- 1¾ cups sliced fresh mushrooms
- 1 medium onion, chopped
- 1 medium green pepper, chopped
- 2 cans (14½ oz. each) Italian diced tomatoes
- 1 jar (23½ oz.) Italian sausage and garlic spaghetti sauce
- 1 jar (16 oz.) chunky mild salsa
- 1 pkg. (8 oz.) sliced pepperoni, chopped
- 1 cup shredded Swiss cheese, divided
- 4 cups shredded part-skim mozzarella cheese, divided
- 1½ cups shredded Parmesan cheese, divided
- 1 jar (24 oz.) 3-cheese spaghetti sauce

1. Cook pasta according to package directions. Meanwhile, in a Dutch oven, cook beef, sausage, mushrooms, onion and green pepper over medium heat until meat is no longer pink, breaking meat into crumbles; drain.
2. Drain pasta; add to the meat mixture. Stir in the tomatoes, spaghetti sauce, salsa and pepperoni.
3. Preheat oven to 350°. Divide half of the pasta mixture between 2 greased 13x9-in. baking dishes. Sprinkle each with ¼ cup Swiss cheese, 1 cup mozzarella cheese and ⅓ cup Parmesan cheese. Spread ¾ cup of the 3-cheese spaghetti sauce over each. Top with remaining pasta mixture and 3-cheese spaghetti sauce. Sprinkle with remaining cheeses.
4. Cover and bake until bubbly, about 25 minutes. Uncover; bake until cheese is melted, about 10 minutes longer.

FREEZE OPTION Cover unbaked casserole and freeze for up to 3 months. To use, thaw in refrigerator overnight. Remove from refrigerator 30 minutes before baking. Preheat oven to 350°. Bake casserole, covered, 45 minutes. Uncover; bake 10 minutes or until cheese is melted.

1½ CUPS 708 cal., 38g fat (16g sat. fat), 106mg chol., 1788mg sod., 54g carb. (18g sugars, 5g fiber), 38g pro.

MEATY PASTA CASSEROLES

ENCHILADA CASSER-OLE!

ENCHILADA CASSER-OLE!

My husband loves this casserole, so it never lasts too long in our house. Packed with black beans, cheese, tomatoes and southwestern flavor, it's an impressive-looking entree that's as simple as it is delicious.
—*Marsha Wills, Homosassa, FL*

Prep: 25 min. • **Bake:** 30 min.
Makes: 8 servings

- 1 lb. lean ground beef (90% lean)
- 1 large onion, chopped
- 2 cups salsa
- 1 can (15 oz.) black beans, rinsed and drained
- ¼ cup reduced-fat Italian salad dressing
- 2 Tbsp. reduced-sodium taco seasoning
- ¼ tsp. ground cumin
- 6 flour tortillas (8 in.)
- ¾ cup reduced-fat sour cream
- 1 cup shredded reduced-fat Mexican cheese blend
- 1 cup shredded lettuce
- 1 medium tomato, chopped
- ¼ cup minced fresh cilantro

1. In a large skillet, cook beef and onion over medium heat until meat is no longer pink, breaking it into crumbles; drain. Stir in the salsa, beans, dressing, taco seasoning and cumin. Place 3 tortillas in an 11x7-in. baking dish coated with cooking spray. Layer with half of the meat mixture, 6 Tbsp. sour cream and ½ cup cheese. Repeat layers.
2. Cover and bake at 400° for 25 minutes. Uncover; bake until heated through, 5-10 minutes longer. Let stand for 5 minutes; top with lettuce, tomato and cilantro.

1 PIECE 357 cal., 12g fat (5g sat. fat), 45mg chol., 864mg sod., 37g carb. (6g sugars, 3g fiber), 23g pro.

BUTTERY GRILLED SHRIMP

BUTTERY GRILLED SHRIMP

This is easy and delicious! These shrimp are great with steak, but for a special occasion, brush the sauce on lobster tails and grill.
—Sheryl Shenberger, Albuquerque, NM

Takes: 25 min. • **Makes:** 8 servings

- ½ cup butter, melted
- 3 Tbsp. lemon juice
- 2 tsp. chili powder
- 1 tsp. ground ginger
- ¼ tsp. salt
- 2 lbs. uncooked shrimp (16-20 per lb.), peeled and deveined

1. In a bowl, combine first 5 ingredients; set aside ¼ cup mixture. Thread shrimp onto 8 metal or soaked wooden skewers.
2. Grill, covered, over medium heat 3-5 minutes on each side or until shrimp turn pink, basting occasionally with butter mixture. Remove from grill; brush with reserved ¼ cup butter mixture.

1 SKEWER 201 cal., 13g fat (8g sat. fat), 168mg chol., 295mg sod., 2g carb. (0 sugars, 0 fiber), 19g pro.

MARINADE MADE EASY

Unlike meats that can marinate for hours, shrimp and other seafood should marinate for only 15 to 30 minutes. Letting it sit any longer, especially when the marinade has an acidic ingredient like lemon juice, will cause the shrimp's flesh to become soft.

WEST AFRICAN CHICKEN STEW

WEST AFRICAN CHICKEN STEW

I really love authentic African flavors, but they can be hard to come by in the U.S. This recipe features a delicious combination of ingredients such as peanut butter, sweet potatoes and black-eyed peas, all of which are readily available.
—Michael Cohen, Los Angeles, CA

Prep: 20 min. • **Cook:** 30 min.
Makes: 8 servings (2½ qt.)

- 1 lb. boneless skinless chicken breasts, cut into 1-in. cubes
- ½ tsp. salt
- ¼ tsp. pepper
- 3 tsp. canola oil, divided
- 1 medium onion, thinly sliced
- 6 garlic cloves, minced
- 2 Tbsp. minced fresh gingerroot
- 2 cans (15½ oz. each) black-eyed peas, rinsed and drained
- 1 can (28 oz.) crushed tomatoes
- 1 large sweet potato, peeled and cut into 1-in. cubes
- 1 cup reduced-sodium chicken broth
- ¼ cup creamy peanut butter
- 1½ tsp. minced fresh thyme or ½ tsp. dried thyme, divided
- ¼ tsp. cayenne pepper
- Hot cooked brown rice, optional

1. Sprinkle chicken with salt and pepper. In a Dutch oven, cook chicken over medium heat in 2 tsp. oil for 4-6 minutes or until no longer pink; remove and set aside.
2. In the same pan, saute onion in remaining 1 tsp. oil until tender. Add garlic and ginger; cook 1 minute longer.
3. Stir in the peas, tomatoes, sweet potato, broth, peanut butter, 1¼ tsp. thyme and cayenne. Bring to a boil. Reduce heat; cover and simmer for 15-20 minutes or until potato is tender. Add chicken; heat through.
4. Serve with rice if desired. Sprinkle with remaining thyme.

1¼ CUPS 275 cal., 7g fat (1g sat. fat), 31mg chol., 636mg sod., 32g carb. (5g sugars, 6g fiber), 22g pro.

COBB SALAD SUB

When we need a quick meal to share, we turn Cobb salad into a sandwich masterpiece. Sometimes I substitute tortillas for the bread and make wraps. *—Kimberly Grusendorf, Medina, OH*

Takes: 15 min. • **Makes:** 12 servings

- 1 loaf (1 lb.) unsliced Italian bread
- ½ cup balsamic vinaigrette or dressing of your choice
- 5 oz. fresh baby spinach (about 6 cups)
- 1½ lbs. sliced deli ham
- 4 hard-boiled large eggs, finely chopped
- 8 bacon strips, cooked and crumbled
- ½ cup crumbled Gorgonzola cheese
- 1 cup cherry tomatoes, chopped

Cut bread loaf in half lengthwise; hollow out top and bottom, leaving a ¾-in. shell (discard removed bread or save for another use). Brush vinaigrette over loaf halves. Layer spinach, ham, eggs, bacon, cheese and cherry tomatoes on bread bottom. Replace top. Cut loaf in half lengthwise from top to bottom; cut crosswise 5 times to make 12 pieces.

1 PIECE 233 cal., 10g fat (3g sat. fat), 97mg chol., 982mg sod., 17g carb. (3g sugars, 1g fiber), 18g pro.

READER RAVES

"We gobbled it down! My husband even went into the fridge to sneak the leftovers after I went to bed! The beauty of this sandwich is that you can really add any topping you would see in a Cobb salad."

—HAVINGFUNWITHMYFAMILY, TASTEOFHOME.COM

COBB SALAD SUB

ZUCCHINI ENCHILADAS

When my garden is bursting with zucchini, I turn to this recipe to make the most of it. My family loves this dish.
—Angela Leinenbach, Mechanicsville, VA

Prep: 1½ hours • **Bake:** 30 min.
Makes: 12 servings

- 1 medium sweet yellow pepper, chopped
- 1 medium green pepper, chopped
- 1 large sweet onion, chopped
- 2 Tbsp. olive oil
- 2 garlic cloves, minced
- 2 cans (15 oz. each) tomato sauce
- 2 cans (14½ oz. each) no-salt-added diced tomatoes, undrained
- 2 Tbsp. chili powder
- 2 tsp. sugar
- 2 tsp. dried marjoram
- 1 tsp. dried basil
- 1 tsp. ground cumin
- ¼ tsp. salt
- ¼ tsp. cayenne pepper
- 1 bay leaf
- 3 lbs. zucchini, shredded (about 8 cups)
- 24 corn tortillas (6 in.), warmed
- 4 cups shredded reduced-fat cheddar cheese
- 2 cans (2¼ oz. each) sliced ripe olives, drained
- ½ cup minced fresh cilantro
- Reduced-fat sour cream, optional

1. In a large saucepan, saute peppers and onion in oil until tender. Add garlic; cook 1 minute longer. Stir in tomato sauce, tomatoes, chili powder, sugar, marjoram, basil, cumin, salt, cayenne and bay leaf. Bring to a boil. Reduce heat; simmer, uncovered, 30-35 minutes or until slightly thickened. Discard bay leaf.
2. Preheat oven to 350°. Place ⅓ cup zucchini down the center of each tortilla; top with 2 Tbsp. cheese and 2 tsp. olives. Roll up and place seam side down in two 13x9-in. baking dishes coated with cooking spray. Pour sauce over the top; sprinkle with remaining cheese.
3. Bake, uncovered, 30-35 minutes or until heated through. Sprinkle with cilantro. Serve with sour cream if desired.

2 ENCHILADAS 326 cal., 13g fat (6g sat. fat), 27mg chol., 846mg sod., 42g carb. (10g sugars, 7g fiber), 16g pro.

SPAGHETTI PIE CASSEROLE

My family adores this casserole. It's old-timey comfort food.
—Patti Lavell, Islamorada, FL

Prep: 30 min. • **Bake:** 30 min.
Makes: 8 servings

- 1 pkg. (8 oz.) spaghetti
- 1 lb. ground beef
- 1 small onion, chopped
- 2 garlic cloves, minced
- 1 jar (14 oz.) spaghetti sauce
- ½ tsp. salt
- ¼ tsp. pepper
- 3 oz. reduced-fat cream cheese
- 1 cup reduced-fat sour cream
- 3 green onions, chopped
- 1½ cups shredded cheddar-Monterey Jack cheese

1. Cook spaghetti according to package directions; drain. Meanwhile, in a large skillet, cook the beef, onion and garlic over medium heat until beef is no longer pink, 6-8 minutes, breaking up beef into crumbles; drain. Stir in the spaghetti sauce, salt and pepper; bring to a boil. Reduce heat; simmer, uncovered, for 20 minutes, stirring occasionally.
2. In a small bowl, mix cream cheese and sour cream until blended; stir in green onions. In a greased 11x7-in. baking dish, layer the spaghetti, cream cheese mixture and meat mixture. Top with shredded cheese.
3. Bake, covered, at 350° for 25 minutes. Uncover; bake until cheese is bubbly, 5-10 minutes longer.

1 PIECE 396 cal., 20g fat (11g sat. fat), 73mg chol., 622mg sod., 31g carb. (7g sugars, 2g fiber), 23g pro.

PRESSURE-COOKER COLA BBQ CHICKEN

This recipe is rich with sweet and smoky deliciousness. The meat is juicy and tender, and I like to add a few tasty toppings, like sliced dill pickles and a layer of pepper jack cheese, for a boost of flavor. This can also be cooked in the slow cooker on low for 8 hours.
—Ashley Lecker, Green Bay, WI

Prep: 10 min. • **Cook:** 10 min.
Makes: 14 servings

- 1 bottle (18 oz.) barbecue sauce
- 1 cup cola
- 2 Tbsp. cider vinegar
- 1 tsp. garlic powder
- 1 tsp. onion powder
- 1 tsp. salt
- ½ tsp. pepper
- 2½ lbs. boneless skinless chicken breasts
- 14 hamburger buns, split
- 14 slices pepper jack cheese
- 1 cup sliced sweet pickles

1. Place the first 7 ingredients in a 6-qt. electric pressure cooker; add chicken. Lock lid; close pressure-release valve. Adjust to pressure-cook on high for 7 minutes. Quick-release pressure. A thermometer inserted into chicken should read at least 165°.
2. Remove chicken; cool slightly. Drain off cooking juices, reserving 2 cups. Shred chicken with 2 forks. Combine with reserved juices. Serve on buns with cheese and pickles.

FREEZE OPTION Freeze cooled meat mixture in freezer containers. To use, partially thaw in refrigerator overnight. Heat through in a saucepan, stirring occasionally; add water if necessary.

1 SANDWICH 367 cal., 10g fat (5g sat. fat), 66mg chol., 971mg sod., 41g carb. (18g sugars, 1g fiber), 26g pro.

PRESSURE-COOKER COLA BBQ CHICKEN

MEDITERRANEAN BULGUR SALAD

Whether it's nutrition or taste you're after, it doesn't get any better than this. Bulgur, beans, tomatoes, pine nuts and olive oil team up in this vegetarian main dish salad.
—Taste of Home *Test Kitchen*

Prep: 15 min. • **Cook:** 20 min.
Makes: 9 servings

- 3 cups vegetable broth
- 1½ cups uncooked bulgur
- 6 Tbsp. olive oil
- 2 Tbsp. lemon juice
- 2 Tbsp. minced fresh parsley
- ½ tsp. salt
- ¼ tsp. pepper
- 1 can (15 oz.) garbanzo beans or chickpeas, rinsed and drained
- 2 cups halved cherry tomatoes
- 1 cup chopped cucumber
- 8 green onions, sliced
- 1 pkg. (4 oz.) crumbled feta cheese
- ½ cup pine nuts, toasted

1. In a large saucepan, bring broth and bulgur to a boil over high heat. Reduce heat; cover and simmer for 20 minutes or until tender and broth is almost absorbed. Remove from the heat; let stand at room temperature, uncovered, until broth is absorbed.
2. In a small bowl, whisk oil, lemon juice, parsley, salt and pepper.
3. In a large serving bowl, combine the bulgur, beans, tomatoes, cucumber and onions. Drizzle with dressing; toss to coat. Sprinkle with cheese and pine nuts.

1 CUP 298 cal., 17g fat (3g sat. fat), 7mg chol., 657mg sod., 31g carb. (4g sugars, 8g fiber), 10g pro.

PIGEON RIVER CHICKEN

For a picnic on the Pigeon River, we made chicken marinated in yogurt with a touch of cayenne. It's delectable warm or cold.
—Lib Jicha, Waynesville, NC

Prep: 25 min. + marinating • **Cook:** 15 min.
Makes: 12 servings

- 2 cups plain yogurt
- 2 Tbsp. hot pepper sauce
- 3 tsp. salt
- 2 broiler/fryer chickens (3 to 4 lbs. each), cut up

COATING

- 2 cups all-purpose flour
- 3 Tbsp. paprika
- 4 tsp. cayenne pepper
- 2 tsp. salt
- 2 tsp. pepper
- 1 tsp. dried thyme
- Oil for deep-fat frying

1. In a large bowl, combine the yogurt, pepper sauce and 3 tsp. salt. Add chicken; turn to coat. Cover and refrigerate 8 hours or overnight.
2. Drain chicken, discarding marinade. In a shallow bowl, mix flour with seasonings. Add chicken, a few pieces at a time, and toss to coat; shake off excess. Transfer to a 15x10x1-in. pan; let stand 20 minutes.
3. In a Dutch oven or deep skillet, heat ½ in. of oil over medium heat to 350°. Fry chicken, uncovered, until coating is dark golden brown and meat is no longer pink, 7-8 minutes per side, turning occasionally. Drain on paper towels.

1 SERVING 608 cal., 42g fat (7g sat. fat), 109mg chol., 1031mg sod., 19g carb. (2g sugars, 1g fiber), 37g pro

CHILE TAMALE PIE

This crowd-pleasing potluck dish packs a little heat, a little sweet and a big-time authentic southwestern flavor. There is no substitute for freshly ground chiles. A small food processor on high speed may be used to grind the chiles and cumin, or use a coffee grinder dedicated for spices. It's a terrific $15 investment for fresh-ground spices anytime—and your palate will thank you!
—Ralph Stamm, Dayton, OH

Prep: 45 min. • **Bake:** 50 min. + standing
Makes: 12 servings

- 1 can (15¼ oz.) whole kernel corn
- 2 cups masa harina
- 1 can (14½ oz.) chicken broth
- 2 Tbsp. butter, melted
- 1 large egg, room temperature, lightly beaten
- 2½ lbs. boneless pork loin roast, cut into ½-in. pieces
- 1 medium onion, chopped
- 1 can (16 oz.) refried beans
- 2 dried Anaheim chiles, chopped
- 2 dried ancho chiles, chopped
- 3 oz. Mexican or semisweet chocolate, grated
- ⅓ cup orange juice
- 2 Tbsp. lime juice
- 1 Tbsp. garlic powder
- 3 tsp. cumin seeds, toasted and crushed
- ¾ cup minced fresh cilantro, optional
- 1 jalapeno pepper, seeded and chopped, optional
- 2 cups shredded cheddar cheese

1. Drain corn, reserving liquid; set corn aside. Place masa harina in a large bowl. In a small bowl, combine the broth, butter, egg and reserved corn liquid; stir into masa harina just until moistened. Set aside.
2. In a large skillet coated with cooking spray, cook pork and onion over medium heat until pork is no longer pink. Add the beans, chiles, chocolate, orange juice, lime juice, garlic powder, cumin, corn and, if desired, cilantro and jalapeno. Bring to a boil. Reduce heat; simmer, uncovered, for 15 minutes. Meanwhile, preheat oven to 325°.
3. Transfer to a greased 13x9-in. baking dish; sprinkle with cheese. Spread masa harina mixture over cheese.
4. Bake, uncovered, until golden brown, 50-60 minutes. Let stand for 10 minutes before serving.

1 CUP 371 cal., 15g fat (8g sat. fat), 93mg chol., 496mg sod., 32g carb. (7g sugars, 6g fiber), 28g pro.

FLAVORFUL MARINATED PORK LOIN

MA

FLAVORFUL MARINATED PORK LOIN

Beautifully glazed with a mouthwatering marinade, this entree is relatively low in fat but still juicy and tender.
—Paula Young, Tiffin, OH

Prep: 20 min. + marinating
Bake: 1 hour + standing
Makes: 12 servings

- 2 Tbsp. plus ¼ cup vegetable broth, divided
- 1 cup orange juice
- ¾ cup apricot preserves
- 3 Tbsp. lemon juice
- 2 Tbsp. olive oil
- 1 Tbsp. curry powder
- 1 Tbsp. Worcestershire sauce
- 1 tsp. dried thyme
- ½ tsp. pepper
- 1 boneless pork loin roast (3 lbs.)
- 1 Tbsp. cornstarch

1. In a bowl, combine 2 Tbsp. vegetable broth and next 8 ingredients. Pour ¾ cup marinade into a large dish; add the pork. Turn to coat; cover and refrigerate overnight, turning occasionally. Set aside 1 cup remaining marinade for sauce; cover and refrigerate. Cover and refrigerate the rest of the marinade for basting.

2. Preheat oven to 350°. Drain pork, discarding marinade; place pork on a rack in a shallow roasting pan. Bake, uncovered, 1 to 1¼ hours or until a thermometer reads 145°, basting occasionally with reserved marinade. Transfer to a serving platter. Let stand 10 minutes before slicing.

3. Meanwhile, in a small saucepan, combine cornstarch with the remaining ¼ cup broth and 1 cup marinade. Bring to a boil; cook and stir until thickened, about 2 minutes. Serve with roast.

3 OZ. COOKED PORK WITH ABOUT 2 TBSP. GRAVY 229 cal., 8g fat (3g sat. fat), 55mg chol., 51mg sod., 15g carb. (8g sugars, 0 fiber), 22g pro.

GARLIC BREAD PASTA TORTE

My kids love to stuff spiral pasta inside bread for a clever dinner torte. We save the bread crusts to make garlicky croutons for salad.
—Melissa Pelkey Hass, Waleska, GA

Prep: 40 min. • **Bake:** 25 min.
Makes: 12 servings

- 1 pkg. (16 oz.) spiral pasta
- 1 pkg. (19½ oz.) Italian turkey sausage links, casings removed
- 8 oz. sliced fresh mushrooms
- 1 medium green pepper, chopped
- 1 medium onion, chopped
- 1 jar (24 oz.) marinara sauce
- 1 Tbsp. minced fresh basil or 1 tsp. dried basil
- 3 tsp. Italian seasoning
- 2½ cups shredded part-skim mozzarella cheese, divided
- 6 Tbsp. butter, cubed
- 6 garlic cloves, minced
- 20 slices white bread, crusts removed
- Additional marinara sauce, warmed, optional

1. Preheat oven to 400°. In a 6-qt. stockpot, cook pasta according to package directions for al dente; drain and return to pot.
2. In a large skillet, cook sausage, mushrooms, green pepper and onion over medium-high heat 7-9 minutes or until sausage is no longer pink, breaking up sausage into crumbles; drain. Stir in sauce, basil and Italian seasoning. Add to pasta; stir in 2 cups cheese.
3. In a microwave, melt butter; stir in garlic. Lightly brush 1 side of bread with garlic butter. Line bottom and side of a greased 10-in. springform pan with bread slices, trimming to fit and facing buttered sides against pan. Fill with pasta mixture; press firmly to pack down. Sprinkle with remaining cheese.
4. Bake, uncovered, 25-30 minutes or until golden brown and cheese is melted. Loosen sides from pan with a knife; remove rim. If desired, serve with additional marinara sauce.

1 PIECE 409 cal., 16g fat (7g sat. fat), 49mg chol., 752mg sod., 48g carb. (7g sugars, 3g fiber), 19g pro.

KENTUCKY GRILLED CHICKEN

This chicken is perfect for an outdoor summer meal, and my family thinks it's fantastic. It takes about an hour on the grill but is worth the wait. I use a new paintbrush to mop on the basting sauce.
—Jill Evely, Wilmore, KY

Prep: 5 min. + marinating • **Grill:** 40 min.
Makes: 10 servings

- 1 cup cider vinegar
- ½ cup canola oil
- 5 tsp. Worcestershire sauce
- 4 tsp. hot pepper sauce
- 2 tsp. salt
- 10 bone-in chicken breast halves (10 oz. each)

1. In a bowl or shallow dish, combine the first 5 ingredients. Pour 1 cup marinade into a separate bowl; add chicken and turn to coat. Cover and refrigerate for at least 4 hours. Cover and refrigerate the remaining marinade for basting.
2. Drain chicken, discarding marinade. Prepare grill for indirect heat, using a drip pan.
3. Place chicken breasts, bone side down, on oiled rack. Grill, covered, over indirect medium heat until a thermometer reads 170°, about 20 minutes on each side, basting occasionally with reserved marinade.

1 CHICKEN BREAST HALF 284 cal., 11g fat (2g sat. fat), 113mg chol., 406mg sod., 0 carb. (0 sugars, 0 fiber), 41g pro.

GRILL IT RIGHT

You can use a charcoal or gas grill to grill the chicken. Just pay attention to doneness cues. If you're limited on outdoor space, you can also try an electric countertop grill or a grill pan.

KENTUCKY GRILLED CHICKEN

IRISH BEEF STEW

Rich and hearty, this stew is a favorite of my husband's. The beef is incredibly tender. Served with crusty bread, it's an ideal cool-weather meal and perfect for any Irish holiday.

—Carrie Karleen, Saint-Nicolas, QC

Prep: 40 min. • **Cook:** 3¼ hours
Makes: 15 servings (3¾ qt.)

- 8 bacon strips, diced
- ⅓ cup all-purpose flour
- 1 tsp. salt
- ½ tsp. pepper
- 3 lbs. beef stew meat, cut into 1-in. cubes
- 1 lb. whole fresh mushrooms, quartered
- 3 medium leeks (white portion only), chopped
- 2 medium carrots, chopped
- ¼ cup chopped celery
- 1 Tbsp. canola oil
- 4 garlic cloves, minced
- 1 Tbsp. tomato paste
- 5 cups reduced-sodium beef broth
- 2 bay leaves
- 1 tsp. dried thyme
- 1 tsp. dried parsley flakes
- 1 tsp. dried rosemary, crushed
- 2 lbs. Yukon Gold potatoes, cut into 1-in. cubes
- 2 Tbsp. cornstarch
- 2 Tbsp. cold water
- 1 cup frozen peas

1. In a stockpot, cook bacon over medium heat until crisp. Using a slotted spoon, remove to paper towels. In a large shallow dish, combine flour, salt and pepper. Add beef, a few pieces at a time, and turn to coat. Brown beef in the bacon drippings. Remove and set aside.
2. In the same pot, saute the mushrooms, leeks, carrots and celery in oil until tender. Add garlic; cook 1 minute longer. Stir in tomato paste until blended. Add the broth, bay leaves, thyme, parsley and rosemary. Return beef and bacon to pot. Bring to a boil. Reduce heat; cover and simmer until beef is tender, about 2 hours.
3. Add potatoes. Return to a boil. Reduce heat; cover and simmer until potatoes are tender, about 1 hour longer. Combine cornstarch and water until smooth; stir into stew. Bring to a boil; cook and stir until thickened, about 2 minutes. Add peas; heat through. Discard bay leaves.

1 CUP 301 cal., 13g fat (4g sat. fat), 66mg chol., 441mg sod., 21g carb. (3g sugars, 2g fiber), 23g pro.

IRISH BEEF STEW

STEW VARIATIONS

BEEF STEW WITH BARLEY Prepare stew as directed, stirring in whole grain mustard and 1 cup quick-cooking barley 1 hour before serving.

ASIAN BEEF STEW Prepare stew as directed, adding hoisin sauce and fish sauce to taste and 1 cup chopped bok choy. Serve over jasmine rice.

CHICKEN SPAGHETTI

CHICKEN SPAGHETTI

Reminiscent of turkey tetrazzini, this creamy casserole serves up nostalgic flavors. Sharp cheddar can be used.
—Taste of Home *Test Kitchen*

Prep: 20 min. • **Bake:** 30 min.
Makes: 10 servings

- 12 oz. uncooked spaghetti, broken into 2-in. pieces
- ¼ cup butter, cubed
- 1 medium onion, chopped
- 2 garlic cloves, minced
- 3 Tbsp. all-purpose flour
- 2 cups 2% milk
- 3 cups cubed cooked chicken breast
- 1 can (10¾ oz.) condensed cream of mushroom soup, undiluted
- 1 jar (4 oz.) diced pimientos, drained
- 4 oz. cream cheese, cubed
- 1½ cups shredded cheddar cheese, divided
- ½ tsp. pepper
- Minced fresh parsley, optional

1. Preheat oven to 350°. Cook spaghetti according to package directions.
2. Meanwhile, in a Dutch oven, melt butter over medium heat. Add the onion; cook and stir until crisp-tender, 6-8 minutes. Add garlic; cook and stir 1 minute longer. Stir in flour until blended; gradually add milk. Bring to a boil; cook and stir until thickened, about 2 minutes. Stir in chicken, soup, pimientos, cream cheese, ¾ cup shredded cheese and pepper.
3. Drain spaghetti, reserving ½ cup pasta water. Add spaghetti to sauce mixture and toss to coat. If needed, add pasta water to loosen sauce to proper consistency. Transfer to a greased 13x9-in. baking dish. Sprinkle with remaining ¾ cup shredded cheese. Cover and bake 20 minutes. Uncover and bake until bubbly, 10-15 minutes longer. If desired, garnish with parsley.

1 CUP 393 cal., 18g fat (9g sat. fat), 76mg chol., 446mg sod., 34g carb. (4g sugars, 2g fiber), 23g pro.

POLENTA
CHILI CASSEROLE

POLENTA CHILI CASSEROLE

This delicious vegetarian bake combines spicy chili, mixed veggies and homemade polenta. It's so hearty that no one seems to miss the meat.

—Dan Kelmenson, West Bloomfield, MI

Prep: 20 min. • **Bake:** 35 min. + standing
Makes: 8 servings

- 4 cups water
- ½ tsp. salt
- 1¼ cups yellow cornmeal
- 2 cups shredded cheddar cheese, divided
- 3 cans (15 oz. each) vegetarian chili with beans
- 1 pkg. (16 oz.) frozen mixed vegetables, thawed and well drained

1. Preheat oven to 350°. In a large heavy saucepan, bring water and salt to a boil. Reduce heat to a gentle boil; slowly whisk in cornmeal. Cook and stir with a wooden spoon until polenta is thickened and pulls away cleanly from side of pan, 15-20 minutes.
2. Remove from heat. Stir in ¼ cup cheddar cheese until melted.
3. Spread into a 13x9-in. baking dish coated with cooking spray. Bake, uncovered, 20 minutes. Meanwhile, heat chili according to package directions.
4. Spread vegetables over polenta; top with chili. Sprinkle with remaining 1¾ cups cheese. Bake until the cheese is melted, 12-15 minutes longer. Let stand 10 minutes before serving.

1 SERVING 397 cal., 12g fat (6g sat. fat), 57mg chol., 922mg sod., 49g carb. (7g sugars, 7g fiber), 21g pro.

MEXICAN CHICKEN ALFREDO

MA

MEXICAN CHICKEN ALFREDO

One family member likes Italian; another likes Mexican. They'll never have to argue when this rich and creamy sensation is on the menu!

—Tia Woodley, Stockbridge, GA

Prep: 25 min. • **Bake:** 30 min.
Makes: 2 casseroles (4 servings each)

- 1 pkg. (16 oz.) gemelli or spiral pasta
- 2 lbs. boneless skinless chicken breasts, cubed
- 1 medium onion, chopped
- ¼ tsp. salt
- ¼ tsp. pepper
- 1 Tbsp. canola oil
- 2 jars (15 oz. each) Alfredo sauce
- 1 cup grated Parmesan cheese
- 1 cup medium salsa
- ¼ cup 2% milk
- 2 tsp. taco seasoning

1. Preheat oven to 350°. Cook pasta according to package directions.
2. Meanwhile, in a large skillet over medium heat, cook chicken, onion, salt and pepper in oil until chicken is no longer pink. Stir in Alfredo sauce; bring to a boil. Stir in cheese, salsa, milk and taco seasoning.
3. Drain pasta; toss with chicken mixture. Divide between 2 greased 8-in. square baking dishes. Cover and bake until bubbly, 30-35 minutes.

FREEZE OPTION Cover and freeze unbaked casserole up to 3 months. To use, thaw in refrigerator overnight. Remove from refrigerator 30 minutes before baking. Preheat oven to 350°. Bake casserole, covered, until bubbly, 50-60 minutes.

1½ CUPS 559 cal., 20g fat (11g sat. fat), 102mg chol., 899mg sod., 55g carb. (4g sugars, 3g fiber), 40g pro.

MA

TURKEY POTPIES

With a golden brown crust and scrumptious filling, these comforting potpies will warm you down to your toes. Because it makes two, you can eat one now and freeze the other for later. They bake and cut beautifully.
—Laurie Jensen, Cadillac, MI

Prep: 40 min. • **Bake:** 40 min. + standing
Makes: 2 pies (6 servings each)

- 2 medium potatoes, peeled and cut into 1-in. pieces
- 3 medium carrots, cut into 1-in. slices
- 1 medium onion, chopped
- 1 celery rib, diced
- 2 Tbsp. butter
- 1 Tbsp. olive oil
- 6 Tbsp. all-purpose flour
- 3 cups chicken broth
- 4 cups cubed cooked turkey
- ⅔ cup frozen peas
- ½ cup plus 1 Tbsp. heavy whipping cream, divided
- 1 Tbsp. minced fresh parsley
- 1 tsp. garlic salt
- ¼ tsp. pepper
- 2 sheets refrigerated pie crust
- 1 large egg

1. Preheat oven to 375°. In a Dutch oven, saute potatoes, carrots, onion and celery in butter and oil until tender. Stir in flour until blended; gradually add broth. Bring to a boil; cook and stir 2 minutes or until thickened. Stir in turkey, peas, ½ cup cream, parsley, garlic salt and pepper.
2. Spoon into 2 ungreased 9-in. pie plates. Unroll crusts; place over filling. Trim crusts and seal to edges of pie plates. Cut out a decorative center or cut slits in crusts. In a small bowl, whisk egg and remaining 1 Tbsp. cream; brush over crusts.
3. Bake until golden brown, 40-45 minutes. Let stand 10 minutes before cutting.

FREEZE OPTION Cover and freeze unbaked potpies up to 3 months. To use, remove from freezer 30 minutes before baking (do not thaw). Preheat oven to 425°. Place pie on a baking sheet; cover edge loosely with foil. Bake 30 minutes. Reduce oven setting to 350°; remove foil. Bake until golden brown and a thermometer inserted in center reads 165°, 55-60 minutes longer.

1 SERVING 287 cal., 15g fat (7g sat. fat), 78mg chol., 542mg sod., 21g carb. (3g sugars, 2g fiber), 17g pro.

READER RAVES

"Absolutely delicious! I froze the second pie and it came out just as delicious as the first one!"

—NANCYPANE, TASTEOFHOME.COM

BARBECUED PICNIC CHICKEN

I like to serve this savory chicken at family picnics. Cooked on a covered grill, the poultry stays so tender and juicy. Everyone loves the zesty, slightly sweet homemade barbecue sauce—and it's so easy to make.

—Priscilla Weaver, Hagerstown, MD

Prep: 15 min. • **Grill:** 45 min.
Makes: 8 servings

- 2 garlic cloves, minced
- 2 tsp. butter
- 1 cup ketchup
- ¼ cup packed brown sugar
- ¼ cup chili sauce
- 2 Tbsp. Worcestershire sauce
- 1 Tbsp. celery seed
- 1 Tbsp. prepared mustard
- ½ tsp. salt
- 2 dashes hot pepper sauce
- 2 broiler/fryer chickens (3½ to 4 lbs. each), cut up

1. In a large saucepan, saute garlic in butter until tender. Add the next 8 ingredients. Bring to a boil, stirring constantly. Remove from heat; set aside.
2. On a lightly greased grill rack, grill chicken, covered, over medium heat for 30 minutes, turning occasionally. Baste with sauce. Grill 15 minutes longer or until a thermometer reaches 170°, basting and turning several times.

1 PIECE 296 cal., 14g fat (4g sat. fat), 79mg chol., 761mg sod., 18g carb. (12g sugars, 1g fiber), 25g pro.

CHUNKY CHICKEN SALAD WITH GRAPES & PECANS

This chicken salad with grapes is ready in a snap when using rotisserie chicken and a few quick chops of pecans, sweet onion and celery.
—Julie Sterchi, Campbellsville, KY

Takes: 25 min. • **Makes:** 8 servings

- ½ cup mayonnaise
- 2 Tbsp. sour cream
- 1 Tbsp. lemon juice
- ⅛ tsp. salt
- ⅛ tsp. pepper
- 4 cups shredded rotisserie chicken
- 1¼ cups seedless red grapes, halved
- ½ cup chopped pecans
- ½ cup chopped celery
- ¼ cup chopped sweet onion, optional
- Optional: Lettuce leaves or whole wheat bread slices

In a large bowl, combine the first 5 ingredients. Add the chicken, grapes, pecans, celery and, if desired, onion; mix lightly to coat. If desired, serve with lettuce leaves or whole wheat bread.

¾ CUP CHICKEN SALAD 311 cal., 22g fat (4g sat. fat), 70mg chol., 180mg sod., 6g carb. (5g sugars, 1g fiber), 21g pro.

READER RAVES

"I used boiled chicken 'cause I had some leftover from another recipe. The grapes and pecans really give this a nice flavor!"

—JCV4, TASTEOFHOME.COM

CHUNKY CHICKEN SALAD WITH GRAPES & PECANS

TACO CORNBREAD CASSEROLE

TACO CORNBREAD CASSEROLE

A whole can of chiles adds fire to this casserole. For less heat, you can use just enough of the can for your taste.
—Lisa A Paul, Terre Haute, IN

Prep: 25 min. • **Bake:** 1 hour
Makes: 8 servings

- 2 lbs. ground beef
- 2 envelopes taco seasoning
- 2 cans (14½ oz. each) diced tomatoes, drained
- 1 cup water
- 1 cup cooked rice
- 1 can (4 oz.) chopped green chiles
- 2 pkg. (8½ oz. each) cornbread/muffin mix
- 1 can (8¾ oz.) whole kernel corn, drained
- 1 cup sour cream
- 2 cups corn chips
- 2 cups shredded Mexican cheese blend or cheddar cheese, divided
- 1 can (2¼ oz.) sliced ripe olives, drained
- Optional: Shredded lettuce, chopped tomatoes and chopped red onion

1. Preheat oven to 400°. In a Dutch oven, cook beef over medium heat until no longer pink, 8-10 minutes, breaking it into crumbles; drain. Stir in the taco seasoning. Add tomatoes, water, rice and green chiles; heat through, stirring occasionally.
2. Meanwhile, prepare cornbread mix according to package directions; stir in corn. Pour half the batter into a greased 13x9-in. baking dish. Layer with half the meat mixture, all the sour cream, half the corn chips and 1 cup cheese. Top with remaining batter, remaining meat mixture and the olives.
3. Bake, uncovered, until cornbread is cooked through, 55-60 minutes. Sprinkle with remaining 1 cup corn chips and 1 cup cheese; bake until cheese is melted, 3-5 minutes longer. If desired, serve with lettuce, tomatoes and red onion.

1½ CUPS 817 cal., 40g fat (17g sat. fat), 183mg chol., 1982mg sod., 74g carb. (20g sugars, 4g fiber), 36g pro.

MA

SUPER SLOPPY JOES

My mother made these sloppy joes many times when I was growing up. She passed the recipe on to me when I got married. My in-laws say they're the best they've ever tasted.
—Ellen Stringer, Bourbonnais, IL

Prep: 15 min. • **Cook:** 35 min.
Makes: 10 servings

- 2 lbs. ground beef
- ½ cup chopped onion
- 2 celery ribs with leaves, chopped
- ¼ cup chopped green pepper
- 1 can (15 oz.) crushed tomatoes
- ¼ cup ketchup
- 2 Tbsp. brown sugar
- 1 Tbsp. white vinegar
- 1 Tbsp. Worcestershire sauce
- 1 Tbsp. steak sauce
- ½ tsp. garlic salt
- ¼ tsp. ground mustard
- ¼ tsp. paprika
- 10 hamburger or hoagie buns, split

1. In a Dutch oven over medium heat, cook the beef, onion, celery and green pepper until meat is no longer pink and the vegetables are tender; drain.
2. Stir in the next 9 ingredients. Simmer, uncovered, for 35-40 minutes or until heated through, stirring occasionally. Spoon about ½ cup meat mixture onto each bun.

FREEZE OPTION Place individual portions cooled meat mixture in freezer containers and freeze. To use, partially thaw in refrigerator overnight. Microwave, covered, on high in a microwave-safe dish until heated through, gently stirring and adding broth or water if necessary.

1 SANDWICH 306 cal., 13g fat (5g sat. fat), 60mg chol., 473mg sod., 25g carb. (7g sugars, 2g fiber), 22g pro.

CHEESEBURGER BOMBS

Instead of enjoying your cheeseburger on a bun, have it in one! These bundles are the perfect take-along option.
—Taste of Home *Test Kitchen*

Prep: 25 min. • **Bake:** 20 min.
Makes: 8 servings

- ½ lb. ground beef
- ¼ cup chopped onion
- ¼ cup crumbled cooked bacon
- ¼ cup ketchup
- 2 Tbsp. prepared mustard
- 2 Tbsp. chopped dill pickle or pickle relish
- 1 tube (16.3 oz.) large refrigerated buttermilk biscuits
- ½ cup shredded cheddar cheese
- 1 large egg, beaten
- ½ tsp. sesame seeds

1. Preheat oven to 350°. In a large skillet, cook beef and onion over medium heat until beef is no longer pink and onion is tender, 3-4 minutes, breaking up beef into crumbles; drain. Stir in the bacon, ketchup, mustard and pickles and cool slightly.
2. On a lightly floured surface, roll each biscuit into a 5-in. circle. Add 1 Tbsp. cheese in the center of each biscuit; top with 2 Tbsp. meat mixture. Bring biscuit dough over filling to center; pinch to seal. Place seam side down on a parchment-lined baking sheet.
3. Brush tops with beaten egg; sprinkle with sesame seeds. Bake until golden brown, 18-20 minutes. Serve warm.

1 CHEESEBURGER BOMB 276 cal., 13g fat (5g sat. fat), 27mg chol., 897mg sod., 28g carb. (5g sugars, 1g fiber), 12g pro.

CHEESEBURGER BOMBS

ITALIAN MEATBALL KABOBS

When the temperature climbs, these deliciously different kabobs are so fun to throw on the grill. Add a green salad and rustic bread to make a complete meal.
—Marie Rizzio, Interlochen, MI

Prep: 30 min. • **Grill:** 10 min.
Makes: 12 kabobs

- 2 large eggs, lightly beaten
- ⅔ cup seasoned bread crumbs
- ½ cup grated Parmesan cheese
- ¼ cup minced fresh parsley
- 4 tsp. Italian seasoning
- ½ tsp. salt
- ½ tsp. garlic powder
- 2½ lbs. ground beef
- 1 medium onion, cut into 1-in. pieces
- 1 medium sweet red pepper, cut into 1-in. pieces
- 1 medium zucchini, cut into 1-in. pieces
- ½ small eggplant, cut into 1-in. pieces
- ½ cup balsamic vinegar
- ½ cup olive oil

1. In a large bowl, combine the first 7 ingredients. Crumble beef over mixture. Mix lightly but thoroughly. Shape into 1½-in. balls.
2. On 12 metal or soaked wooden skewers, alternately thread meatballs and vegetables. In a small bowl, combine vinegar and oil.
3. Grill kabobs, covered, over medium heat for 8-10 minutes or until meatballs are no longer pink and vegetables are tender, basting frequently with vinegar mixture and turning occasionally.

1 KABOB 325 cal., 22g fat (6g sat. fat), 97mg chol., 315mg sod., 10g carb. (4g sugars, 2g fiber), 21g pro.

MA

GRILLED PICNIC CHICKEN

This tasty chicken marinates overnight. The next day, I just pop it on the grill for dinner in no time.
—Cindy DeRoos, Iroquois, ON

Prep: 5 min. + marinating • **Grill:** 40 min.
Makes: 12 servings

- 1½ cups white vinegar
- ¾ cup canola oil
- 6 Tbsp. water
- 4½ tsp. salt
- 1½ tsp. poultry seasoning
- ¾ tsp. garlic powder
- ¾ tsp. pepper
- 3 broiler/fryer chickens (3 to 4 lbs. each), quartered or cut up

1. In a bowl, combine first 7 ingredients. Remove 1 cup for basting; cover and refrigerate. Pour remaining marinade into a large shallow dish; add chicken. Turn chicken to coat; refrigerate 4 hours or overnight, turning once or twice.
2. Drain chicken, discarding marinade in bag. Grill chicken, uncovered, over medium heat for 15 minutes on each side. Baste with the reserved marinade.
3. Grill 10-20 minutes longer or until the juices run clear, turning and basting several times.

7 OZ. COOKED CHICKEN 522 cal., 34g fat (8g sat. fat), 157mg chol., 725mg sod., 0 carb. (0 sugars, 0 fiber), 50g pro.

BUTTERNUT & PORTOBELLO LASAGNA

Lasagna gets fresh flavor and color when you make it with roasted butternut squash, portobello mushrooms, basil and spinach. We feast on this.
—Edward and Danielle Walker, Traverse City, MI

Prep: 1 hour • **Bake:** 45 min. + standing
Makes: 12 servings

- 1 pkg. (10 oz.) frozen cubed butternut squash, thawed
- 2 tsp. olive oil
- 1 tsp. brown sugar
- ¼ tsp. salt
- ⅛ tsp. pepper

MUSHROOMS

- 4 large portobello mushrooms, coarsely chopped
- 2 tsp. balsamic vinegar
- 2 tsp. olive oil
- ¼ tsp. salt
- ⅛ tsp. pepper

SAUCE

- 2 cans (28 oz. each) whole tomatoes, undrained
- 2 tsp. olive oil
- 2 garlic cloves, minced
- 1 tsp. crushed red pepper flakes
- ½ cup fresh basil leaves, thinly sliced
- ¼ tsp. salt
- ⅛ tsp. pepper

LASAGNA

- 9 no-cook lasagna noodles
- 4 oz. fresh baby spinach (about 5 cups)
- 3 cups part-skim ricotta cheese
- 1½ cups shredded part-skim mozzarella cheese

1. Preheat oven to 350°. In a large bowl, combine the first 5 ingredients. In another bowl, combine ingredients for mushrooms. Transfer vegetables to 2 separate foil-lined 15x10x1-in. baking pans. Roast 14-16 minutes or until tender, stirring occasionally.
2. Meanwhile, for sauce, drain tomatoes, reserving juices; coarsely chop the tomatoes. In a large saucepan, heat oil over medium heat. Add garlic and pepper flakes; cook 1 minute. Stir in chopped tomatoes, reserved tomato juices, basil, salt and pepper; bring to a boil. Reduce heat; simmer, uncovered, 35-45 minutes or until thickened, stirring occasionally.
3. Spread 1 cup sauce into a greased 13x9-in. baking dish. Layer with 3 noodles, 1 cup sauce, spinach and mushrooms. Continue layering with 3 noodles, 1 cup sauce, ricotta cheese and roasted squash. Top with remaining noodles and sauce. Sprinkle with mozzarella cheese.
4. Bake, covered, 30 minutes. Bake, uncovered, 15-20 minutes longer or until bubbly. Let stand 15 minutes before serving.

1 PIECE 252 cal., 10g fat (5g sat. fat), 27mg chol., 508mg sod., 25g carb. (5g sugars, 4g fiber), 15g pro.

BUTTERNUT & PORTOBELLO LASAGNA

ROADSIDE DINER CHEESEBURGER QUICHE

Here is an unforgettable quiche that tastes just like its burger counterpart. Easy and appealing, it's perfect for guests and fun for the whole family.

Barbara J. Miller, Oakdale, MN

Prep: 20 min. • **Bake:** 50 min. + standing
Makes: 8 servings

- 1 sheet refrigerated pie crust
- ¾ lb. ground beef
- 2 plum tomatoes, seeded and chopped
- 1 medium onion, chopped
- ½ cup dill pickle relish
- ½ cup crumbled cooked bacon
- 5 large eggs
- 1 cup heavy whipping cream
- ½ cup 2% milk
- 2 tsp. prepared mustard
- 1 tsp. hot pepper sauce
- ½ tsp. salt
- ¼ tsp. pepper
- 1½ cups shredded cheddar cheese
- ½ cup shredded Parmesan cheese
- Optional: Mayonnaise, additional pickle relish, crumbled cooked bacon, chopped onion and chopped tomato

1. Preheat oven to 375°. Unroll crust into a 9-in. deep-dish pie plate; flute edges. In a large skillet, cook beef over medium heat until no longer pink, breaking it into crumbles; drain. Stir in the tomatoes, onion, relish and bacon. Transfer to prepared crust.
2. In a large bowl, whisk the eggs, cream, milk, mustard, pepper sauce, salt and pepper. Pour over beef mixture. Sprinkle with cheeses.
3. Bake until a knife inserted in center comes out clean, 50-60 minutes. If necessary, cover edges with foil during the last 15 minutes in order to prevent overbrowning. Let stand for 10 minutes before cutting. Garnish with optional ingredients as desired.

1 PIECE 502 cal., 35g fat (19g sat. fat), 236mg chol., 954mg sod., 24g carb. (8g sugars, 1g fiber), 23g pro.

TEST KITCHEN TIP

In Europe, Parmigiano-Reggiano and Parmesan are one and the same. Here in the U.S., though, Parmesan is a broad term and may not actually come from Italy's Parmigiano-Reggiano region. For the best flavor in this lighter recipe, choose authentic Parmigiano-Reggiano—you'll need less than the original ½ cup, but still get that signature cheesy richness with fewer calories and less fat.

SPINACH PENNE SALAD

SPINACH PENNE SALAD

You can always double the vinaigrette for this recipe and use half of it to marinate and grill chicken breasts. Slice and add to the salad for a substantial salad offering.
—Benice Silver, Carmel, IN

Takes: 30 min. • **Makes:** 10 servings

- 1 pkg. (16 oz.) uncooked whole wheat penne pasta

VINAIGRETTE
- ½ cup olive oil
- ½ cup white wine vinegar
- ⅓ cup grated Parmesan cheese
- 1 Tbsp. Dijon mustard
- 2 garlic cloves, minced
- 1 tsp. dried oregano
- ¼ tsp. salt
- ¼ tsp. pepper

SALAD
- 1 pkg. (6 oz.) fresh baby spinach
- 3 medium tomatoes, seeded and chopped
- ¾ cup (6 oz.) crumbled feta cheese
- 4 green onions, thinly sliced
- ½ cup sliced ripe or Greek olives

1. In a Dutch oven, cook pasta according to package directions. Drain and rinse in cold water; drain again.
2. Meanwhile, in a small bowl, whisk the vinaigrette ingredients. In a large bowl, combine the pasta, spinach, tomatoes, feta cheese, onions and olives. Add vinaigrette; toss to coat. Serve salad immediately.

1½ CUPS 327 cal., 15g fat (3g sat. fat), 7mg chol., 233mg sod., 38g carb. (2g sugars, 7g fiber), 11g pro.

BREADED CURRY CHICKEN DRUMMIES

BREADED CURRY CHICKEN DRUMMIES

These drumsticks are crispy with just the right amount of zing to get your mouth watering for more! They are super easy to make and are baked rather than fried, so they save on fat but not on flavor. Boneless, skinless chicken breasts or assorted chicken pieces can be used instead of all drumsticks.
—Lynn Kaufman, Mount Morris, IL

Prep: 20 min. • **Bake:** 45 min.
Makes: 8 servings

- 1½ cups seasoned bread crumbs
- 1½ tsp. kosher salt
- 1½ tsp. onion powder
- 1½ tsp. garlic powder
- 1 tsp. curry powder
- 1 tsp. smoked paprika
- 1 tsp. dried parsley flakes
- ½ tsp. ground turmeric
- ¼ tsp. pepper
- ⅛ tsp. cayenne pepper
- ½ cup butter, cubed
- 3 Tbsp. lemon juice
- 16 chicken drumsticks (about 4 lbs.)

1. Preheat oven to 375°. In a shallow bowl, mix bread crumbs and seasonings. In a microwave, melt butter with lemon juice. Brush drumsticks with butter mixture, then coat with crumb mixture. Place on greased racks set into two 15x10x1-in. pans.
2. Bake until golden brown and a thermometer reads 170°-175°, 45-55 minutes, rotating pans halfway through baking.

2 DRUMSTICKS 380 cal., 24g fat (11g sat. fat), 125mg chol., 535mg sod., 9g carb. (1g sugars, 1g fiber), 31g pro.

CREAMY CAVATAPPI & CHEESE

Dive fork-first into oodles of noodles coated with a to-die-for sharp cheddar cheese sauce in this grown-up mac and cheese. Hot sauce lends a mild heat that's delectable with the smoky topping.
—Barbara Colucci, Rockledge, FL

Prep: 30 min. • **Bake:** 20 min.
Makes: 10 servings

- 6 cups uncooked cavatappi or spiral pasta
- 3 garlic cloves, minced
- 1/3 cup butter
- 1/4 cup all-purpose flour
- 1 Tbsp. hot pepper sauce
- 4 cups 2% milk
- 6 cups shredded sharp cheddar cheese
- 1 cup cubed Velveeta
- 3 green onions, chopped

TOPPINGS

- 1/2 cup panko bread crumbs
- 3 thick-sliced bacon strips, cooked and coarsely crumbled
- 1 Tbsp. butter, melted
- 1 green onion, chopped
- Coarsely ground pepper, optional

1. Cook cavatappi according to package directions.
2. Meanwhile, saute garlic in butter in a Dutch oven. Stir in flour and pepper sauce until blended; gradually add milk. Bring to a boil; cook and stir until thickened, about 2 minutes.
3. Stir in cheeses until melted; add green onions. Drain cavatappi; stir into cheese mixture.
4. Transfer to a greased 13x9-in. baking dish. Combine the bread crumbs, bacon and melted butter; sprinkle over the top.
5. Bake, uncovered, at 350° until bubbly, 20-25 minutes. Sprinkle with green onion and, if desired, pepper.

1 CUP 706 cal., 38g fat (21g sat. fat), 110mg chol., 782mg sod., 60g carb. (8g sugars, 3g fiber), 32g pro.

CREAMY CAVATAPPI & CHEESE

SAUCY GRILLED BABY BACK RIBS

The root beer in the sauce adds a subtle sweetness to this savory rib recipe.
—Terri Kandell, Addison, MI

Prep: 2 hours • **Grill:** 15 min.
Makes: 8 servings

- 2 cups ketchup
- 2 cups cider vinegar
- 1 cup corn syrup
- ¼ cup packed brown sugar
- ¼ cup root beer
- ½ tsp. salt
- ½ tsp. garlic powder
- ½ tsp. onion powder
- ½ tsp. hot pepper sauce
- 4 lbs. pork baby back ribs

1. In a large saucepan, combine first 9 ingredients. Bring to a boil. Reduce heat; simmer, uncovered, 20-25 minutes or until slightly thickened, stirring occasionally.
2. Meanwhile, preheat oven to 325°. Set aside 3 cups of sauce for basting and serving.
3. Brush remaining sauce over ribs. Place bone side down on a rack in a large shallow roasting pan. Cover tightly with foil and bake 1½ to 2 hours or until tender.
4. On a greased grill, cook ribs, covered, over medium heat 15-25 minutes or until browned, turning and brushing occasionally with some of the reserved sauce. Cut into serving-size pieces; serve with sauce.
1 SERVING 603 cal., 31g fat (11g sat. fat), 122mg chol., 1046mg sod., 56g carb. (35g sugars, 0 fiber), 25g pro.

CRANBERRY-WALNUT CHICKEN SALAD SANDWICHES

I made these simple yet special sandwiches for a birthday party. Tangy cranberries and crunchy celery pep up the chicken. Leftover turkey works well, too.
—Shannon Tucker, Land O Lakes, FL

Takes: 15 min. • **Makes:** 8 servings

- ½ cup mayonnaise
- 2 Tbsp. honey Dijon mustard
- ¼ tsp. pepper
- 2 cups cubed rotisserie chicken
- 1 cup shredded Swiss cheese
- ½ cup chopped celery
- ½ cup dried cranberries
- ¼ cup chopped walnuts
- ½ tsp. dried parsley flakes
- 8 lettuce leaves
- 16 slices pumpernickel bread

1. In a large bowl, combine mayonnaise, mustard and pepper. Stir in the chicken, cheese, celery, cranberries, walnuts and parsley.
2. Place lettuce on 8 slices of bread; top each with ½ cup chicken salad. Top with remaining bread.
1 SANDWICH 411 cal., 22g fat (5g sat. fat), 49mg chol., 469mg sod., 35g carb. (7g sugars, 5g fiber), 20g pro.

BUFFALO CHICKEN ENCHILADAS

BUFFALO CHICKEN ENCHILADAS

These buffalo chicken enchiladas, filled with tender rotisserie chicken and lots of cheese—and, of course, Buffalo sauce—will be the most craveable, easy and delicious meal you've ever tasted.
—Becky Hardin, St. Peters, MO

Prep: 15 min. • **Bake:** 25 min.
Makes: 10 servings

- 3 cups shredded rotisserie chicken
- 2 cups shredded cheddar cheese, divided
- 1 can (10 oz.) diced tomatoes and green chiles, drained
- 1 can (10 oz.) enchilada sauce
- ½ cup Buffalo wing sauce
- 1 can (10½ oz.) condensed cream of celery soup, undiluted
- 4 oz. reduced-fat cream cheese, cubed
- ½ cup blue cheese salad dressing
- 10 flour tortillas (8 in.)
- ⅓ cup crumbled blue cheese
- Optional: Chopped tomatoes, sliced celery, shredded lettuce, sliced green onions, minced fresh cilantro and additional cheddar cheese

1. Preheat oven to 350°. In a large bowl, combine chicken, 1¾ cups shredded cheese, diced tomatoes and green chiles, enchilada sauce and wing sauce. In a small saucepan, heat soup, cream cheese, dressing and remaining ¼ cup shredded cheese over low heat until cheeses are melted, 5-10 minutes. Remove from heat.
2. Place ⅓ cup chicken mixture off center on each tortilla. Roll up and place in a greased 13x9-in. baking dish, seam side down. Top with sauce.
3. Bake, uncovered, until enchiladas are heated through and cheese is melted, 25-30 minutes. Sprinkle with blue cheese and additional toppings of your choice.

1 ENCHILADA 472 cal., 26g fat (10g sat. fat), 76mg chol., 1387mg sod., 34g carb. (2g sugars, 3g fiber), 25g pro.

SAUSAGE BREAD SANDWICHES

MA

SAUSAGE BREAD SANDWICHES

I make these sandwiches in my spare time and freeze them so they're ready when needed, such as for tailgating parties when we attend Kansas State football games.
—Donna Roberts, Manhattan, KS

Prep: 30 min. • **Bake:** 20 min.
Makes: 4 sandwich loaves (3 pieces each)

- 1 pkg. (16 oz.) hot roll mix
- 2 lbs. reduced-fat bulk pork sausage
- 2 Tbsp. dried parsley flakes
- 2 tsp. garlic powder
- 1 tsp. onion powder
- ½ tsp. dried oregano
- 2 cups shredded part-skim mozzarella cheese
- ½ cup grated Parmesan cheese
- 1 large egg
- 1 Tbsp. water

1. Preheat oven to 350°. Prepare roll mix dough according to package directions.
2. Meanwhile, in a large skillet, cook sausage over medium heat 8-10 minutes or until no longer pink, breaking into crumbles; drain. Stir in seasonings.
3. Divide dough into 4 portions. On a lightly floured surface, roll each into a 14x8-in. rectangle. Top each with 1¼ cups sausage mixture to within 1 in. of edges; sprinkle with ½ cup mozzarella cheese and 2 Tbsp. Parmesan cheese. Roll up jelly-roll style, starting with a long side; pinch seams and ends to seal.
4. Transfer to greased baking sheets, seam side down. In a small bowl, whisk egg with water; brush over loaves. Bake 20-25 minutes or until golden brown and heated through. Cool 5 minutes before slicing.

FREEZE OPTION Cool cooked sandwiches 1 hour on wire racks. Cut each sandwich into thirds; wrap each securely in foil. Freeze until serving. To reheat sandwiches in the oven, place wrapped frozen sandwiches on a baking sheet. Heat in a preheated 375° oven for 20-25 minutes or until heated through.

1 PIECE 432 cal., 25g fat (10g sat. fat), 103mg chol., 926mg sod., 27g carb. (5g sugars, 1g fiber), 24g pro.

CHICKEN & ASPARAGUS BAKE

Greet guests with a taste of springtime with this chicken and asparagus casserole on the menu. It bakes in just half an hour. People savor the rich cheesy sauce, and it freezes well, too.
—Ramona Ruskell, Columbia, MO

Prep: 20 min. • **Bake:** 25 min.
Makes: 10 servings

- ¼ cup butter
- 1 medium onion, chopped
- 1 can (10½ oz.) condensed cream of mushroom soup, undiluted
- 1 can (8 oz.) mushroom stems and pieces, drained
- 1 can (5 oz.) evaporated milk
- 2 Tbsp. chopped pimientos
- 2 tsp. soy sauce
- ½ tsp. pepper
- ¼ tsp. hot pepper sauce
- 2 cups shredded cheddar cheese
- 5 cups cubed cooked chicken
- 1 pkg. (10 oz.) frozen cut asparagus, thawed
- 3 Tbsp. sliced almonds

1. Preheat oven to 350°. In a large saucepan, melt butter over medium heat; add onion. Cook and stir until tender, 3-5 minutes. Stir in soup, mushrooms, milk, pimientos, soy sauce, pepper and pepper sauce. Stir in cheese until melted.
2. In a greased shallow 2½-qt. baking dish, layer half each of the chicken, asparagus and cheese sauce. Repeat layers. Sprinkle with almonds. Bake, uncovered, until bubbly, 25-30 minutes.

1 SERVING 335 cal., 21g fat (10g sat. fat), 103mg chol., 604mg sod., 8g carb. (3g sugars, 1g fiber), 28g pro.

CHICKEN & ASPARAGUS BAKE

VEGGIE NICOISE SALAD

More and more people in my workplace are becoming vegetarians. When we cook or eat together, the focus is on fresh produce. This salad combines some of our favorite ingredients in one dish—and with the hard-boiled eggs and kidney beans, it also delivers enough protein to satisfy those who are skeptical of vegetarian fare.
—Elizabeth Kelley, Chicago, IL

Prep: 40 min. • **Cook:** 25 min.
Makes: 8 servings

- ⅓ cup olive oil
- ¼ cup lemon juice
- 2 tsp. minced fresh oregano
- 2 tsp. minced fresh thyme
- 1 tsp. Dijon mustard
- 1 garlic clove, minced
- ¼ tsp. coarsely ground pepper
- ⅛ tsp. salt
- 1 can (16 oz.) kidney beans, rinsed and drained
- 1 small red onion, halved and thinly sliced
- 1 lb. small red potatoes (about 9), halved
- 1 lb. fresh asparagus, trimmed
- ½ lb. fresh green beans, trimmed
- 12 cups torn romaine (about 2 small bunches)
- 6 hard-boiled large eggs, quartered
- 1 jar (6½ oz.) marinated quartered artichoke hearts, drained
- ½ cup Nicoise or kalamata olives

1. For vinaigrette, whisk together first 8 ingredients. In another bowl, toss kidney beans and onion with 1 Tbsp. vinaigrette. Set aside bean mixture and remaining vinaigrette.
2. Place potatoes in a saucepan and cover with water. Bring to a boil. Reduce the heat; simmer, covered, until tender, 10-15 minutes. Drain. While potatoes are warm, toss with 1 Tbsp. vinaigrette.
3. In a pot of boiling water, cook the asparagus just until crisp-tender, 2-4 minutes. Remove with tongs and immediately drop into ice water. Drain and pat dry. In same pot of boiling water, cook green beans until crisp-tender, 3-4 minutes. Remove beans; place in ice water. Drain and pat dry.
4. To serve, toss asparagus with 1 Tbsp. vinaigrette; toss green beans with 2 tsp. vinaigrette. Toss romaine with remaining vinaigrette; place on a platter. Arrange vegetables, kidney bean mixture, eggs, artichoke hearts and olives on the top.

1 SERVING 329 cal., 19g fat (4g sat. fat), 140mg chol., 422mg sod., 28g carb. (6g sugars, 7g fiber), 12g pro.

READER RAVES

"Delicious 'meat-free Monday' dish that my whole family enjoyed. The vinaigrette is the best! I couldn't find fresh oregano, so I swapped out the fresh oregano for fresh basil—it works!"

—CYANMAGNET, TASTEOFHOME.COM

SIDES & SALADS

P. 152

P. 174

P. 172

LOADED TWICE-BAKED POTATO CASSEROLE

Creamy, cheesy and loaded with bacon, this comforting casserole immediately makes guests feel at home.
—Cyndy Gerken, Naples, FL

Prep: 1½ hours • **Bake:** 30 min.
Makes: 16 servings

- 8 large baking potatoes (about 6½ lbs.)
- 2 Tbsp. olive oil
- 1½ tsp. salt, divided
- 1½ tsp. pepper, divided
- ½ cup butter, cubed
- 1⅓ cups heavy whipping cream
- ½ cup sour cream
- 4 cups shredded cheddar cheese, divided
- 12 bacon strips, cooked and crumbled, divided
- 4 green onions, sliced, divided
- Additional sour cream, optional

1. Preheat oven to 375°. Scrub potatoes; pierce several times with a fork. Brush with oil; sprinkle with 1 tsp. salt and ½ tsp. pepper. Place on a foil-lined baking pan; bake 1 to 1¼ hours or until tender. Cool slightly.
2. In a small saucepan, melt butter over medium heat. Whisk in whipping cream and ½ cup sour cream. Add 3 cups cheese; stir until melted. Remove from heat; cover to keep warm.
3. When potatoes are cool enough to handle, cut each potato lengthwise in half. Scoop out pulp and place in a large bowl. Cut 2 potato skin shells into 1-in. pieces; save remaining skins for another use.
4. Mash pulp with remaining ½ tsp. salt and 1 tsp. pepper. Stir in cheese mixture, half the bacon and 4 Tbsp. green onion. Transfer to a greased 3-qt. baking dish. Top with the cut-up potato skins. Sprinkle with remaining bacon and 1 cup cheese.
5. Bake until heated through and lightly browned, 30-35 minutes. Sprinkle with remaining green onion. If desired, serve with additional sour cream.

½ CUP 367 cal., 27g fat (16g sat. fat), 84mg chol., 458mg sod., 20g carb. (2g sugars, 2g fiber), 12g pro.

PULL-APART GARLIC BREAD

People go wild over this golden, garlicky loaf whenever I serve it. There's intense flavor in every bite.
—Carol Shields, Summerville, PA

Prep: 10 min. + rising • **Bake:** 30 min.
Makes: 16 servings

- ¼ cup butter, melted
- 1 Tbsp. dried parsley flakes
- 1 tsp. garlic powder
- ¼ tsp. garlic salt
- 1 loaf (1 lb.) frozen white bread dough, thawed

1. In a small bowl, combine the butter, parsley, garlic powder and garlic salt. Cut dough into 1-in. pieces; dip into butter mixture. Layer in a greased 9x5-in. loaf pan. Cover and let rise until doubled, about 1 hour.
2. Bake at 350° for 30 minutes or until golden brown.

1 SERVING 104 cal., 4g fat (2g sat. fat), 8mg chol., 215mg sod., 15g carb. (1g sugars, 1g fiber), 3g pro.

READER RAVES

"I made this bread for a family gathering and found it to be very easy and tasty! Since it uses frozen bread dough, there's no mess from making 'from scratch' yeast dough."

—BICKTASW, TASTEOFHOME.COM

SICILIAN BRUSSELS SPROUTS

I love to make this dish because the flavors jumping around in your mouth keep you coming back bite after bite. Other nuts can be used in place of the pine nuts.
—Marsha Gillett, Yukon, OK

Prep: 30 min. • **Bake:** 15 min.
Makes: 12 servings

- 12 oz. pancetta, diced
- 2 lbs. fresh Brussels sprouts, halved
- 3 Tbsp. capers, drained
- ¼ cup olive oil
- 3 Tbsp. champagne vinegar
- 1 tsp. lemon juice
- ¼ tsp. salt
- ¼ tsp. pepper
- ¾ cup golden raisins
- ½ cup pine nuts, toasted
- 1 tsp. grated lemon zest

1. In a large cast-iron or other ovenproof skillet, cook pancetta over medium heat until browned. Remove to paper towels with a slotted spoon.
2. Add Brussels sprouts to pan; cook and stir until lightly browned. Remove from heat. Stir in capers, oil, vinegar, lemon juice, salt and pepper.
3. Bake, uncovered, at 350° until caramelized, stirring occasionally, 15-20 minutes. Add raisins, pine nuts, lemon zest and pancetta; toss to coat.

¾ CUP 235 cal., 17g fat (4g sat. fat), 23mg chol., 723mg sod., 15g carb. (8g sugars, 4g fiber), 9g pro.

BALSAMIC GREEN BEAN SALAD

Serve up those green beans in a whole new way! The tangy flavors and crunch of this tasty-looking side complement any special meal or potluck.
—Megan Spencer, Farmington Hills, MI

Prep: 30 min. + chilling
Makes: 16 servings (¾ cup each)

- 2 lbs. fresh green beans, trimmed and cut into 1½-in. pieces
- ¼ cup olive oil
- 3 Tbsp. lemon juice
- 3 Tbsp. balsamic vinegar
- ¼ tsp. salt
- ¼ tsp. garlic powder
- ¼ tsp. ground mustard
- ⅛ tsp. pepper
- 1 large red onion, chopped
- 4 cups cherry tomatoes, halved
- 1 cup (4 oz.) crumbled feta cheese

1. Place beans in a 6-qt. stockpot; add water to cover. Bring to a boil. Cook, covered, 8-10 minutes or until crisp-tender. Drain and immediately place in ice water. Drain and pat dry.
2. In a small bowl, whisk oil, lemon juice, vinegar, salt, garlic powder, mustard and pepper. Drizzle over beans. Add onion; toss to coat. Refrigerate, covered, at least 1 hour. Just before serving, stir in tomatoes and cheese.

¾ CUP 77 cal., 5g fat (1g sat. fat), 4mg chol., 112mg sod., 7g carb. (3g sugars, 3g fiber), 3g pro.

TEST KITCHEN TIP

To trim beans for a salad in seconds, gather beans in a small pile, lining up the tips on 1 side. Cut off tips with a single slice using a chef's knife. Flip the pile over and do the same on the other side.

BALSAMIC
GREEN BEAN SALAD

CREAMY MAKE-AHEAD MASHED POTATOES

CREAMY MAKE-AHEAD MASHED POTATOES

My recipe takes mashed potatoes to the next level with a savory topping of cheese, onions and bacon.
—JoAnn Koerkenmeier, Damiansville, IL

Prep: 35 min. + chilling • **Bake:** 40 min.
Makes: 10 servings

- 3 lbs. potatoes (about 9 medium), peeled and cubed
- 8 oz. cream cheese, softened
- ½ cup sour cream
- ½ cup butter, cubed
- ¼ cup 2% milk
- 1½ tsp. onion powder
- 1 tsp. salt
- 1 tsp. garlic powder
- ½ tsp. pepper
- Optional: Shredded cheddar cheese, crumbled cooked bacon and chopped green onions

1. Place potatoes in a Dutch oven; cover with water. Bring to a boil. Reduce heat; cook, uncovered, 10-15 minutes or until tender. Drain potatoes; return to pan.
2. Mash potatoes, gradually adding cream cheese, sour cream and butter. Stir in milk and seasonings. Transfer to a greased 13x9-in. baking dish. If desired, sprinkle with cheese and bacon. Refrigerate, covered, up to 1-2 days.
3. Preheat oven to 350°. Remove potatoes from refrigerator and let stand while oven heats. Bake, covered, 30 minutes. Uncover; bake 10 minutes longer or until heated through. If desired, sprinkle with green onions.

¾ CUP 354 cal., 20g fat (12g sat. fat), 56mg chol., 400mg sod., 40g carb. (3g sugars, 5g fiber), 7g pro.

FRIED ONIONS & APPLES

FRIED ONIONS & APPLES

Because a lot of delicious onions are grown in our state, they are always part of my menu. This tangy side dish is good with pork and beef. The inspiration for this unusual combination was a prolific apple tree!
—Janice Mitchell, Aurora, CO

Takes: 30 min. • **Makes:** 12 servings

- 3 large yellow onions, sliced
- 3 Tbsp. butter
- 6 large tart red apples, sliced
- ½ cup packed brown sugar
- 1 tsp. salt
- ½ tsp. paprika
- ⅛ tsp. ground nutmeg

1. In a large cast-iron or other heavy skillet, saute onions in butter until tender. Place apples on top of onions. Combine remaining ingredients; sprinkle over apples.
2. Cover and simmer for 10 minutes. Uncover and simmer until apples are tender, about 5 minutes longer. Serve with a slotted spoon.

1 CUP 137 cal., 3g fat (2g sat. fat), 8mg chol., 230mg sod., 28g carb. (24g sugars, 4g fiber), 1g pro.

HASH BROWN BROCCOLI BAKE

Here's a perfect dish for a potluck or holiday buffet. It goes well with fish, poultry, pork or beef. Cheddar cheese can be substituted for Swiss. Often, I double the recipe to serve a crowd.
—Jeanette Volker, Walton, NE

Prep: 25 min. • **Bake:** 50 min.
Makes: 14 servings

- 4 Tbsp. butter, divided
- 2 Tbsp. all-purpose flour
- 1 tsp. salt
- ⅛ tsp. ground nutmeg
- ⅛ tsp. pepper
- 2 cups 2% milk
- 1 pkg. (8 oz.) cream cheese, cubed
- 2 cups shredded Swiss cheese
- 6 cups frozen shredded hash brown potatoes (about 20 oz.), thawed
- 1 pkg. (16 oz.) frozen chopped broccoli, thawed
- ½ cup dry bread crumbs

1. Preheat oven to 350°. In a large saucepan, melt 2 Tbsp. butter. Stir in flour, salt, nutmeg and pepper until smooth; gradually add milk. Bring to a boil; cook and stir until thickened, about 2 minutes. Remove from heat. Add cream cheese and Swiss cheese; stir until melted. Stir in potatoes.
2. Spoon half the potato mixture into a greased 2-qt. baking dish. Top with broccoli and remaining potato mixture. Bake, covered, 35 minutes.
3. Melt remaining 2 Tbsp. butter; toss with bread crumbs. Sprinkle over the casserole. Bake, covered, until casserole is heated through and topping is golden, 15-20 minutes.

¾ CUP 216 cal., 15g fat (9g sat. fat), 42mg chol., 334mg sod., 13g carb. (3g sugars, 2g fiber), 9g pro.

HASH BROWN BROCCOLI BAKE

GRANDMOTHER'S ORANGE SALAD

This slightly sweet gelatin salad is a little bit tangy, too. It adds beautiful color to any meal and appeals to all ages.
—Ann Eastman, Santa Monica, CA

Prep: 20 min. + chilling
Makes: 10 servings

- 1 can (11 oz.) mandarin oranges
- 1 can (8 oz.) crushed pineapple
- Water
- 1 pkg. (6 oz.) orange gelatin
- 1 pint orange sherbet, softened
- 2 bananas, sliced

1. Drain oranges and pineapple, reserving juices. Set oranges and pineapple aside. Add water to juices to measure 2 cups. Place in a saucepan and bring to a boil; pour over gelatin in a large bowl. Stir until gelatin is dissolved. Stir in sherbet until smooth.
2. Chill until partially set (watch it carefully). Fold in oranges, pineapple and bananas. Pour into an oiled 6-cup mold. Chill until firm.

1 PIECE 161 cal., 1g fat (0 sat. fat), 2mg chol., 55mg sod., 39g carb. (35g sugars, 1g fiber), 2g pro.

JAZZED-UP FRENCH BREAD

JAZZED-UP FRENCH BREAD

Fire up the grill right away for this recipe! It takes seconds to prepare and then cooks away over indirect heat, giving you plenty of time to assemble the rest of the meal.

—Lori LeCroy, East Tawas, MI

Prep: 10 min. • **Grill:** 25 min.
Makes: 10 servings

- 2 cups shredded Colby-Monterey Jack cheese
- ⅔ cup mayonnaise
- 6 green onions, chopped
- 1 loaf (1 lb.) French bread, halved lengthwise

1. In a small bowl, combine cheese, mayonnaise and onions. Spread over cut sides of bread and reassemble loaf. Wrap in a double thickness of heavy-duty foil (about 28x18 in.); seal tightly.
2. Grill, covered, over indirect medium heat for 25-30 minutes or until cheese is melted, turning once. Let stand for 5 minutes before cutting into slices.

1 PIECE 313 cal., 19g fat (7g sat. fat), 25mg chol., 491mg sod., 25g carb. (2g sugars, 1g fiber), 10g pro.

MUSHROOM CHEESE BREAD Combine 1 cup shredded mozzarella cheese, a 4-oz. can of drained mushroom stems and pieces, ⅓ cup mayonnaise and 2 Tbsp. each shredded Parmesan cheese and chopped green onion. Proceed as directed.

BACON GARLIC BREAD Combine ⅓ cup each mayonnaise and softened butter. Stir in 1 cup shredded Italian cheese blend, 4 crumbled cooked bacon strips and 5 minced garlic cloves. Proceed as directed.

ITALIAN RICOTTA EASTER BREAD

I changed our family's traditional Easter bread by adding ricotta and a few other ingredients. The almond flavoring works wonders!

—Tina Mirilovich, Johnstown, PA

Prep: 30 min. • **Bake:** 45 min.
Makes: 18 servings

- ¾ cup plain or butter-flavored shortening, room temperature
- 1½ cups sugar
- 3 large eggs, room temperature
- 3 large egg yolks, room temperature
- 1 cup whole-milk ricotta cheese
- 1 tsp. almond extract (or flavor of choice)
- 6 cups all-purpose flour
- 1 Tbsp. baking powder
- 1 tsp. salt
- ½ cup 2% milk

GLAZE

- 1½ cups confectioners' sugar
- 3 Tbsp. 2% milk
- ½ tsp. almond extract (or flavor of choice)
- Sliced toasted almonds or assorted sprinkles

1. Preheat oven to 350°. Cream the shortening and sugar until light and fluffy, 5-7 minutes. Add eggs and egg yolks, 1 at a time, beating well after each addition. Beat in ricotta and extract. In another bowl, whisk 5 cups flour, baking powder and salt; add to creamed mixture alternately with milk, beating well after each addition. Stir in final 1 cup flour by hand.
2. Turn out onto a lightly floured surface; divide into thirds. Roll each into an 18-in. rope. Place ropes on a parchment-lined baking sheet and braid. Pinch ends to seal; tuck under braid. Bake until a toothpick inserted in center comes out clean, 45-55 minutes (do not overbake). Remove to wire rack to cool.
3. Meanwhile, beat confectioners' sugar, milk and extract until smooth. Brush on bread while still warm; top with sliced almonds or sprinkles.

NOTE To toast nuts, bake in a shallow pan in a 350°; oven for 5-10 minutes or cook in a skillet over low heat until lightly browned, stirring occasionally.

1 PIECE 376 cal., 11g fat (4g sat. fat), 68mg chol., 247mg sod., 60g carb. (28g sugars, 1g fiber), 8g pro.

READER RAVES

"Wow, amazing! This will be an Easter tradition from now on. It is easy to make and perfect for hostess gifts!"

—SUEFALK, TASTEOFHOME.COM

GRILLED PEACH COUSCOUS SALAD

GRILLED PEACH COUSCOUS SALAD

You'll feel inspired at the farmers market with the recipe for this couscous salad in tow. Grilled peaches and limes plus a subtly sweet dressing bring pizazz.
—Emily King, Fayetteville, AR

Takes: 30 min. • **Makes:** 8 servings

- ½ cup uncooked couscous
- 1 medium lime
- 2 medium firm ripe peaches, halved and pitted
- 1 tsp. plus ¼ cup canola oil, divided
- 1 English cucumber, halved and sliced
- 1 cup cherry tomatoes, halved
- ¼ medium red onion, thinly sliced
- 1 Tbsp. agave nectar
- 2 tsp. white wine vinegar
- ½ tsp. salt
- ¼ tsp. pepper

1. Prepare couscous according to package directions; fluff. Transfer to a large bowl; let cool. Meanwhile, finely grate enough zest from lime to measure 1½ tsp.; set aside for dressing. Slice lime in half. Brush peach and lime halves with 1 tsp. oil. Grill peaches, covered, over medium heat until tender, 3-4 minutes on each side. Remove to a cutting board. Grill lime halves just until tender, about 1 minute.
2. When cool enough to handle, chop peaches and add to couscous. Stir in cucumber, tomatoes and red onion. Squeeze juice from lime into a small bowl. Add agave, vinegar, salt, pepper, reserved lime zest and remaining ¼ cup oil. Whisk until blended. Pour over salad; toss to coat.

¾ CUP 144 cal., 8g fat (1g sat. fat), 0 chol., 150mg sod., 18g carb. (7g sugars, 2g fiber), 2g pro.

BROCCOLI RICE CASSEROLE

BROCCOLI RICE CASSEROLE

This hearty broccoli rice casserole is my usual choice to make for a potluck. With the green of the broccoli and the rich cheese sauce, it's pretty to serve, and it makes a tasty side dish for almost any kind of meat.

—Margaret Mayes, La Mesa, CA

Prep: 10 min. • **Bake:** 25 min.
Makes: 8 servings

- 1 Tbsp. butter
- 1 small onion, chopped
- ½ cup chopped celery
- 3 cups frozen chopped broccoli, thawed
- 1 jar (8 oz.) cheese dip
- 1 can (10½ oz.) condensed cream of mushroom soup, undiluted
- 1 can (5 oz.) evaporated milk
- 3 cups cooked rice

Preheat oven to 325°. In a large skillet, melt butter over medium-high heat. Add onion, celery and broccoli; cook and stir until crisp-tender, 3-5 minutes. Stir in the cheese dip, soup and milk until smooth. Spoon rice into a greased 8-in. square baking dish. Pour cheese mixture over rice; do not stir. Bake, uncovered, until bubbly, 25-30 minutes.

1 CUP 241 cal., 11g fat (6g sat. fat), 32mg chol., 782mg sod., 28g carb. (5g sugars, 3g fiber), 8g pro.

READER RAVES

"I've made this many times and everyone likes it, even those who don't like broccoli."

—SJACNSMITH, TASTEOFHOME.COM

GERMAN RED CABBAGE

GERMAN RED CABBAGE

Sunday afternoons were a time for family gatherings when I was a kid. While the uncles played cards, the aunts made German treats such as this traditional red cabbage.

—Jeannette Heim, Dunlap, TN

Prep: 10 min. • **Cook:** 65 min.
Makes: 10 servings

- 1 medium onion, halved and sliced
- 1 medium apple, sliced
- 1 medium head red cabbage, shredded (about 8 cups)
- ⅓ cup sugar
- ⅓ cup white vinegar
- ¾ tsp. salt, optional
- ¼ tsp. pepper

In a large Dutch oven coated with cooking spray, cook and stir onion and apple over medium heat until onion is tender, about 5 minutes. Stir in remaining ingredients and cook, covered, until cabbage is tender, about 1 hour, stirring occasionally. Serve warm or cold.

1 CUP 64 cal., 0 fat (0 sat. fat), 0 chol., 23mg sod., 16g carb. (12g sugars, 2g fiber), 1g pro.

ARTICHOKE CAPRESE PLATTER

I dressed up the classic Italian trio of mozzarella, tomatoes and basil with marinated artichokes. It looks so yummy on a pretty platter set out on a buffet. Using fresh mozzarella is the key to its great taste.
—Margaret Wilson, San Bernardino, CA

Takes: 15 min. • **Makes:** 12 servings

- 2 jars (7½ oz. each) marinated artichoke hearts
- 2 Tbsp. red wine vinegar
- 2 Tbsp. olive oil
- 6 plum tomatoes, sliced
- 1 lb. fresh mozzarella cheese, sliced
- 2 cups loosely packed fresh basil leaves
- Coarsely ground pepper, optional

1. Drain artichokes, reserving ½ cup marinade. In a small bowl, whisk vinegar, oil and reserved marinade.
2. On a large serving platter, arrange artichokes, tomatoes, mozzarella and basil. Drizzle with vinaigrette. If desired, sprinkle with coarsely ground pepper.

½ CUP 192 cal., 16g fat (7g sat. fat), 30mg chol., 179mg sod., 5g carb. (2g sugars, 1g fiber), 7g pro.

COLORFUL CORNBREAD SALAD

When my garden comes in, I harvest the veggies for potluck dishes. I live in the South, and we think bacon and cornbread make everything better, even salad!
—Rebecca Clark, Warrior, AL

Prep: 30 min. + chilling
Bake: 15 min. + cooling
Makes: 14 servings

- 1 pkg. (8½ oz.) cornbread/muffin mix
- 1 cup mayonnaise
- ½ cup sour cream
- 1 envelope ranch salad dressing mix
- 1 to 2 Tbsp. adobo sauce from canned chipotle peppers
- 4 to 6 cups torn romaine
- 4 medium tomatoes, chopped
- 1 medium green pepper, chopped
- 1 medium onion, chopped
- 1 lb. bacon strips, cooked and crumbled
- 4 cups shredded cheddar cheese

1. Preheat oven to 400°. Prepare the cornbread batter according to package directions. Pour into a greased 8-in. square baking pan. Bake until a toothpick inserted in center comes out clean, 15-20 minutes. Cool completely in pan on a wire rack.
2. Coarsely crumble cornbread into a large bowl. In a small bowl, mix the mayonnaise, sour cream, salad dressing mix and adobo sauce.
3. In a 3-qt. trifle bowl or glass bowl, layer a third of the cornbread and half each of the romaine, tomatoes, pepper, onion, bacon, cheese and mayonnaise mixture in the listed order. Repeat layers. Top with remaining cornbread, and additional chopped tomato and bacon if desired. Refrigerate, covered, 2-4 hours before serving.

¾ CUP 407 cal., 31g fat (11g sat. fat), 61mg chol., 821mg sod., 18g carb. (6g sugars, 2g fiber), 14g pro.

COLORFUL
CORNBREAD SALAD

BUTTERNUT & CHARD PASTA BAKE

This recipe is made for butternut squash lovers, with pureed squash in the sauce and squash pieces in the casserole alongside an ideal companion, Swiss chard. This is a hybrid of ever-popular holiday veggie sides.
—Arlene Erlbach, Morton Grove, IL

Prep: 25 min. • **Bake:** 30 min.
Makes: 9 servings

- 3 cups uncooked bow tie pasta
- 2 cups fat-free ricotta cheese
- 4 large eggs
- 3 cups frozen cubed butternut squash, thawed and divided
- 1 tsp. dried thyme
- ½ tsp. salt, divided
- ¼ tsp. ground nutmeg
- 1 cup coarsely chopped shallots
- 1½ cups chopped Swiss chard, stems removed
- 2 Tbsp. olive oil
- 1½ cups panko bread crumbs
- ⅓ cup coarsely chopped fresh parsley
- ¼ tsp. garlic powder

1. Preheat oven to 375°. Cook pasta according to package directions for al dente; drain. Meanwhile, place ricotta, eggs, 1½ cups squash, thyme, ¼ tsp. salt and nutmeg in a food processor; process until smooth. Pour into a large bowl. Stir in pasta, shallots, Swiss chard and remaining 1½ cups squash. Transfer to a greased 13x9-in. baking dish.
2. In a large skillet, heat oil over medium-high heat. Add bread crumbs; cook and stir until golden brown, 2-3 minutes. Stir in parsley, garlic powder and remaining ¼ tsp. salt. Sprinkle over pasta mixture.
3. Bake, uncovered, until set and topping is golden brown, 30-35 minutes.

1 CUP 223 cal., 6g fat (1g sat. fat), 83mg chol., 209mg sod., 33g carb. (4g sugars, 2g fiber), 9g pro.

BUTTERNUT & CHARD PASTA BAKE

ORANGE GELATIN PRETZEL SALAD

Salty pretzels pair nicely with the sweet fruit in this refreshing layered salad. A family favorite, it's also a pretty potluck dish.

—Peggy Boyd, Northport, AL

Prep: 20 min. + chilling
Bake: 10 min. + cooling
Makes: 12 servings

- ¾ cup butter, melted
- 1 Tbsp. plus ¾ cup sugar, divided
- 2 cups finely crushed pretzels
- 2 cups boiling water
- 2 pkg. (3 oz. each) orange gelatin
- 2 cans (8 oz. each) crushed pineapple, drained
- 1 can (11 oz.) mandarin oranges, drained
- 1 pkg. (8 oz.) cream cheese, softened
- 2 cups whipped topping
- Optional: Additional whipped topping and mandarin oranges

1. Preheat oven to 350°. Mix melted butter and 1 Tbsp. sugar; stir in pretzels. Press onto bottom of an ungreased 13x9-in. baking dish. Bake 10 minutes. Cool completely on a wire rack.
2. In a large bowl, add boiling water to gelatin; stir 2 minutes to completely dissolve. Stir in fruit. Refrigerate until partially set, about 30 minutes.
3. Meanwhile, in a bowl, beat cream cheese and remaining ¾ cup sugar until smooth. Fold in whipped topping. Spread over crust.
4. Gently spoon gelatin mixture over the top. Refrigerate, covered, until firm, 2-4 hours. To serve, cut into squares. If desired, top with additional whipped topping and oranges.

1 SERVING 400 cal., 21g fat (13g sat. fat), 50mg chol., 402mg sod., 51g carb. (38g sugars, 1g fiber), 4g pro.

PARTY POTATOES

These creamy tasty potatoes can be made the day before and stored in the refrigerator until you're ready to pop them in the oven (I often do that). The garlic powder and chives add zip, and the shredded cheese adds color.

—Sharon Mensing, Greenfield, IA

Prep: 15 min. • **Bake:** 50 min.
Makes: 12 servings

- 4 cups mashed potatoes (8 to 10 large) or 4 cups prepared instant potatoes
- 1 cup sour cream
- 1 pkg. (8 oz.) cream cheese, softened
- 1 tsp. minced chives
- ¼ tsp. garlic powder
- ¼ cup dry bread crumbs
- 1 Tbsp. butter, melted
- ½ cup shredded cheddar cheese

1. In a large bowl, combine potatoes, sour cream, cream cheese, chives and garlic powder. Turn out into a greased 2-qt. casserole. Combine bread crumbs with butter; sprinkle over potatoes.
2. Bake at 350° for 50-60 minutes. Top with cheese and serve immediately.

¾ CUP 207 cal., 13g fat (8g sat. fat), 43mg chol., 305mg sod., 16g carb. (1g sugars, 0 fiber), 5g pro.

TARRAGON ASPARAGUS

STRAWBERRY-PINEAPPLE COLESLAW

Sweet fruit, tangy coleslaw dressing and colorful, crisp cabbage make a wonderful combination to share with others. I like to include the nuts because they add a healthy crunch.
—Victoria Pederson, Ham Lake, MN

Prep: 15 min. + chilling
Makes: about 14 servings

- 2 pkg. (14 oz. each) coleslaw mix
- 1 jar (13 oz.) coleslaw salad dressing
- 1 cup salted cashews or macadamia nuts
- 1 cup dried cranberries
- 1 cup chopped fresh or canned pineapple
- 1 cup chopped fresh sugar snap peas
- 1 cup chopped fresh strawberries
- ½ cup sweetened shredded coconut
- ½ cup chopped green onions

Combine all ingredients in a large bowl; toss to coat. Cover and refrigerate until serving.

¾ CUP 244 cal., 15g fat (3g sat. fat), 3mg chol., 272mg sod., 26g carb. (19g sugars, 3g fiber), 3g pro.

TARRAGON ASPARAGUS

I grow purple asparagus, so I'm always looking for new ways to prepare it. Recently, my husband and I discovered how wonderful any color of asparagus tastes when it's grilled.
—Sue Gronholz, Beaver Dam, WI

Takes: 15 min. • **Makes:** 8 servings

- 2 lbs. fresh asparagus, trimmed
- 2 Tbsp. olive oil
- 1 tsp. salt
- ½ tsp. pepper
- ¼ cup honey
- 2 to 4 Tbsp. minced fresh tarragon

On a large plate, toss asparagus with oil, salt and pepper. Grill, covered, over medium heat 6-8 minutes or until crisp-tender, turning occasionally and basting frequently with honey during the last 3 minutes. Sprinkle with tarragon.

1 SERVING 76 cal., 4g fat (1g sat. fat), 0 chol., 302mg sod., 11g carb. (10g sugars, 1g fiber), 2g pro.

STRAWBERRY-PINEAPPLE COLESLAW

SUMMER ORZO

SUMMER ORZO

I'm always looking for fun ways to use up the fresh veggies that come in my Community Supported Agriculture box, and this salad is one of my favorite creations. I like to improvise with whatever I have on hand.
—Shayna Marmar, Philadelphia, PA

Prep: 30 min. + chilling
Makes: 16 servings

- 1 pkg. (16 oz.) orzo pasta
- ¼ cup water
- 1½ cups fresh or frozen corn
- 24 cherry tomatoes, halved
- 2 cups crumbled feta cheese
- 1 medium cucumber, seeded and chopped
- 1 small red onion, finely chopped
- ¼ cup minced fresh mint
- 2 Tbsp. capers, drained and chopped, optional
- ½ cup olive oil
- ¼ cup lemon juice
- 1 Tbsp. grated lemon zest
- 1½ tsp. salt
- 1 tsp. pepper
- 1 cup sliced almonds, toasted

1. Cook orzo according to package directions for al dente. Drain orzo; rinse with cold water and drain well. Transfer to a large bowl.
2. In a large nonstick skillet, heat ¼ cup water over medium heat. Add corn; cook and stir until crisp-tender, 3-4 minutes. Add to orzo; stir in tomatoes, feta cheese, cucumber, onion, mint and, if desired, capers. In a small bowl, whisk oil, lemon juice, lemon zest, salt and pepper until blended. Pour over orzo mixture; toss to coat. Refrigerate 30 minutes.
3. Just before serving, stir in almonds.

NOTE To toast nuts, bake in a shallow pan in a 350° oven for 5-10 minutes or cook in a skillet over low heat until lightly browned, stirring occasionally.

¾ CUP 291 cal., 15g fat (4g sat. fat), 15mg chol., 501mg sod., 28g carb. (3g sugars, 3g fiber), 11g pro.

FARMHOUSE APPLE COLESLAW

FARMHOUSE APPLE COLESLAW

A friend from church gave me this apple coleslaw recipe that her grandmother handed down to her. All the flavors complement each other well, while the fruit creates a refreshing change of pace from the usual coleslaw.
—Jan Myers, Atlantic, IA

Prep: 20 min. + chilling
Makes: 12 servings

- 4 cups shredded cabbage
- 1 large apple, chopped
- ¾ cup raisins
- ½ cup chopped celery
- ¼ cup chopped onion
- ¼ cup mayonnaise
- 2 Tbsp. lemon juice
- 1 Tbsp. sugar
- 1 Tbsp. olive oil
- ½ tsp. salt
- ⅛ tsp. pepper

In a serving bowl, combine the cabbage, apple, raisins, celery and onion. In a small bowl, combine the remaining ingredients. Pour over cabbage mixture and toss to coat. Cover and refrigerate for at least 30 minutes.

⅔ CUP 87 cal., 5g fat (1g sat. fat), 0 chol., 131mg sod., 12g carb. (8g sugars, 1g fiber), 1g pro.

TEST KITCHEN TIP

For this recipe, choose apples with a firm, crisp texture, like Cortland, Granny Smith or Honeycrisp. These apples will maintain their shape and give this salad a nice crunch. If you opt for an apple that's sweet (rather than very tart like Granny Smith), you can reduce the amount of sugar in this dressing by half.

GREAT GRAIN SALAD

I can't think of a better dish to round out a meal. My grain salad features all of my favorite nuts, seeds and fruits. Try adding grilled chicken to make it a meal on its own.
—Rachel Dueker, Gervais, OR

Prep: 15 min. • **Cook:** 1 hour + chilling
Makes: 12 servings (¾ cup each)

- 3 cups water
- ½ cup medium pearl barley
- ½ cup uncooked wild rice
- ⅔ cup uncooked basmati rice
- ½ cup slivered almonds
- ½ cup sunflower kernels
- ½ cup salted pumpkin seeds or pepitas
- ½ cup each golden raisins, chopped dried apricots and dried cranberries
- ⅓ cup minced fresh parsley
- 4 tsp. grated orange zest

VINAIGRETTE

- ⅔ cup walnut oil
- ⅔ cup raspberry vinegar
- 2 tsp. orange juice
- 2 tsp. pepper
- 1 tsp. salt

1. In a large saucepan, bring water to a boil. Add barley and wild rice. Reduce heat; cover and simmer for 55-65 minutes or until tender. Meanwhile, cook basmati rice according to package directions. Cool barley and rices to room temperature.
2. In a large bowl, combine the almonds, sunflower kernels, pumpkin seeds, dried fruit, parsley and orange zest; add barley and rices.
3. In a small bowl, whisk the vinaigrette ingredients. Pour over salad and toss to coat. Cover and refrigerate for at least 2 hours.

¾ CUP 368 cal., 22g fat (3g sat. fat), 0 chol., 281mg sod., 39g carb. (11g sugars, 4g fiber), 8g pro.

RED POTATO & EGG SALAD

This flavorful red potato salad with egg is the perfect side for summer cookouts. The red potatoes really dress it up.
—Margaret (Peggy) Blomquist, Newfield, NY

Prep: 40 min. + chilling
Makes: 17 servings

- 5 lbs. medium red potatoes, halved
- 5 hard-boiled large eggs, chopped
- 1 celery rib, finely chopped
- ½ medium onion, finely chopped
- 1½ cups mayonnaise
- ¼ cup sweet pickle relish
- 3 Tbsp. sugar
- 2 Tbsp. dried parsley flakes
- 2 tsp. prepared mustard
- 1 tsp. salt
- 1 tsp. cider vinegar
- ⅛ tsp. pepper

1. Place potatoes in a large kettle; cover with water. Bring to a boil. Reduce heat; cover and cook until tender, 15-20 minutes. Drain and cool. Cut potatoes into ¾-in. cubes.
2. In a large bowl, combine potatoes, eggs, celery and onion. In a small bowl, combine remaining ingredients. Pour over potato mixture and stir gently to coat. Cover and refrigerate for 6 hours or overnight.

¾ CUP 276 cal., 17g fat (3g sat. fat), 69mg chol., 309mg sod., 25g carb. (5g sugars, 2g fiber), 5g pro.

READER RAVES

"I love this recipe. I make it a least once a month. The added flavor of relish really gives it a nice taste."

—LUANDA, TASTEOFHOME.COM

RED POTATO & EGG SALAD

YOU'RE-BACON-ME-CRAZY POTATO SALAD

My kids and I always want potato salad when we grill or barbecue, but we don't like the store-bought versions. I toyed with many combinations until I developed this one. Now if I mention grilling to the family, this is their top side-dish request.
—Paul Cogswell, League City, TX

Prep: 10 min. • **Cook:** 25 min. + chilling
Makes: 12 servings

- 2½ lbs. small red potatoes, cut into 1-in. pieces
- 3 tsp. salt
- 1 lb. bacon strips, finely chopped
- 1 large onion, chopped
- 3 celery ribs, finely chopped
- 2 cups mayonnaise
- 2 Tbsp. Dijon or yellow mustard
- ¾ tsp. dill weed
- ½ tsp. celery salt
- ¼ tsp. celery seed

1. Place potatoes in a 6-qt. stockpot; add water to cover. Add salt; bring to a boil. Reduce heat; cook, uncovered, until potatoes are tender, 12-15 minutes.
2. Meanwhile, in a large skillet, cook bacon over medium heat until crisp, stirring occasionally. Remove with a slotted spoon and drain on paper towels; reserve 4 Tbsp. bacon drippings. Cook and stir onion in reserved drippings until browned, 6-8 minutes.
3. Reserve ¼ cup cooked bacon for topping. Add onion, drippings, celery and remaining bacon to potatoes.
4. In a small bowl, mix mayonnaise, mustard and seasonings. Pour over potato mixture; toss to coat. Refrigerate, covered, until chilled, about 1 hour. Just before serving, sprinkle salad with reserved bacon.

¾ CUP 424 cal., 36g fat (7g sat. fat), 20mg chol., 1147mg sod., 17g carb. (2g sugars, 2g fiber), 7g pro.

YOU'RE-BACON-ME-CRAZY POTATO SALAD

SPICY SWEET POTATO CHIPS & CILANTRO DIP

This irresistible combo could become your new signature snack food. Park the spicy baked chips next to a bowl of the cool, creamy dip and let the gang have at it. What a fantastic twist on traditional chips and dip!
—Elizabeth Godecke, Chicago, IL

Prep: 20 min. • **Bake:** 25 min./batch
Makes: 12 servings (1½ cups dip)

- 2 to 3 large sweet potatoes (1¾ lbs.), peeled and cut into ⅛-in. slices
- 2 Tbsp. canola oil
- 1 tsp. chili powder
- ½ tsp. garlic powder
- ½ tsp. taco seasoning
- ¼ tsp. salt
- ¼ tsp. ground cumin
- ¼ tsp. pepper
- ⅛ tsp. cayenne pepper

DIP

- ¾ cup mayonnaise
- ½ cup sour cream
- 2 oz. cream cheese, softened
- 4½ tsp. minced fresh cilantro
- 1½ tsp. lemon juice
- ½ tsp. celery salt
- ⅛ tsp. pepper

1. Preheat oven to 400°. Place sweet potatoes in a large bowl. In a small bowl, mix oil and seasonings; drizzle over potatoes and toss to coat.
2. Arrange half the sweet potatoes in a single layer in 2 ungreased 15x10x1-in. baking pans. Bake 25-30 minutes or until golden brown, turning once. Repeat with remaining sweet potatoes.
3. In a small bowl, beat dip ingredients until blended. Serve with chips.

½ CUP CHIPS WITH ABOUT 1 TBSP. DIP 285 cal., 16g fat (4g sat. fat), 8mg chol., 217mg sod., 33g carb. (14g sugars, 4g fiber), 3g pro.

HOLIDAY CRANBERRY GELATIN SALAD

HOLIDAY CRANBERRY GELATIN SALAD

My family has requested this delicious holiday salad every year since the first time I served it. The not-too-sweet flavor is a perfect pairing with just about any meat.

—Jennifer Mastnick-Cook, Hartville, OH

Prep: 30 min. + chilling
Makes: 12 servings

- 2 pkg. (3 oz. each) raspberry gelatin
- 2 cups boiling water, divided
- 1 can (14 oz.) whole-berry cranberry sauce
- 2 Tbsp. lemon juice
- 1 cup heavy whipping cream
- 1 pkg. (8 oz.) cream cheese, softened
- ½ cup chopped pecans

1. In a small bowl, dissolve gelatin in 1 cup boiling water. In another bowl, combine cranberry sauce and remaining 1 cup water; add gelatin mixture and lemon juice. Pour into a 13x9-in. dish coated with cooking spray; refrigerate until firm, about 1 hour.
2. In a large bowl, beat cream until stiff peaks form. In another bowl, beat cream cheese until smooth. Stir ½ cup whipped cream into cream cheese; fold in remaining whipped cream. Spread over gelatin mixture; sprinkle with pecans. Refrigerate for at least 2 hours.

1 PIECE 241 cal., 14g fat (7g sat. fat), 34mg chol., 100mg sod., 28g carb. (22g sugars, 1g fiber), 3g pro.

CHEDDAR & CHIVE MASHED POTATOES

CHEDDAR & CHIVE MASHED POTATOES

My husband swears my cheddar mashed potatoes are the world's best. We always have some in the freezer. Sometimes I dollop individual servings in muffin cups and reheat them that way instead.
—Cyndy Gerken, Naples, FL

Prep: 45 min. • **Bake:** 1 hour
Makes: 16 servings

- 5 lbs. Yukon Gold potatoes, peeled and cut into 1-in. pieces (about 10 cups)
- 1 cup butter, cubed
- 1 cup sour cream
- 2 tsp. salt
- ¾ tsp. pepper
- ½ cup heavy whipping cream
- 1½ cups shredded cheddar cheese
- 1½ cups shredded Monterey Jack cheese
- ¼ cup grated Parmesan cheese
- 2 Tbsp. minced fresh chives

TOPPINGS

- 1 cup shredded cheddar cheese
- 1 can (6 oz.) french-fried onions

1. Preheat oven to 350°. Place potatoes in a 6-qt. stockpot; add water to cover. Bring to a boil. Reduce heat to medium; cook, uncovered, until tender, 10-15 minutes. Drain; transfer to a large bowl.
2. Add butter, sour cream, salt and pepper; beat until blended. Beat in whipping cream. Stir in the cheeses and chives.
3. Bake, covered, 45 minutes, stirring after 30 minutes. Sprinkle with toppings; bake, uncovered, until heated through, about 15 minutes.

¾ CUP 474 cal., 32g fat (18g sat. fat), 70mg chol., 693mg sod., 37g carb. (3g sugars, 2g fiber), 11g pro.

THREE-BEAN BAKED BEANS

MA

THREE-BEAN BAKED BEANS

I got this recipe from my aunt and made a couple of changes to suit my taste. With ground beef and bacon mixed in, these satisfying beans are a big hit at backyard barbecues and church picnics. I'm always asked to bring my special beans.
—Julie Currington, Gahanna, OH

Prep: 20 min. • **Bake:** 1 hour
Makes: 12 servings

- ½ lb. ground beef
- 5 bacon strips, diced
- ½ cup chopped onion
- ⅓ cup packed brown sugar
- ¼ cup sugar
- ¼ cup ketchup
- ¼ cup barbecue sauce
- 2 Tbsp. molasses
- 2 Tbsp. prepared mustard
- ½ tsp. chili powder
- ½ tsp. salt
- 2 cans (15 oz. each) pork and beans, undrained
- 1 can (16 oz.) butter beans, rinsed and drained
- 1 can (16 oz.) kidney beans, rinsed and drained

1. Preheat oven to 350°. In a large skillet, cook and crumble beef with bacon and onion over medium heat until beef is no longer pink; drain.
2. Stir in sugars, ketchup, barbecue sauce, molasses, mustard, chili powder and salt until blended. Stir in beans. Transfer to a greased 2½-qt. baking dish. Bake, covered, 1 hour or until beans reach desired thickness.

FREEZE OPTION Freeze cooled bean mixture in freezer containers. To use, partially thaw in refrigerator overnight. Heat through in a saucepan, stirring occasionally; add water if necessary.

¾ CUP 269 cal., 8g fat (2g sat. fat), 19mg chol., 708mg sod., 42g carb. (21g sugars, 7g fiber), 13g pro.

GARLIC HERB BUBBLE LOAF

GARLIC HERB BUBBLE LOAF

I adapted an old sour cream bread recipe for this deliciously different pull-apart loaf that smells heavenly while baking. It has a light crust, tender interior and lots of herb and butter flavor. We think it's wonderful with a hot bowl of potato soup.
—Katie Crill, Priest River, ID

Prep: 25 min. + rising • **Bake:** 35 min.
Makes: 18 servings

- ½ cup water (70° to 80°)
- ½ cup sour cream
- 2 Tbsp. butter, softened
- 3 Tbsp. sugar
- 1½ tsp. salt
- 3 cups bread flour
- 2¼ tsp. active dry yeast

GARLIC HERB BUTTER

- ¼ cup butter, melted
- 4 garlic cloves, minced
- ¼ tsp. each dried oregano, thyme and rosemary, crushed

1. In bread machine pan, place the first 7 ingredients in order suggested by manufacturer. Select dough setting (check dough after 5 minutes of mixing; add 1-2 Tbsp. of water or flour if needed).
2. When cycle is completed, turn out dough onto a lightly floured surface. Cover and let rest for 15 minutes. Divide dough into 36 pieces. Shape each piece into a ball. In a shallow bowl, combine butter, garlic and herbs. Dip each ball in mixture; place in an ungreased 9x5-in. loaf pan. Cover and let rise in a warm place until doubled, about 45 minutes.
3. Bake at 375° for 35-40 minutes or until golden brown (cover loosely with foil if bread browns too quickly). Remove from pan to a wire rack. Serve warm.

NOTE We recommend you do not use a bread machine's time-delay feature for this recipe.

1 SERVING 141 cal., 6g fat (3g sat. fat), 12mg chol., 230mg sod., 19g carb. (2g sugars, 1g fiber), 3g pro.

ORANGE-PISTACHIO QUINOA SALAD

Add this fresh and healthy salad to your holiday spread. Its citrusy, nutty taste is simply delicious.
—Jean Greenfield, San Anselmo, CA

Prep: 15 min. • **Cook:** 15 min. + cooling
Makes: 8 servings

- 1⅓ cups water
- ⅔ cup quinoa, rinsed
- 2 cups chopped romaine lettuce
- 1 can (15 oz.) garbanzo beans or chickpeas, rinsed and drained
- 1 can (15 oz.) mandarin oranges, drained
- 1 medium cucumber, halved and sliced
- 1 cup shelled pistachios, toasted
- ½ cup finely chopped red onion
- 1 medium navel orange
- 2 Tbsp. olive oil
- ½ tsp. salt
- Pinch pepper

1. In a large saucepan, bring water to a boil. Add quinoa. Reduce heat; simmer, covered, 12-14 minutes or until liquid is absorbed. Remove from heat; fluff with a fork. Cool.
2. In a large bowl, combine romaine, garbanzo beans, mandarin oranges, cucumber, pistachios, onion and cooled quinoa. In a small bowl, finely grate zest from orange. Cut orange crosswise in half; squeeze juice from orange and add to zest. Whisk in oil, salt and pepper. Drizzle over salad; toss to coat.

1 CUP 257 cal., 12g fat (1g sat. fat), 0 chol., 287mg sod., 31g carb. (10g sugars, 6g fiber), 8g pro.

ORANGE-PISTACHIO QUINOA SALAD

SOUR CREAM POTATO SALAD

Italian dressing and horseradish make this creamy potato salad different from most, plus those ingredients really add some zip! It's perfect for picnics or potlucks.

—Veda Luttrell, Sutter, CA

Prep: 20 min. • **Cook:** 25 min. + chilling.
Makes: 8 servings

- 2 lbs. medium red potatoes
- ½ cup Italian salad dressing
- 4 hard-boiled large eggs
- ¾ cup sliced celery
- ⅓ cup thinly sliced green onions
- 1 cup mayonnaise
- ½ cup sour cream
- 1½ tsp. prepared horseradish
- 1½ tsp. prepared mustard
- 1½ tsp. celery seed
- ¾ tsp. salt

1. Place potatoes in a large saucepan and cover with water. Bring to a boil. Reduce heat; cover and cook until tender, 15-20 minutes. Drain.
2. When cool enough to handle, peel and slice potatoes. Place in a large bowl; add salad dressing and toss gently. Cover and refrigerate for 2 hours.
3. Slice eggs in half; remove yolks and set aside. Chop egg whites; add to potatoes with celery and green onion.
4. In another bowl, combine mayonnaise, sour cream, horseradish, mustard, celery seed and salt. Crumble egg yolks; add to mayonnaise mixture and whisk until blended. Spoon over potatoes; toss gently to coat. Cover and refrigerate for at least 2 hours before serving.

¾ CUP 366 cal., 28g fat (6g sat. fat), 114mg chol., 577mg sod., 21g carb. (3g sugars, 2g fiber), 6g pro.

POTATO SALAD TIPS

Can you peel the potatoes before boiling them, instead of boiling them and then peeling? Yes! But red potatoes are easier to peel when they're cooked, so you're better off peeling potatoes after cooking them. (Bonus: potatoes boiled whole also tend to keep their shape.) Or just leave the peel on for more fiber and a hint of color!

Can you use other kinds of potatoes to make sour cream potato salad? We love red potatoes in potato salad, but other waxy or semi-waxy types also work well. Yukon Golds, or a mix of red, gold, and purple potatoes would also be nice in this recipe.

MANGO SALAD WITH MINT YOGURT DRESSING

An abundant planter full of mint inspired me to create this summery salad. The flavors pair so well and really let the freshness of the mint shine.
—Natalie Klein, Albuquerque, NM

Prep: 25 min. + chilling
Makes: 8 servings

- 3 medium mangoes, peeled and cut into ¼-in. slices
- 3 medium Gala apples, cut into ¼-in. slices
- 2 Tbsp. lime juice, divided
- ½ cup plain yogurt
- 2 Tbsp. honey
- 1 tsp. minced fresh gingerroot
- ¼ tsp. salt
- ¼ cup fresh mint leaves, thinly sliced

1. In a large bowl, combine the mangoes and apples. Drizzle with 1 Tbsp. lime juice; toss to coat.
2. In a small bowl, combine the yogurt, honey, ginger, salt and remaining 1 Tbsp. lime juice. Stir into mango mixture. Sprinkle with mint and toss to coat. Refrigerate for at least 15 minutes before serving.

1 CUP 105 cal., 1g fat (0 sat. fat), 2mg chol., 84mg sod., 26g carb. (22g sugars, 3g fiber), 1g pro.

READER RAVES

"Killer dressing! We've made this a few times now and love it, very versatile."

—SHEHAUNESSY, TASTEOFHOME.COM

CAULIFLOWER PARMESAN CASSEROLE

A lighter version of a classic white sauce coats the cauliflower in this perfect potluck buffet dish. Thick and creamy with a golden brown top layer, it's a super side dish that tastes as comforting as it looks.
—Taste of Home *Test Kitchen*

Prep: 30 min. • **Bake:** 30 min.
Makes: 12 servings

- 3 pkg. (16 oz. each) frozen cauliflower, thawed
- 1 large onion, chopped
- ⅓ cup butter, cubed
- ⅓ cup all-purpose flour
- ½ tsp. salt
- ¼ tsp. ground mustard
- ¼ tsp. pepper
- 2 cups fat-free milk
- ½ cup grated Parmesan cheese

TOPPING

- ½ cup soft whole wheat bread crumbs
- 2 Tbsp. butter, melted
- ¼ tsp. paprika

1. Preheat oven to 350°. Place 1 in. water in a Dutch oven; add cauliflower. Bring to a boil. Reduce heat; cover and cook until crisp-tender, 4-6 minutes. Drain and pat dry.
2. Meanwhile, in a large saucepan, saute onion in butter until tender. Stir in flour, salt, mustard and pepper until blended; gradually add milk. Bring to a boil; cook and stir until thickened, 1-2 minutes. Remove from the heat. Add cheese; stir until melted.
3. Place cauliflower in a greased 13x9-in. baking dish. Pour the sauce on top.
4. Combine the bread crumbs, butter and paprika. Sprinkle over sauce. Bake, uncovered, 30-35 minutes or until bubbly.

¾ CUP 142 cal., 8g fat (5g sat. fat), 22mg chol., 257mg sod., 13g carb. (5g sugars, 3g fiber), 6g pro.

CAULIFLOWER PARMESAN CASSEROLE

CANDY BAR APPLE SALAD

CANDY BAR APPLE SALAD

This creamy, sweet Snickers salad with a crisp apple crunch is amazing. The recipe makes a lot, which is good, because it will go fast!
—Cyndi Fynaardt, Oskaloosa, IA

Takes: 15 min. • **Makes:** 12 servings

- 1½ cups cold 2% milk
- 1 pkg. (3.4 oz.) instant vanilla pudding mix
- 1 carton (8 oz.) frozen whipped topping, thawed
- 4 large apples, chopped (about 6 cups)
- 4 Snickers candy bars (1.86 oz. each), cut into ½-in. pieces

In a large bowl, whisk milk and pudding mix for 2 minutes. Let stand until it's soft-set, about 2 minutes. Fold in the whipped topping. Fold in apples and candy bars. Refrigerate until serving.

¾ CUP 218 cal., 9g fat (6g sat. fat), 6mg chol., 174mg sod., 31g carb. (24g sugars, 2g fiber), 3g pro.

TEST KITCHEN TIP

Switch up this recipe by using a different pudding mix—butterscotch, chocolate or caramel—and finish with crunchy toppings like chopped peanuts, mini chocolate chips or extra apple and candy pieces.

LEMON ROASTED FINGERLINGS & BRUSSELS SPROUTS

I've tried this recipe with other veggie combinations, too. The trick is choosing ones that roast in about the same amount of time. Try skinny green beans and thinly sliced onions, cauliflower florets and baby carrots, or okra and cherry tomatoes.
—Courtney Gaylord, Columbus, IN

Prep: 15 min. • **Bake:** 20 min.
Makes: 8 servings

- 1 lb. fingerling potatoes, halved
- 1 lb. Brussels sprouts, trimmed and halved
- 6 Tbsp. olive oil, divided
- ¾ tsp. salt, divided
- ¼ tsp. pepper
- 3 Tbsp. lemon juice
- 1 garlic clove, minced
- 1 tsp. Dijon mustard
- 1 tsp. honey

1. Preheat oven to 425°. Place potatoes and Brussels sprouts in a greased 15x10x1-in. baking pan. Drizzle with 2 Tbsp. oil; sprinkle with ½ tsp. salt and pepper. Toss to coat. Roast 20-25 minutes or until tender, stirring once.
2. In a small bowl, whisk lemon juice, garlic, mustard, honey and remaining oil and salt until blended. Transfer vegetables to a large bowl; drizzle with vinaigrette and toss to coat. Serve warm.

¾ CUP 167 cal., 10g fat (1g sat. fat), 0 chol., 256mg sod., 17g carb. (3g sugars, 3g fiber), 3g pro.

CREAMY HASH BROWN CASSEROLE

MA

CREAMY HASH BROWN CASSEROLE

This versatile side dish is so good and goes with almost any entree. A creamy cheese sauce and crunchy topping make this casserole a top pick for all kinds of gatherings.

—Teresa Stutzman, Adair, OK

Prep: 10 min. • **Bake:** 50 min.
Makes: 8 servings

- 1 pkg. (32 oz.) frozen cubed hash brown potatoes, thawed
- 1 lb. Velveeta, cubed
- 2 cups sour cream
- 1 can (10 ¾ oz.) condensed cream of chicken soup, undiluted
- ¾ cup butter, melted, divided
- 3 Tbsp. chopped onion
- ¼ tsp. paprika
- 2 cups cornflakes, lightly crushed
- Fresh savory, optional

1. Preheat oven to 350°. In a large bowl, combine hash browns, Velveeta, sour cream, soup, ½ cup butter and onion. Spread into a greased 13x9-in. baking dish. Sprinkle with paprika.
2. Combine cornflakes and remaining ¼ cup butter; sprinkle over the top. Bake, covered, until heated through, 40-50 minutes. Uncover, bake until top is golden brown, 10 minutes longer. If desired, garnish with savory.

FREEZE OPTION Cover and freeze unbaked casserole. To use, partially thaw in refrigerator overnight. Remove from refrigerator 30 minutes before baking. Preheat oven to 350°. Bake casserole as directed, increasing time as necessary to heat through and for a thermometer inserted in center to read 165°.

¾ CUP 663 cal., 43g fat (27g sat. fat), 125mg chol., 1359mg sod., 49g carb. (9g sugars, 3g fiber), 19g pro.

MAKEOVER CHEDDAR BISCUITS

These biscuits have a cheesy richness that everyone will love. I like to serve them with steaming bowls of chili or hearty beef soup.

—Alicia Rooker, Milwaukee, WI

Takes: 30 min. • **Makes:** 15 biscuits

- 1 cup all-purpose flour
- 1 cup cake flour
- 1½ tsp. baking powder
- ¾ tsp. salt
- ½ tsp. garlic powder, divided
- ¼ tsp. baking soda
- 4 Tbsp. cold butter, divided
- ⅓ cup finely shredded cheddar cheese
- 1 cup buttermilk
- ½ tsp. dried parsley flakes

1. In a large bowl, combine the flours, baking powder, salt, ¼ tsp. garlic powder and baking soda. Cut in 3 Tbsp. butter until mixture resembles coarse crumbs; add cheese. Stir in buttermilk just until moistened.
2. Drop by 2 tablespoonfuls 2 in. apart onto baking sheets coated with cooking spray. Bake at 425° until golden brown, 10-12 minutes. Melt remaining 1 Tbsp. butter; stir in parsley and remaining ¼ tsp. garlic powder. Brush over biscuits. Serve warm.

1 BISCUIT 106 cal., 4g fat (3g sat. fat), 11mg chol., 233mg sod., 14g carb. (1g sugars, 0 fiber), 3g pro.

READER RAVES

"These biscuits were not only easy to make but also delicious. I added Old Bay seasoning to my butter mixture as well as in the biscuit batter."

—LDBRELAND, TASTEOFHOME.COM

MAKEOVER
CHEDDAR BISCUITS

CHEESY CORN SPOON BREAD

Homey and comforting, this custardlike side dish is a much-requested recipe at potlucks and holiday dinners. The jalapeno pepper adds just the right bite. Second helpings of this tasty casserole are common—leftovers aren't.
—Katherine Franklin, Carbondale, IL

Prep: 15 min. • **Bake:** 35 min.
Makes: 15 servings

- ¼ cup butter, cubed
- 1 medium onion, chopped
- 2 large eggs
- 2 cups sour cream
- 1 can (15¼ oz.) whole kernel corn, drained
- 1 can (14¾ oz.) cream-style corn
- ¼ tsp. salt
- ¼ tsp. pepper
- 1 pkg. (8½ oz.) cornbread/muffin mix
- 2 medium jalapeno peppers, divided
- 2 cups shredded cheddar cheese, divided

1. Preheat oven to 375°. In a large skillet, heat butter over medium-high heat. Add onion; saute until tender.
2. Beat eggs; add sour cream, both cans of corn, salt and pepper. Stir in the cornbread mix just until blended. Mince 1 jalapeno pepper; fold into corn mixture with sauteed onion and 1½ cups cheese.
3. Transfer to a greased shallow 3-qt. baking dish. Sprinkle with remaining ½ cup cheese. Bake, uncovered, until a toothpick inserted in center comes out clean, 35-40 minutes; cool slightly. Slice remaining jalapeno; sprinkle over dish.

NOTE Wear disposable gloves when cutting hot peppers; the oils can burn skin. Avoid touching your face.

1 SERVING 266 cal., 17g fat (9g sat. fat), 56mg chol., 470mg sod., 21g carb. (7g sugars, 2g fiber), 8g pro.

CHEESY CORN SPOON BREAD

GRILLED POTATO & CORN SALAD

Corn salad and potato salad are two summer classics. I smashed them together for a crowd-pleasing side that we love with burgers. Locally sourced ingredients from the farmers market make it extra special.
—Donna Gribbins, Shelbyville, KY

Prep: 45 min. + chilling • **Grill:** 25 min.
Makes: 10 servings

- 2 lbs. medium Yukon Gold potatoes, cut into ¼-in. thick slices
- 2 Tbsp. olive oil, divided
- 2 poblano peppers
- 4 medium ears sweet corn, husked
- 6 green onions
- ⅔ cup sour cream
- ¼ cup mayonnaise
- 2 Tbsp. lime juice
- 1 cup crumbled Cotija cheese
- ¼ cup chopped fresh cilantro
- 1½ tsp. grated lime zest
- ½ tsp. salt
- ¼ tsp. pepper
- Optional: Lime wedges, fresh cilantro leaves and additional crumbled Cotija cheese

1. Place potatoes in a large saucepan; add water to cover. Bring to a boil. Reduce heat; cook, uncovered, 5 minutes. Drain potatoes and toss with 1 Tbsp. oil.

2. Grill poblanos, covered, over high heat until skins are blistered and blackened on all sides, 8-10 minutes, turning occasionally. Immediately place peppers in a small bowl; let stand, covered, for 20 minutes. Reduce grill temperature to medium heat.

3. Meanwhile, brush corn with remaining 1 Tbsp. oil. Place potatoes in a grill basket. Grill corn and potatoes, covered, over medium heat until tender and lightly browned, 12-15 minutes, turning them occasionally. Cool slightly. Grill green onions until blackened, 5-6 minutes. Cut into 1-in. pieces and place in a large bowl. Peel off and discard charred skin from poblanos; remove stems and seeds. Cut peppers into ½-in. pieces and add to onions. Cut corn from cobs; add corn and potatoes to peppers.

4. In a small bowl, whisk sour cream, mayonnaise and lime juice until blended; stir in cheese, cilantro, zest, salt and pepper. Add to potato mixture, stir to coat. Refrigerate, covered, at least 1 hour before serving. If desired, top with additional Cotija cheese or cilantro and serve with lime wedges.

NOTE Wear disposable gloves when cutting hot peppers; the oils can burn skin. Avoid touching your face.

¾ CUP 260 cal., 14g fat (5g sat. fat), 25mg chol., 347mg sod., 28g carb. (5g sugars, 3g fiber), 7g pro.

RESURRECTION ROLLS

A jumbo marshmallow buried inside a triangle of crescent dough makes for a unique and sweet breakfast treat. Serve warm, coated with a glaze and chopped pecans.
—Taste of Home *Test Kitchen*

Takes: 30 min. • **Makes:** 16 servings

- 2 tubes (8 oz. each) refrigerated crescent rolls
- ¼ cup sugar
- 1 tsp. ground cinnamon
- ¼ cup butter, melted
- 16 large marshmallows

GLAZE

- ½ cup confectioners' sugar
- ½ tsp. vanilla extract
- 2 to 3 tsp. 2% milk
- ¼ cup chopped pecans

1. Preheat oven to 400°. Unroll both tubes of crescent dough; separate into 16 triangles. Combine the sugar and cinnamon in a shallow bowl. Place melted butter in another shallow bowl. Dip marshmallows into butter, then roll in cinnamon sugar and place 1 coated marshmallow at wide end of each triangle of dough.
2. Fold corners of dough over marshmallow and roll up. (You might need to stretch and pat the dough as you wrap it around each marshmallow.) Pinch seems to seal tightly. Dip bottoms in butter and place, buttered side down, into ungreased regular-size muffin cups.
3. Bake until golden brown and rolls pull away from the pans slightly, 7-9 minutes. Immediately remove from pans to a wire rack.
4. For glaze, combine confectioners' sugar, vanilla and enough milk to reach desired consistency. Drizzle over rolls; sprinkle with nuts. Serve warm.

1 ROLL 190 cal., 9g fat (4g sat. fat), 8mg chol., 242mg sod., 25g carb. (14g sugars, 0 fiber), 3g pro.

RESURRECTION ROLLS

INTERNATIONAL POTATO CAKE

Over the years, I've made this potato cake with lamb, ham and hard salami. It's a perfect side for a lunch or dinner party.
—Judy Batson, Tampa, FL

Prep: 40 min. • **Bake:** 35 min. + cooling
Makes: 12 servings

- ¼ cup seasoned bread crumbs
- 3 lbs. potatoes (about 9 medium), peeled and cubed
- ½ cup heavy whipping cream
- ¼ cup butter, cubed
- 3 large eggs, beaten
- 1 tsp. Greek seasoning
- ¼ tsp. garlic salt
- ¼ tsp. lemon-pepper seasoning
- ¼ lb. thinly sliced fontina cheese
- ¼ lb. thinly sliced hard salami, coarsely chopped

TOPPING

- ⅓ cup grated Parmesan cheese
- 1 Tbsp. seasoned bread crumbs
- 1 Tbsp. butter, melted

1. Sprinkle bread crumbs onto the bottom of a greased 9-in. springform pan.
2. Place potatoes in a large saucepan and cover with water. Bring to a boil. Reduce heat; cover and simmer 10-15 minutes or until tender. Drain; transfer to a large bowl. Mash potatoes with cream, butter, eggs and seasonings.
3. Preheat oven to 350°. Spoon half the potatoes into prepared pan. Layer with cheese and salami; top with remaining potatoes. Combine topping ingredients; spoon over potatoes.
4. Cover and bake 30 minutes. Uncover; bake 5-10 minutes longer or until topping is golden brown and a thermometer reads 160°. Cool on a wire rack 10 minutes. Carefully run a knife around edge of pan to loosen; remove side of pan. Serve warm.

1 PIECE 252 cal., 16g fat (9g sat. fat), 101mg chol., 526mg sod., 18g carb. (2g sugars, 1g fiber), 9g pro.

ORANGE FLUFF SALAD

My sister gave me this fluffy salad recipe that whips up in a jiffy. Unlike many gelatin recipes, there's no need to have the salad set for hours, so it's wonderful for unexpected company.
—Stacey Meyer, Merced, CA

Takes: 15 min. • **Makes:** 8 servings

- 1 cup sour cream
- 1 pkg. (3 oz.) lemon gelatin
- 2 cans (11 oz. each) mandarin oranges, drained
- 1 can (21 oz.) pineapple tidbits, drained
- 1 carton (8 oz.) frozen whipped topping, thawed
- Pastel miniature marshmallows, optional

Place sour cream in a large bowl. Sprinkle with gelatin and stir until blended. Fold in the oranges, pineapple and whipped topping. Sprinkle with marshmallows if desired.

1 CUP 225 cal., 9g fat (8g sat. fat), 19mg chol., 44mg sod., 30g carb. (26g sugars, 1g fiber), 2g pro.

PICKLED BEETS

I grew up with my mother's pickled beets. The beets she used came from our garden and were canned for the winter months. Even as a child I loved beets because they brought so much color to our table. Their tangy flavor is a great complement to the rest of the foods in a meal.

—Sara Lindler, Irmo, SC

Prep: 35 min. + chilling, • **Cook:** 5 min.
Makes: 8 servings

- 8 medium fresh beets
- 1 cup vinegar
- ½ cup sugar
- 1½ tsp. whole cloves
- 1½ tsp. whole allspice
- ½ tsp. salt

1. Scrub beets and trim tops to 1 in. Place in a Dutch oven; add water to cover. Bring to a boil. Reduce heat; simmer, covered, 25-30 minutes or until tender. Remove from water; cool. Peel beets and slice; place in a bowl.
2. In a small saucepan, combine vinegar, sugar, cloves, allspice and salt. Bring to a boil; boil 5 minutes. Pour over beets. Refrigerate at least 1 hour. Drain before serving.

1 CUP 71 cal., 0 fat (0 sat. fat), 0 chol., 186mg sod., 18g carb. (16g sugars, 1g fiber), 1g pro.

CUBAN BLACK BEANS

This hearty side dish starts with sofrito, a combination of finely minced onions and green peppers. The tomato puree gives the beans a distinctive flavor.

—Marina Castle Kelley, Canyon Country, CA

Prep: 20 min. + soaking • **Cook:** 1¾ hours
Makes: 9 servings

- 2 cups dried black beans, rinsed
- 1 bay leaf
- 3 medium green peppers, chopped
- 2 medium onions, chopped
- ½ cup olive oil
- 6 garlic cloves, minced
- 1 can (15 oz.) tomato puree
- ½ cup chicken broth
- 2 Tbsp. sugar
- ¾ tsp. salt

1. Rinse and sort beans; soak according to package directions. Drain and rinse beans, discarding liquid.
2. Place beans in a large saucepan; add 6 cups water and bay leaf. Bring to a boil. Reduce heat; cover and simmer until tender, 1½ to 2 hours.
3. Meanwhile, in a large skillet, saute peppers and onions in oil until tender. Add garlic; cook 1 minute longer. Stir in the tomato puree, chicken broth, sugar and salt. Bring to a boil. Reduce heat; simmer, uncovered, until thickened, 8-10 minutes. Drain beans; discard bay leaf. Stir beans into tomato mixture.

¾ CUP 312 cal., 13g fat (2g sat. fat), 0 chol., 214mg sod., 38g carb. (8g sugars, 8g fiber), 11g pro.

READER RAVES

"Delicious! I paired this with pork chops and yellow rice and what a wonderful flavor!"

—AUG-95, TASTEOFHOME.COM

AUTHENTIC GERMAN POTATO SALAD

This recipe came from Speck's Restaurant, which was a famous eating establishment in St. Louis from the 1920s through the '50s. I ate lunch there almost every day and always ordered the potato salad. When the owner learned I was getting married, he gave me the recipe as a wedding gift!
—Violette Klevorn, Washington, MO

Prep: 30 min. + cooling • **Cook:** 20 min.
Makes: 8 servings

- 3 lbs. medium red potatoes
- 5 bacon strips, diced
- 1 medium onion, chopped
- ¼ cup all-purpose flour
- 2 tsp. salt
- ¼ tsp. celery seed
- ¼ tsp. pepper
- 1¼ cups sugar
- 1 cup cider vinegar
- ¾ cup water
- 3 Tbsp. minced fresh parsley

1. Place potatoes in a Dutch oven; cover with water. Bring to a boil. Reduce heat; cover and simmer for 25-30 minutes or until tender. Drain and cool.
2. In a large skillet, cook bacon over medium heat until crisp; using a slotted spoon, remove to paper towels. Drain, reserving 4 Tbsp. drippings in pan. Add onion, saute until tender.
3. Stir in the flour, salt, celery seed and pepper until blended. Gradually add the sugar, vinegar and water. Bring to a boil over medium-high heat; cook and stir for 2 minutes or until thickened.
4. Cut potatoes into ¼-in. slices. Add potatoes and bacon to the skillet; cook and stir gently over low heat until heated through. Sprinkle with parsley and serve warm.

¾ CUP 344 cal., 7g fat (2g sat. fat), 12mg chol., 719mg sod., 63g carb. (34g sugars, 3g fiber), 6g pro.

CARROTS LYONNAISE

CARROTS LYONNAISE

This recipe from a junior high home economics class was brought home by my sister Laurie. My family liked it so much that it became a part of our Christmas dinner tradition.
—Elizabeth Plants, Kirkwood, MO

Takes: 30 min. • **Makes:** 8 servings

- 2 lbs. fresh carrots, cut into 2-in. pieces
- 1 medium onion, thinly sliced
- ⅓ cup butter
- 2 Tbsp. all-purpose flour
- 2 tsp. chicken bouillon granules
- ¼ tsp. salt
- ⅛ tsp. pepper
- 1 cup water
- Minced fresh parsley

1. In a Dutch oven, bring 1 in. of water to a boil. Add carrots; cover and cook until crisp-tender, 5-8 minutes.
2. Meanwhile, in a large cast-iron or other heavy skillet, saute onion in butter until tender. Stir in the flour, bouillon, salt and pepper until blended; gradually add water. Bring to a boil; cook and stir until thickened, 2 minutes. Drain carrots; stir into sauce. Sprinkle with parsley.

¾ CUP 128 cal., 8g fat (5g sat. fat), 20mg chol., 423mg sod., 14g carb. (6g sugars, 3g fiber), 2g pro.

READER RAVES

"I was pleasantly surprised with this recipe! Really great flavors for a kicked-up carrot side dish! I will be bringing these for my family's Easter dinner this year."

—SLT220YAHOO441, TASTEOFHOME.COM

SOUR CREAM CUCUMBERS

SOUR CREAM CUCUMBERS

It's been a tradition at our house to serve this dish with the other Hungarian specialties my mom learned to make from the women at church. It's especially good during the summer when the cucumbers are fresh-picked from the garden.
—Pamela Eaton, Monclova, OH

Prep: 15 min. + chilling
Makes: 8 servings

- ½ cup sour cream
- 3 Tbsp. white vinegar
- 1 Tbsp. sugar
- Pepper to taste
- 4 medium cucumbers, peeled if desired, and thinly sliced
- 1 small sweet onion, thinly sliced and separated into rings

In a large bowl, whisk sour cream, vinegar, sugar and pepper until blended. Add cucumbers and onion; toss to coat. Refrigerate, covered, at least 4 hours. Serve with a slotted spoon.

¾ CUP 62 cal., 3g fat (2g sat. fat), 10mg chol., 5mg sod., 7g carb. (5g sugars, 2g fiber), 2g pro.

BIG-BATCH DISHES

P. 201

P. 202

P. 195

FRENCH CANADIAN TOURTIERES

FRENCH CANADIAN TOURTIERES

This recipe comes from my big sister. Each fall, we get together and make about 20 of these pies to serve at Christmas, give as gifts or save in the freezer for unexpected company.
—Pat Menee, Carberry, MB

Prep: 1¼ hours • **Bake:** 40 min.
Makes: 4 pies (8 servings each)

- 4 celery ribs
- 4 medium carrots
- 2 large onions
- 2 garlic cloves, peeled
- 4 lbs. ground pork
- 2 lbs. ground veal
- 2 lbs. bulk pork sausage
- 1 can (14½ oz.) chicken broth
- ½ cup minced fresh parsley
- 1 Tbsp. salt
- 1 tsp. pepper
- 1 tsp. dried basil
- 1 tsp. dried rosemary, crushed
- 1 tsp. cayenne pepper
- 1 tsp. ground mace
- 1 tsp. ground cloves
- 1 cup dry bread crumbs
- Dough for 4 double-crust pies

1. Coarsely chop celery, carrots and onions; place in a food processor with garlic. Cover and process until finely chopped.

2. In a stockpot or 2 Dutch ovens, cook vegetables, pork, veal and sausage until meat is no longer pink; drain. Stir in broth, parsley and seasonings. Cover and cook over low heat 20 minutes. Stir in bread crumbs.

3. Preheat oven to 400°. On a lightly floured surface, roll out half of dough into four ⅛-in.-thick circles; transfer to four 9-in. pie plates. Trim even with rims. Add about 4 cups filling to each crust. Roll out remaining dough into four ⅛-in.-thick circles. Place over filling. Trim, seal and flute edges. Cut slits in the tops.

4. Cover edges of pies loosely with foil. Bake 25 minutes. Reduce oven setting to 350°. Remove foil and bake pies until crusts are golden brown, 15-20 minutes longer.

FREEZE OPTION Cover and freeze unbaked pies. To use, remove from freezer 30 minutes before baking (do not thaw). Preheat oven to 400°. Place pie on a baking sheet; cover edge loosely with foil. Bake 25 minutes. Reduce heat to 350°. Remove foil. Bake until crust is golden brown and a thermometer inserted in center reads 165°, 50-60 minutes longer.

DOUGH FOR DOUBLE-CRUST PIE Combine 2½ cups all-purpose flour and ½ tsp. salt; cut in 1 cup cold butter until crumbly. Gradually add ⅓-⅔ cup ice water, tossing with a fork until the dough holds together when pressed. Divide the dough in half. Shape each into a disk; wrap disks and refrigerate 1 hour.

1 PIECE 469 cal., 29g fat (12g sat. fat), 76mg chol., 672mg sod., 31g carb. (4g sugars, 1g fiber), 19g pro.

BURGOO

A Kentucky Derby favorite, this hearty, comforting meat-and-vegetable stew will feed a large crowd. It takes a bit of effort but is worth it.
—Taste of Home *Test Kitchen*

Prep: 30 min. • **Cook:** 2½ hours
Makes: 24 servings (7½ qt.)

- 3 Tbsp. olive oil, divided
- 2 lbs. boneless pork shoulder butt roast, cut into 1½-in. cubes
- 2 lbs. boneless beef chuck roast, cut into 1½-in. cubes
- 2 lbs. bone-in chicken thighs
- 3 medium carrots, cut into 1-in. pieces
- 2 celery ribs, cut into 1-in. pieces
- 1 large onion, chopped
- 1 large green pepper, chopped
- 3 garlic cloves, minced
- 2 cartons (32 oz. each) reduced-sodium beef broth
- 1 can (28 oz.) crushed tomatoes
- 3 bay leaves
- 2 tsp. salt
- 2 tsp. dried thyme
- 1 tsp. pepper
- 2 medium potatoes, peeled and cubed
- 2½ cups frozen lima beans (about 12 oz.)
- 2½ cups frozen corn (about 12 oz.)
- 2 cups finely chopped cabbage
- ¼ cup Worcestershire sauce
- 3 Tbsp. cider vinegar
- Hot pepper sauce, optional

1. In a large stockpot, heat 2 Tbsp. oil over medium heat. Brown pork in batches; remove and set aside. Repeat with beef and chicken. In same pan, heat remaining 1 Tbsp. oil over medium heat. Add carrots, celery, onion and green pepper; cook and stir until tender, 5-7 minutes. Add garlic; cook 1 minute longer.
2. Add broth, stirring to loosen browned bits from pan. Add tomatoes, bay leaves, salt, thyme and pepper. Return pork, beef and chicken to pan. Bring to a boil. Reduce heat; cover and simmer until meat is very tender, about 2 hours.
3. Remove chicken to a plate. When cool enough to handle, remove meat from bones; discard skin and bones. Using 2 forks, shred meat into bite-sized pieces. Return meat to stockpot.
4. Add potatoes, lima beans, corn and cabbage; cover and cook for 30 minutes. Discard the bay leaves. Stir in the Worcestershire sauce and vinegar. If desired, serve with hot sauce.
1¼ CUPS 265 cal., 13g fat (4g sat. fat), 67mg chol., 404mg sod., 15g carb. (4g sugars, 3g fiber), 22g pro.

MA

PIZZA PASTA CASSEROLE

Kids will line up for this zippy pizza-flavored dish. The recipe makes two casseroles, so you can serve one to your family right away and keep the other in the freezer for another night.
—Nancy Scarlett, Graham, NC

Prep: 20 min. • **Bake:** 25 min.
Makes: 2 casseroles (10 servings each)

- 2 lbs. ground beef
- 1 large onion, chopped
- 3½ cups spaghetti sauce
- 1 pkg. (16 oz.) spiral or cavatappi pasta, cooked and drained
- 4 cups shredded part-skim mozzarella cheese
- 8 oz. sliced pepperoni

1. Preheat oven to 350°. In a large skillet, cook beef and onion over medium heat until meat is no longer pink; drain. Stir in spaghetti sauce and pasta.
2. Transfer to 2 greased 13x9-in. baking dishes. Sprinkle with cheese. Arrange pepperoni over the top.
3. Bake, uncovered, 25-30 minutes or until heated through.
FREEZE OPTION Cool unbaked casseroles; cover and freeze up to 3 months. To use, partially thaw in refrigerator overnight. Remove from refrigerator 30 minutes before baking. Preheat oven to 350°. Bake as directed, increasing time to 35-40 minutes or until heated through and a thermometer inserted in center reads 165°.
1 SERVING 301 cal., 15g fat (6g sat. fat), 46mg chol., 545mg sod., 22g carb. (4g sugars, 1g fiber), 19g pro.

PIZZA PASTA CASSEROLE

MA

BEST ITALIAN BEEF SANDWICHES

I love having friends over for a winter picnic each year, and these sandwiches are really a hit with potato salad and baked beans. The beef freezes well, which makes it handy to have on hand for last-minute meals.
—Marjorie Libby, Madison, WI

Prep: 30 min. + chilling • **Bake:** 2½ hours
Makes: 20 sandwiches

- 1 beef sirloin tip roast (4 to 5 lbs.)
- Water
- ½ tsp. salt
- 2 to 3 onions, thinly sliced
- 1 tsp. onion salt
- 1 tsp. garlic salt
- 1 tsp. dried oregano
- 2 tsp. Italian seasoning
- 1 tsp. seasoned salt
- 1 tsp. dried basil
- 3 beef bouillon cubes
- 7 to 8 hot banana peppers, seeded and sliced
- 20 hard rolls, split
- Giardiniera, optional

1. In a deep baking pan, place roast in 1 in. water. Sprinkle with salt and cover with onions. Cover and bake at 350° for 1½ hours or until meat is tender. Remove meat from baking pan; reserve and refrigerate broth. Refrigerate meat until firm. Cut into thin slices. Place in a 13x9-in. baking pan.

2. Meanwhile, in a saucepan, combine broth with remaining ingredients except rolls. Bring to a boil; reduce heat and simmer 10 minutes. Pour over meat. Cover and refrigerate for 24 hours. Reheat, covered, at 325° for 1 hour. Serve on hard rolls. If desired, top with giardiniera.

1 SANDWICH 288 cal., 7g fat (2g sat. fat), 58mg chol., 827mg sod., 31g carb. (2g sugars, 2g fiber), 24g pro.

BEST ITALIAN BEEF SANDWICHES

CUCUMBER TEA SANDWICHES

My children wanted to plant a garden, and we ended up with buckets of cucumbers. When I tired of making pickles, I came up with these pretty little sandwiches. We made 200 of them for a family gathering, and everyone wanted the recipe.
—Kimberly Smith, Brighton, TN

Prep: 30 min. + chilling • **Makes:** 4 dozen

- 1 pkg. (8 oz.) cream cheese, softened
- ¼ cup mayonnaise
- 1 Tbsp. snipped fresh dill
- 1 Tbsp. lemon juice
- ½ tsp. Worcestershire sauce
- ¼ tsp. salt
- ⅛ tsp. cayenne pepper
- ⅛ tsp. pepper
- 2 large cucumbers, seeded and chopped
- ½ cup chopped sweet red pepper
- ¼ cup chopped onion
- ¼ cup pimiento-stuffed olives, chopped
- ¼ cup minced fresh parsley
- 12 slices whole wheat bread
- Cucumber slices and fresh dill sprigs, optional

1. In a small bowl, beat the first 8 ingredients until blended. Stir in cucumbers, red pepper, onion, olives and parsley. Chill for up to 2 hours.
2. Remove crusts from bread; cut each slice into 4 triangles. Spread with cream cheese mixture. If desired, garnish with cucumber slices and dill sprigs.
1 TEA SANDWICH 46 cal., 3g fat (1g sat. fat), 5mg chol., 81mg sod., 4g carb. (1g sugars, 1g fiber), 1g pro.

HAM & CHEESE PUFF

For brunch, lunch or anytime, people really seem to go for the big chunks of ham combined with the flavors of mustard and cheese. Assembled the night before, it's a great make-ahead potluck dish.
—Nina Clark, Wareham, MA

Prep: 15 min. + chilling • **Bake:** 55 min.
Makes: 2 casseroles (12 servings each)

- 2 loaves (1 lb. each) Italian bread, cut into 1-in. cubes
- 6 cups cubed fully cooked ham
- 1½ lbs. Monterey Jack or Muenster cheese, cubed
- 1 medium onion, chopped
- ¼ cup butter
- 16 large eggs
- 7 cups whole milk
- ½ cup prepared mustard

1. Toss bread, ham and cheese; divide between 2 greased 13x9-in. baking dishes. In a skillet, saute onion in butter until tender; transfer to a bowl. Add eggs, milk and mustard; mix well. Pour over bread mixture. Cover and refrigerate overnight.
2. Remove from refrigerator 30 minutes before baking. Bake, uncovered, at 350° for 55-65 minutes or until a knife inserted in the center comes out clean. Serve immediately.
1 PIECE 369 cal., 19g fat (9g sat. fat), 187mg chol., 949mg sod., 24g carb. (5g sugars, 1g fiber), 25g pro.

CARROT SHEET CAKE

We sold pieces of this to-die-for carrot cake at an art show. Before long, we sold all 10 cakes we had made!
—Dottie Cosgrove, South El Monte, CA

Prep: 20 min. • **Bake:** 35 min. + cooling
Makes: 30 servings

- 4 large eggs, room temperature
- 1 cup canola oil
- 2 cups sugar
- 2 cups all-purpose flour
- ½ tsp. baking soda
- ½ tsp. baking powder
- 2 tsp. ground cinnamon
- ½ tsp. salt
- 3 cups shredded carrots
- ⅔ cup chopped walnuts

FROSTING

- 1 pkg. (8 oz.) cream cheese, softened
- ½ cup butter, softened
- 1 tsp. vanilla extract
- 4 cups confectioners' sugar
- ⅔ cup chopped walnuts

1. Preheat oven to 350°. In a bowl, beat eggs, oil and sugar until smooth. In another bowl, combine flour, baking soda, baking powder, cinnamon and salt; add to egg mixture and beat well. Stir in carrots and walnuts. Pour into a greased 15x10x1-in. baking pan. Bake 35 minutes or until a toothpick inserted in center comes out clean. Cool on a wire rack.
2. For frosting, beat cream cheese, butter and vanilla in a bowl until smooth; beat in confectioners' sugar. Spread over cake. Sprinkle with chopped walnuts. Decorate as desired. Store cake in the refrigerator.
1 PIECE 311 cal., 17g fat (5g sat. fat), 45mg chol., 193mg sod., 38g carb. (29g sugars, 1g fiber), 4g pro.

GROUND BEEF BAKED BEANS

I serve this satisfying ground beef and bean bake when I need to feed a crowd. I keep an extra pan of it in my freezer for occasions when there's no time to cook.
—Louann Sherbach, Wantagh, NY

Prep: 15 min. • **Bake:** 45 min.
Makes: 2 casseroles (12 servings each)

- 3 lbs. ground beef
- 4 cans (15¾ oz. each) pork and beans
- 2 cups ketchup
- 1 cup water
- 2 envelopes onion soup mix
- ¼ cup packed brown sugar
- ¼ cup ground mustard
- ¼ cup molasses
- 1 Tbsp. white vinegar
- 1 tsp. garlic powder
- ½ tsp. ground cloves
- Sliced green onions, optional

1. Preheat oven to 400°. In a Dutch oven, cook beef over medium heat until no longer pink, breaking into crumbles; drain. Stir in the remaining ingredients; heat through. Transfer to 2 greased 2-qt. baking dishes.
2. Cover and bake for 30 minutes. Uncover and bake until bubbly, 10-15 minutes longer.
⅔ CUP 157 cal., 6g fat (2g sat. fat), 28mg chol., 544mg sod., 15g carb. (8g sugars, 1g fiber), 12g pro.

MIX & MATCH

For some variation, top these baked beans with crisply cooked bacon. For a spicier flavor, add 1 Tbsp. of chili powder as you brown the beef, to bloom the flavor. Taste as you go and add more chili powder if you like. You can also experiment with stirring in cumin, coriander or cayenne pepper.

GROUND BEEF
BAKED BEANS

MA

PEAR WALDORF PITAS

Here's a guaranteed table brightener for a shower, luncheon or party. Just stand back and watch these sandwiches vanish. For an eye-catching presentation, I tuck each one into a colorful folded napkin.

—Roxann Parker, Dover, DE

Prep: 20 min. + chilling
Makes: 20 mini pitas halves

- 2 medium ripe pears, diced
- ½ cup thinly sliced celery
- ½ cup halved seedless red grapes
- 2 Tbsp. finely chopped walnuts
- 2 Tbsp. lemon yogurt
- 2 Tbsp. mayonnaise
- ⅛ tsp. poppy seeds
- 20 miniature pita pocket halves
- Lettuce leaves

1. In a large bowl, combine pears, celery, grapes and walnuts. In another bowl, whisk yogurt, mayonnaise and poppy seeds. Add to pear mixture; toss to coat. Refrigerate 1 hour or overnight.
2. Line pita halves with lettuce; fill each with 2 Tbsp. pear mixture.

1 PITA HALF 67 cal., 2g fat (0 sat. fat), 0 chol., 86mg sod., 12g carb. (3g sugars, 1g fiber), 2g pro.

READER RAVES

"This recipe exceeded my expectations. The lemon flavor from the yogurt really added to the pear and grapes. I added shredded chicken to the mixture and then topped each pita with a mint leaf. Delectable!"

—AMY0818, TASTEOFHOME.COM

PEAR WALDORF PITAS

BARBECUED TURKEY

BARBECUED TURKEY

I don't remember where my sister found this recipe, but it quickly became a family favorite. From the zesty, flavorful sauce and crispy skin to the juicy and tender meat, it's the best Thanksgiving turkey I've ever tried.
—Valerie Delano, Cascade, MT

Prep: 70 min. • **Grill:** 2 hours + standing
Makes: 24 servings (1½ cups sauce)

- 2 large onions, chopped
- 2 garlic cloves, minced
- ¼ cup plus 2 Tbsp. canola oil, divided
- 2 cups ketchup
- ½ cup water
- ½ cup maple syrup
- ¼ cup cider vinegar
- ¼ cup molasses
- ¼ cup Dijon mustard
- ¼ cup Worcestershire sauce
- 1 tsp. celery seed
- 1 tsp. crushed red pepper flakes
- 4 tsp. pepper, divided
- ½ tsp. ground ginger
- 1 turkey (12 to 14 lbs.)
- 1 Tbsp. salt

1. In a large saucepan, saute onions and garlic in ¼ cup oil until tender. Stir in the ketchup, water, syrup, vinegar, molasses, mustard, Worcestershire sauce, celery seed, pepper flakes, 1 tsp. pepper and ginger. Bring to a boil. Reduce heat; simmer, uncovered, for 30 minutes or until slightly thickened. Set aside 1½ cups for serving.
2. Remove giblets from turkey (discard or save for another use). Lightly oil the grill rack. Prepare grill for indirect heat, using a drip pan. Skewer turkey openings; tie drumsticks together. Rub remaining 2 Tbsp. oil over skin of turkey. Sprinkle salt and remaining 3 tsp. pepper over turkey and inside cavity.
3. Place turkey over drip pan, breast side up; grill, covered, over indirect medium heat 1 hour. Brush with some of the sauce mixture. Grill until a thermometer inserted in thickest part of thigh reads 170°-175°, 1½ to 2 hours longer, basting frequently with remaining sauce. Cover and let stand for 20 minutes before carving. Serve with reserved sauce.

5 OZ. COOKED TURKEY WITH 1 TBSP. SAUCE 355 cal., 16g fat (4g sat. fat), 123mg chol., 726mg sod., 15g carb. (13g sugars, 0 fiber), 36g pro.

SWEET & SALTY PARTY MIX

These crunchy munchies are sure to rank high with your family and friends. The combination of sweet and salty flavors is just right.
—Candice Lumley, Charles City, IA

Prep: 10 min. • **Bake:** 1¼ hours + cooling
Makes: about 10 qt.

- 1 pkg. (12 oz.) Corn Chex
- 1 pkg. (10 oz.) Cheerios
- 1 pkg. (10 oz.) Honeycomb cereal
- 1 pkg. (10 oz.) pretzel sticks
- 1¾ cups sugar
- 1½ cups canola oil
- 1¼ cups butter, melted
- 3 Tbsp. soy sauce
- 2 Tbsp. garlic salt

1. Preheat oven to 275°. In a very large bowl, combine cereals and pretzels. In another bowl, mix the remaining ingredients until sugar is dissolved. Pour over cereal mixture; toss to coat.
2. Transfer to a large roasting pan. Bake, uncovered, 1¼ hours or until cereal is crisp, stirring every 15 minutes. Cool completely. Store in an airtight container.

¾ CUP 227 cal., 13g fat (4g sat. fat), 13mg chol., 560mg sod., 28g carb. (11g sugars, 1g fiber), 2g pro.

SEAFOOD GUMBO

Gumbo is one of the dishes that makes Louisiana cuisine so famous. We live across the border in Texas and can't get enough of this traditional Cajun dish featuring okra, shrimp, spicy seasonings and what is called the holy trinity—onions, green peppers and celery. This recipe calls for seafood, but you could also use chicken, duck or sausage.
—Ruth Aubey, San Antonio, TX

Prep: 20 min. • **Cook:** 30 min.
Makes: 24 servings (6 qt.)

- 1 cup all-purpose flour
- 1 cup canola oil
- 4 cups chopped onion
- 2 cups chopped celery
- 2 cups chopped green pepper
- 1 cup sliced green onions
- 4 cups chicken broth
- 8 cups water
- 4 cups sliced okra
- 2 Tbsp. paprika
- 1 Tbsp. salt
- 2 tsp. oregano
- 1 tsp. ground black pepper
- 6 cups small shrimp, rinsed and drained, or seafood of your choice
- 1 cup minced fresh parsley
- 2 Tbsp. Cajun seasoning

1. In a heavy Dutch oven, combine the flour and oil until smooth. Cook over medium-high heat for 5 minutes, stirring constantly. Reduce heat to medium. Cook and stir for 10 minutes longer or until mixture is reddish brown.
2. Add the onion, celery, green pepper and green onions; cook and stir for 5 minutes. Add the chicken broth, water, okra, paprika, salt, oregano and pepper. Bring to a boil; reduce heat and simmer, covered, for 10 minutes.
3. Add shrimp and parsley. Simmer, uncovered, about 5 minutes longer or until shrimp is done. Remove from heat; stir in Cajun seasoning.
1 CUP 166 cal., 10g fat (1g sat. fat), 96mg chol., 900mg sod., 10g carb. (2g sugars, 2g fiber), 10g pro.

BLT DIP

Fans of bacon, lettuce and tomato sandwiches will fall for this creamy dip. It's easy to transport to different functions and always draws recipe requests.
—Emalee Payne, Eau Claire, WI

Takes: 10 min. • **Makes:** 6 cups

- 2 cups sour cream
- 2 cups mayonnaise
- 2 lbs. sliced bacon, cooked and crumbled
- 6 plum tomatoes, chopped
- 3 green onions, chopped
- Additional crumbled cooked bacon and chopped green onions, optional
- Assorted crackers or chips

In a large bowl, combine the sour cream, mayonnaise, bacon, tomatoes and onions. Refrigerate until serving. Garnish with bacon and onions if desired. Serve with crackers or chips.
1 SERVING (2 TBSP.) 123 cal., 12g fat (3g sat. fat), 15mg chol., 155mg sod., 1g carb., trace fiber, 2g pro.

READER RAVES

"My very picky husband loved this dip and couldn't stop eating it. He raved about it to all our friends!"

—VJBREN, TASTEOFHOME.COM

BLT DIP

TACO SALAD FOR A LARGE CROWD

TACO SALAD FOR A LARGE CROWD

I made this huge taco salad to bring to a party and people were scrambling to figure out who made it. Needless to say, I brought home only an empty bowl, and the guests all went home with a full stomach! Everyone loves this taco salad recipe.
—Lisa Homer, Avon, NY

Prep: 25 min. • **Cook:** 10 min.
Makes: 26 servings

- 1½ lbs. ground beef
- 2 envelopes taco seasoning, divided
- 1 medium head iceberg lettuce
- 1 pkg. (10 oz.) nacho-flavored tortilla chips, coarsely crushed
- 2 pints grape tomatoes, halved
- 2 cans (16 oz. each) kidney beans, rinsed and drained
- 3 cans (2¼ oz. each) sliced ripe olives, drained
- 1½ cups shredded cheddar cheese
- 1 large sweet onion, chopped
- 2 cans (4 oz. each) chopped green chiles
- 1½ cups Thousand Island salad dressing
- 1⅓ cups salsa
- ⅓ cup sugar

1. In a Dutch oven over medium heat, cook and crumble beef with 1 envelope plus 2 Tbsp. taco seasoning, until meat is no longer pink; drain.
2. In a very large serving bowl, combine the lettuce, chips, tomatoes, beans, olives, cheese, onion, chiles and beef mixture.
3. In a small bowl, combine the salad dressing, salsa, sugar and remaining taco seasoning; pour over salad and toss to coat.
1⅓ CUPS 262 cal., 15g fat (4g sat. fat), 24mg chol., 696mg sod., 23g carb. (7g sugars, 3g fiber), 10g pro.

BREAKFAST SAUSAGE BREAD

MA

BREAKFAST SAUSAGE BREAD

Any time we take this savory, satisfying bread to a potluck, it goes over very well. We never bring any home. My husband usually makes it. He prides himself on the beautiful golden loaves.
—Shirley Caldwell, Northwood, OH

Prep: 25 min. + rising • **Bake:** 25 min.
Makes: 2 loaves (16 pieces each)

- 2 loaves (1 lb. each) frozen white bread dough, thawed
- ½ lb. mild pork sausage
- ½ lb. bulk spicy pork sausage
- 1½ cups diced fresh mushrooms
- ½ cup chopped onion
- 3 large eggs, divided use
- 2½ cups shredded mozzarella cheese
- 1 tsp. dried basil
- 1 tsp. dried parsley flakes
- 1 tsp. dried rosemary, crushed
- 1 tsp. garlic powder

1. Cover dough and let rise in a warm place until doubled. Preheat oven to 350°. In a large skillet, cook sausage, mushrooms and onion over medium-high heat until sausage is no longer pink, breaking up sausage into crumbles, 6-8 minutes. Drain. Transfer to a bowl; cool.
2. Stir in 2 eggs, cheese and seasonings. Roll out each loaf of dough into a 16x12-in. rectangle. Spread half of the sausage mixture over each rectangle to within 1 in. of edges. Roll up jelly-roll style, starting with a short side; pinch seams to seal. Place on a greased baking sheet.
3. In a small bowl, whisk remaining egg. Brush over tops. Bake until golden brown, 25-30 minutes. Serve warm.
FREEZE OPTION Securely wrap and freeze cooled loaves in foil and place in airtight containers. To use, place foil-wrapped loaf on a baking sheet and reheat in a 450° oven until heated through, 10-15 minutes. Carefully remove foil; return to oven a few minutes longer until crust is crisp.
1 PIECE 102 cal., 6g fat (2g sat. fat), 32mg chol., 176mg sod., 8g carb. (1g sugars, 1g fiber), 5g pro.

TURTLE CANDIES

I am a self-taught candy maker through trial and error. These turtles are a favorite of friends and family.
—Carole Wiese, New Berlin, WI

Prep: 40 min. + chilling
Cook: 20 min. + standing • **Makes:** 4 dozen

- 1 lb. pecan halves, toasted
- 1 can (14 oz.) sweetened condensed milk
- ¾ cup light corn syrup
- ½ cup sugar
- ⅓ cup packed brown sugar
- ¼ cup butter, cubed
- 1½ tsp. vanilla extract
- 1 lb. milk chocolate candy coating, chopped
- Flake sea salt, optional

1. On waxed paper-lined baking sheets, arrange pecans in small clusters of 4-5 pecans each.
2. For caramel, in a small saucepan, combine the milk, corn syrup and sugars. Cook and stir over medium heat until a candy thermometer reads 238° (soft-ball stage). Remove from the heat. Stir in butter and vanilla. Working quickly, spoon caramel onto pecan clusters. Let stand until set.
3. In a microwave, melt candy coating; stir until smooth. Spoon over caramel. If desired, top with flake sea salt. Chill for 10 minutes or until set. Store in an airtight container.
NOTE We recommend that you test your candy thermometer before each use by bringing water to a boil; the thermometer should read 212°. Adjust your recipe temperature up or down based on your test.
1 TURTLE 171 cal., 11g fat (4g sat. fat), 5mg chol., 20mg sod., 19g carb. (15g sugars, 1g fiber), 2g pro.

TURTLE CANDIES

ANGEL BISCUITS

Light, airy biscuits are a spooktacular Halloween treat when you serve them with butter and honey.
—Faye Hintz, Springfield, MO

Prep: 20 min. + rising • **Bake:** 10 min.
Makes: 2½ dozen

- 2 pkg. (¼ oz. each) active dry yeast
- ¼ cup warm water (110° to 115°)
- 2 cups warm buttermilk (110° to 115°)
- 5 to 5½ cups all-purpose flour
- ⅓ cup sugar
- 2 tsp. salt
- 2 tsp. baking powder
- 1 tsp. baking soda
- 1 cup shortening
- Melted butter

1. In a small bowl, dissolve yeast in warm water. Let stand 5 minutes. Stir in warm buttermilk.
2. In a large bowl, combine the flour, sugar, salt, baking powder and baking soda. Cut in shortening with a pastry blender until mixture resembles coarse crumbs. Stir in yeast mixture.
3. Turn out onto a lightly floured surface; knead lightly 3-4 times. Roll out to ½-in. thickness; cut with a 2½-in. biscuit cutter. Place 2 in. apart on lightly greased baking sheets. Cover with kitchen towels and let rise in a warm place until almost doubled, about 1 hour.
4. Bake at 450° for 8-10 minutes or until golden brown. Lightly brush tops with melted butter. Serve warm.

NOTE To substitute for each cup of buttermilk, use 1 Tbsp. white vinegar or lemon juice plus enough milk to measure 1 cup. Stir, then let stand 5 min. Or, use 1 cup plain yogurt or 1¾ tsp. cream of tartar plus 1 cup milk.

1 BISCUIT 150 cal., 7g fat (2g sat. fat), 1mg chol., 244mg sod., 19g carb. (3g sugars, 1g fiber), 3g pro.

MUSTARD BARBECUE SHAVED HAM

This recipe makes enough ham sandwiches to feed a crowd and is so easy to put together. Have your butcher slice the ham very thin. I like to make this on the stovetop and serve it from my slow cooker.
—Joyce Moynihan, Lakeville, MN

Takes: 30 min. • **Makes:** 20 servings

- 1 cup cider vinegar
- 1 cup yellow mustard
- 1 cup ketchup
- ⅓ cup packed brown sugar
- ¼ cup butter, cubed
- 1 Tbsp. Worcestershire sauce
- 2 tsp. onion powder
- 1 tsp. garlic powder
- ½ tsp. cayenne pepper
- ½ tsp. pepper
- 5 lbs. shaved deli ham
- 20 sandwich rolls, split

In a Dutch oven, combine the first 10 ingredients. Cook and stir over medium heat until butter is melted. Bring to a boil; reduce heat. Simmer, covered, for 15 minutes. Add ham; heat through. Serve on rolls.

1 SANDWICH 382 cal., 10g fat (2g sat. fat), 57mg chol., 1761mg sod., 46g carb. (15g sugars, 2g fiber), 29g pro.

REUBEN WAFFLE POTATO APPETIZERS

I love Reubens, so I turned the classic sandwich into a fun appetizer with corned beef and sauerkraut on waffle fries.

—Gloria Bradley, Naperville, IL

Prep: 30 min. • **Bake:** 10 min./batch
Makes: about 4 dozen

- 1 pkg. (22 oz.) frozen waffle-cut fries
- 4 oz. cream cheese, softened
- 2 cups shredded fontina cheese, divided
- ⅓ cup Thousand Island salad dressing
- 3 Tbsp. chopped sweet onion
- 1½ tsp. prepared horseradish
- 12 oz. sliced deli corned beef, coarsely chopped
- 1 cup sauerkraut, rinsed, well drained and chopped
- 2 Tbsp. minced fresh chives

1. Prepare waffle fries according to package directions for baking. Meanwhile, in a small bowl, beat cream cheese, 1 cup fontina cheese, salad dressing, onion and horseradish until blended.

2. Remove fries from oven; set oven to 400°. Top each waffle fry with about ¼ oz. corned beef and 1 tsp. each cream cheese mixture, sauerkraut and remaining 1 cup fontina cheese. Bake until cheese is melted, 8-10 minutes. Sprinkle with chives.

1 APPETIZER 62 cal., 4g fat (2g sat. fat), 12mg chol., 168mg sod., 4g carb. (0 sugars, 0 fiber), 3g pro.

REUBEN WAFFLE POTATO APPETIZERS

MELON & GRAPE SALAD

Fruit salad is a nice way to round out a potluck. This one—with an easy-to-prepare refreshing citrus dressing—makes a nice addition to any buffet.

—Mary Etta Buran, Olmsted Township, OH

Prep: 20 min. + chilling
Makes: 54 servings (about 1 cup each)

- 1 medium-large watermelon, cut into cubes or balls
- 3 honeydew melons, cut into cubes or balls
- 3 cantaloupe melons, cut into cubes or balls
- 1½ lbs. seedless green grapes
- 1½ lbs. seedless red grapes
- 3 cups sugar
- ⅓ cup lemon juice
- ⅓ cup lime juice
- ⅓ cup orange juice

Combine melons and grapes. Combine sugar and juices; pour over fruit and toss to coat. Cover and chill for 1 hour. Serve with a slotted spoon.

1 CUP 119 cal., 1g fat (0 sat. fat), 0 chol., 11mg sod., 30g carb. (28g sugars, 1g fiber), 1g pro.

MA

SWEET HOOSIER DOG SAUCE

In our area of Indiana, we love sweet Coney sauce on our hot dogs! Our town still has an old drive-in that is famous for theirs.
—Jill Thomas, Washington, IN

Takes: 30 min. • **Makes:** 5 cups

- 2 lbs. ground beef
- 1 can (6 oz.) tomato paste
- 1 cup water
- 1 can (8 oz.) tomato sauce
- ½ cup sweet pickle relish
- ¼ cup dried minced onion
- 2 Tbsp. sugar
- 1 Tbsp. chili powder
- 2 tsp. Worcestershire sauce
- 1 tsp. salt
- 1 tsp. cider vinegar
- 1 tsp. yellow mustard
- ½ tsp. celery salt
- ¼ tsp. garlic powder
- ¼ tsp. onion powder
- Hot dogs and buns
- Optional: Diced onion, sliced pickles and shredded cheddar cheese

In a Dutch oven, cook beef over medium heat until no longer pink, breaking into crumbles, 8-10 minutes; drain. Stir in tomato paste; cook and stir 3 minutes. Stir in next 13 ingredients. Bring to a boil; reduce heat. Simmer, uncovered, until thickened, 15-20 minutes, stirring occasionally. Serve sauce over hot dogs in buns. Add optional toppings as desired.

FREEZE OPTION Freeze cooled sauce in freezer containers. To use, partially thaw in refrigerator overnight. Heat through in a covered saucepan, stirring occasionally; add water if necessary.

¼ CUP 111 cal., 5g fat (2g sat. fat), 28mg chol., 298mg sod., 7g carb. (4g sugars, 1g fiber), 9g pro.

PATRIOTIC PEPPER PLATTER

PATRIOTIC PEPPER PLATTER

Cream cheese stuffed peppers are simple to make, easy to travel with and wonderful to eat at room temperature. This platter can be made all summer long for each red, white and blue holiday! The dish accommodates those who eat meat as well as those who don't. With or without the bacon, these peppers are delish!
—Tina Martino, Hewitt, NJ

Prep: 30 min. • **Bake:** 25 min.
Makes: 4 dozen

- 24 miniature sweet red peppers
- 1 pkg. (8 oz.) cream cheese, softened
- ½ cup grated Parmesan cheese
- 12 bacon strips
- 2 slices white cheddar cheese
- 1 jar (9½ oz.) pitted Greek olives, drained
- Crushed red pepper flakes, optional

1. Preheat oven 400°. Cut red peppers in half lengthwise and remove seeds. In a small bowl, beat cream cheese and Parmesan cheese until blended. Spoon into pepper halves. Cut bacon in half lengthwise. Wrap half-strips of bacon around 24 pepper halves; place in a greased 15x10x1-in. baking pan. Place unwrapped pepper halves in another 15x10x1-in. baking pan.
2. Bake until bacon is cooked and filling is bubbly, 25-30 minutes. Meanwhile, using a star cookie cutter, cut stars out of cheese slices. Arrange peppers, olives and cheese stars on a serving platter to resemble an American flag. If desired, sprinkle bacon-wrapped peppers with red pepper flakes.

1 SERVING 50 cal., 4g fat (2g sat. fat), 8mg chol., 162mg sod., 1g carb. (0 sugars, 0 fiber), 2g pro.

MA

MAKE-AHEAD SAUSAGE PINWHEELS

Filled with sausage, sweet pepper and cream cheese, these roll-ups are excellent for unexpected visitors, a cocktail party or a halftime snack. Besides being easy to make, they can be done way ahead and kept in the freezer. All you have to do is pop them into a hot oven!
—Cindy Nerat, Menominee, MI

Prep: 30 min. + freezing • **Bake:** 15 min.
Makes: about 6½ dozen

- 1 lb. bulk regular or spicy pork sausage
- ½ cup diced sweet red pepper
- 1 green onion, chopped
- 1 pkg. (8 oz.) cream cheese, cubed
- 2 tubes (8 oz. each) refrigerated crescent rolls

1. In a large skillet, cook and crumble sausage over medium-high heat until no longer pink, 5-7 minutes; drain. Add pepper and green onion; cook and stir 2 minutes. Transfer to a bowl; cool for 10 minutes. Stir in cream cheese until blended; cool completely.
2. Unroll 1 can of crescent dough and separate into 4 rectangles; pinch perforations to seal. Press each rectangle to 6x4½ in.; spread each with ⅓ cup filling to within ¼ in. of edges. Roll up jelly-roll style, starting with a short side; pinch seam to seal. Roll gently to make logs smooth. Place on a waxed paper-lined baking sheet, seam side down. Repeat with remaining crescent dough. Freeze, covered, until firm, about 1 hour.
3. Preheat oven to 350°. Cut each log into 10 slices. Bake on parchment-lined baking sheets until golden brown, 15-18 minutes. Serve warm.

FREEZE OPTION Freeze pinwheels in freezer containers, separating layers with waxed paper. To use, bake frozen pinwheels as directed, increasing time by 3-5 minutes.

1 APPETIZER 46 cal., 3g fat (1g sat. fat), 6mg chol., 89mg sod., 2g carb. (1g sugars, 0 fiber), 1g pro.

TANGY PARTY PUNCH

As social chair one year during college, I tried to come up with a more interesting beverage than the usual mixture of cranberry juice and lemon-lime soda. This pastel punch was always a hit at receptions and parties.
—Jennifer Bangerter, Nixa, MO

Takes: 10 min. • **Makes:** 32 servings (8 qt.)

- 1 can (46 oz.) pineapple juice, chilled
- 1 can (46 oz.) orange juice, chilled
- 1 can (12 oz.) frozen limeade concentrate, thawed
- 1 can (12 oz.) frozen lemonade concentrate, thawed
- 3 liters ginger ale, chilled
- 1 pint lemon or pineapple sherbet
- 1 pint lime sherbet
- 1 pint orange sherbet

In a large punch bowl, combine the first 4 ingredients. Stir in ginger ale. Add scoops of sherbet. Serve immediately.

1 CUP 155 cal., 1g fat (0 sat. fat), 2mg chol., 20mg sod., 38g carb. (34g sugars, 0 fiber), 1g pro.

WATERMELON BASKET

I cut a watermelon into a basket shape and then fill it with melon balls to serve with a creamy dip.
—Christine Johnson, Ricetown, KY

Prep: 30 min. + chilling
Makes: 32 servings (about 1⅓ cups dip)

- 1 large watermelon (10 lbs.)
- 1 medium honeydew, cut into balls
- 3 cups white cranberry juice
- 1 cup light corn syrup
- 2 Tbsp. lime juice

FRUIT DIP

- 1 pkg. (8 oz.) cream cheese, softened
- ¼ cup 2% milk
- 3 Tbsp. sugar
- 3 Tbsp. lemon juice
- ¾ tsp. ground cardamom

1. With a sharp knife, cut a thin slice from the bottom of the watermelon so it sits flat. Mark a horizontal cutting line 2 in. above center and around the melon.
2. For handle, score a 1½-in.-wide strip across the top of melon, connecting both sides to the horizontal line. With a long sharp knife, cut all the way through the rind above the cutting line in a zigzag pattern.
3. Carefully lift off the side pieces. Remove fruit from both sections and cut into balls. Refrigerate the basket.
4. In a large bowl, combine watermelon and honeydew balls. In another bowl, whisk cranberry juice, corn syrup and lime juice until blended; pour over melon balls. Cover and chill for 3 hours.
5. Drain; spoon melon into watermelon basket. In a small bowl, beat the cream cheese and milk until smooth. Beat in sugar, lemon juice and cardamom; serve with melon.

¾ CUP WITH 2 TSP. DIP 127 cal., 3g fat (2g sat. fat), 8mg chol., 41mg sod., 25g carb. (22g sugars, 1g fiber), 2g pro.

WATERMELON BASKET

CHEESY CHICKEN TACO DIP

CHEESY CHICKEN TACO DIP

We're huge college football fans (go Irish!), and my chicken taco dip hasn't missed a season opener in many years. A slow cooker keeps the dip warm for the whole game—if it lasts that long!
—Deanna Garretson, Yucaipa, CA

Prep: 15 min. • **Cook:** 4 hours 10 min.
Makes: 8 cups

- 1 jar (16 oz.) salsa
- 1 can (30 oz.) refried beans
- 1½ lbs. boneless skinless chicken breasts
- 1 Tbsp. taco seasoning
- 2 cups shredded cheddar cheese
- 3 green onions, chopped
- 1 medium tomato, chopped
- ¼ cup chopped fresh cilantro
- Tortilla chips

1. In a greased 3- or 4-qt. slow cooker, mix salsa and beans. Top with chicken; sprinkle with taco seasoning. Cook, covered, on low until chicken is tender, 4-5 hours.
2. Remove chicken; shred finely using 2 forks. Return to slow cooker; stir in cheese. Cook, covered, on low until cheese is melted, 10-15 minutes, stirring occasionally.
3. To serve, top with green onions, tomato and cilantro. Serve with chips.

HEALTH TIP Skip the chips and serve with crunch celery sticks for a lighter bite.

¼ CUP DIP 82 cal., 3g fat (2g sat. fat), 19mg chol., 238mg sod., 5g carb. (1g sugars, 1g fiber), 7g pro.

BACON CHEESEBURGER SLIDER BAKE

MA

BACON CHEESEBURGER SLIDER BAKE

I created this dish to fill two pans because these sliders disappear fast. Just cut the recipe in half if you want to make only one batch.
—Nick Iverson, Denver, CO

Prep: 20 min. • **Bake:** 20 min.
Makes: 2 dozen

- 2 pkg. (17 oz. each) Hawaiian sweet rolls
- 22 slices American or cheddar cheese, divided
- 2 lbs. ground beef
- 1 cup chopped onion
- 1 can (14½ oz.) diced tomatoes with garlic and onion, drained
- 1 Tbsp. Dijon mustard
- 1 Tbsp. Worcestershire sauce
- ¾ tsp. salt
- ¾ tsp. pepper
- 24 bacon strips, cooked and broken into 1-in. pieces

GLAZE

- 1 cup butter, cubed
- ¼ cup packed brown sugar
- 4 tsp. Worcestershire sauce
- 2 Tbsp. Dijon mustard
- 2 Tbsp. sesame seeds

1. Preheat oven to 350°. Without separating rolls, cut each package of rolls horizontally in half; arrange bottom halves in 2 greased 13x9-in. baking pans. In each pan, place 5 slices of cheese on bottom halves of rolls. Bake until cheese is melted, 3-5 minutes.
2. In a large skillet, cook beef and onion over medium heat until beef is no longer pink and onion is tender, breaking beef into crumbles, 6-8 minutes; drain. Stir in tomatoes, mustard, Worcestershire sauce, salt and pepper. Cook and stir until combined, 1-2 minutes.
3. Spoon beef mixture evenly over rolls; top with bacon and remaining cheese. Replace tops.
4. For the glaze, in a microwave-safe bowl, combine butter, brown sugar, Worcestershire sauce and mustard. Microwave, covered, on high until butter is melted, stirring occasionally. Drizzle or brush over rolls; sprinkle with sesame seeds. Bake, uncovered, until golden brown and heated through, 20-25 minutes.

1 SLIDER 380 cal., 24g fat (13g sat. fat), 86mg chol., 628mg sod., 21g carb. (9g sugars, 2g fiber), 18g pro.

MA

RASPBERRY-RHUBARB SLAB PIE

Slab pie is a pastry baked in a jelly-roll pan and cut into slabs like a bar cookie—or a pie bar, if you will. My grandfather was a professional baker and served pieces of slab pie to his customers back in the day. Here is my spin, featuring rhubarb and gorgeous red raspberries.
—Jeanne Ambrose, Des Moines, IA

Prep: 30 min. + chilling
Bake: 45 min. + cooling
Makes: 24 servings

- 3¼ cups all-purpose flour
- 1 tsp. salt
- 1 cup butter
- ¾ cup plus 1 to 2 Tbsp. 2% milk
- 1 large egg yolk
- 2 cups sugar
- ⅓ cup cornstarch
- 5 cups fresh or frozen unsweetened raspberries, thawed and drained
- 3 cups sliced fresh or frozen rhubarb, thawed and drained

VANILLA ICING

- 1¼ cups confectioners' sugar
- ½ tsp. vanilla extract
- 5 to 6 tsp. 2% milk

1. In a large bowl, combine flour and salt; cut in butter until crumbly. Whisk ¾ cup milk and egg yolk; gradually add to flour mixture, tossing with a fork until dough forms a ball. Add additional milk, 1 Tbsp. at a time, if necessary.
2. Divide dough into 2 portions so that 1 is slightly larger than the other; cover each and refrigerate 1 hour or until easy to handle.
3. Preheat oven to 375°. Roll out larger portion of dough between 2 large sheets of lightly floured waxed paper into an 18x13-in. rectangle. Transfer to an ungreased 15x10x1-in. baking pan. Press onto the bottom and up sides of pan; trim crust to edges of pan.
4. In a large bowl, combine sugar and cornstarch. Add raspberries and rhubarb; toss to coat. Spoon into crust.
5. Roll out remaining dough; place over filling. Fold bottom crust over edges of top crust; seal with a fork. Prick top with a fork.
6. Bake until golden brown, 45-55 minutes. Cool completely on a wire rack.
7. For icing, combine confectioners' sugar, vanilla and enough milk to achieve a drizzling consistency; drizzle over pie. Cut pie into squares.

NOTE If using frozen rhubarb, measure rhubarb while still frozen, then thaw completely. Drain in a colander, but do not press liquid out.

1 PIECE 247 cal., 8g fat (5g sat. fat), 29mg chol., 159mg sod., 42g carb. (25g sugars, 2g fiber), 3g pro.

BRIE CHERRY PASTRY CUPS

BRIE CHERRY PASTRY CUPS

Golden brown and flaky, these bite-sized puff pastries with creamy Brie and sweet cherry preserves could easily double as a scrumptious dessert.
—Marilyn McSween, Mentor, OH

Takes: 30 min. • **Makes:** 3 dozen

- 1 sheet frozen puff pastry, thawed
- ½ cup cherry preserves
- 4 oz. Brie cheese, cut into ½-in. cubes
- ¼ cup chopped pecans or walnuts
- 2 Tbsp. minced chives

1. Unfold puff pastry; cut into 36 squares. Gently press squares onto the bottoms of 36 greased miniature muffin cups.
2. Bake at 375° for 10 minutes. Using the end of a wooden spoon handle, make a ½-in.-deep indentation in the center of each. Bake until golden brown, 6-8 minutes longer. With spoon handle, press squares down again.
3. Spoon ½ rounded tsp. preserves into each cup. Top with cheese; sprinkle with nuts and chives. Bake until cheese is melted, 3-5 minutes.

1 PASTRY CUP 61 cal., 3g fat (1g sat. fat), 3mg chol., 42mg sod., 7g carb. (3g sugars, 1g fiber), 1g pro.

READER RAVES

"These are a perfect balance of flavors. The cherry preserves give a perfect touch of sweetness to go with the cheese. Everyone devours these."

—DOCKGIRL, TASTEOFHOME.COM

SOUTHWESTERN BEAN DIP

Just by using different types of beans, you can make this dip as spicy as you like. My family could eat this as a complete meal.
—Jeanne Shear, Sabetha, KS

Prep: 20 min. • **Bake:** 30 min.
Makes: about 9 cups

- 2 lbs. ground beef
- 1 Tbsp. dried minced onion
- 1 can (8 oz.) tomato sauce
- 1 can (16 oz.) kidney beans, rinsed and drained
- 1 can (16 oz.) chili beans, undrained
- 4 cups shredded cheddar cheese
- Sliced jalapeno pepper
- Tortilla chips

1. Preheat oven to 350°. In a large skillet, cook beef over medium heat until no longer pink; drain. Transfer to a bowl; add the onion. Mash with a fork until crumbly.
2. In a blender, process tomato sauce and beans until chunky. Add to beef mixture and mix well. Spoon half into a greased 13x9-in. baking dish; top with half of the cheese. Repeat layers.
3. Bake, uncovered until cheese is melted, about 30 minutes. Top with sliced jalapeno. Serve warm with chips.
2 TBSP. 53 cal., 3g fat (2g sat. fat), 13mg chol., 88mg sod., 3g carb. (0 sugars, 1g fiber), 4g pro.

SOUTHWESTERN BEAN DIP

CUBANO PORK SANDWICHES

CUBANO PORK SANDWICHES

MA

When a hungry crowd is coming over, we plan to make our juicy pork a day ahead. I call the sauce Mojo because it's loaded with zingy flavors.
—Theresa Yardas, Sheridan, IN

Prep: 1¾ hours + marinating
Cook: 8 hours • **Makes:** 24 servings

- ⅓ cup ground cumin
- ¼ cup sugar
- 2 Tbsp. onion powder
- 1 Tbsp. kosher salt
- ½ tsp. pepper
- 1 boneless pork shoulder roast (6 to 7 lbs.)
- 2 tsp. olive oil
- 1 large onion, quartered
- 1 cup beef broth
- ⅔ cup lime juice
- ⅓ cup lemon juice
- ⅓ cup orange juice
- 1 bay leaf
- 1 tsp. dried cilantro flakes
- 1 tsp. dried oregano
- 1 tsp. dried thyme
- 1 tsp. ground allspice
- 4 tsp. olive oil

SANDWICHES

- 2 loaves unsliced French bread (1 lb. each)
- ¼ cup sweet pickle relish
- ¼ cup Dijon mustard
- 8 slices Swiss cheese

1. In a small bowl, mix the first 5 ingredients. Cut roast into thirds; rub with oil. Rub spice mixture over meat. Cover and refrigerate 24 hours.
2. In a large saucepan, combine onion, broth, juices, bay leaf and seasonings. Bring to a boil. Reduce heat; simmer, covered, 45 minutes. Strain sauce, discarding onion and seasonings.
3. In a large skillet, heat oil over medium heat. Brown roast on all sides; drain. Transfer to a 6-qt. slow cooker. Pour sauce over meat. Cook, covered, on low 8-10 hours or until meat is tender. Remove roast; cool slightly. Skim fat from cooking juices. Shred pork with 2 forks. Return pork to slow cooker; heat through.
4. Preheat oven to 325°. Split bread horizontally. Hollow out bottoms of loaves, leaving ¾-in. shells. Spread relish and mustard inside shells. Layer with meat and cheese. Replace tops.
5. Wrap sandwiches tightly in heavy-duty foil. Place on baking sheets. Bake 20-25 minutes or until heated through. Cut each crosswise into 12 slices.

1 PIECE 368 cal., 16g fat (6g sat. fat), 76mg chol., 648mg sod., 28g carb. (5g sugars, 2g fiber), 26g pro.

WHITE GRAPE PUNCH

This mix-ahead drink never sticks around long once I set it out. The refill requests come quickly!
—Debra Fraaken, Fort Collins, CO

Prep/Total Time: 15 min. • **Makes:** 6 qt.

- 2 cans (12 oz. each) frozen apple juice concentrate, thawed
- 2 cans (11½ oz. each) frozen white grape juice concentrate
- 6 cups cold water
- 12 cups lemon-lime soda (about 3 liters), chilled
- Lemon and lime slices

1. In a large pitcher, combine apple juice concentrate, white grape concentrate and water. Refrigerate until serving.
2. Just before serving, pour mixture into 2 pitchers or a punch bowl. Stir in soda and top with lemon and lime slices.

¾ CUP 109 cal., 0 fat (0 sat. fat), 0 chol., 17mg sod., 27g carb. (27g sugars, 0 fiber), 0 pro.

ROASTED TURKEY WITH MAPLE CRANBERRY GLAZE

I prepare turkey with a taste of Canada in mind. The sweet maple flavor comes through even in the breast meat. You may start to notice a caramelized color after about two hours. That's when I cover the bird loosely with foil while it finishes cooking. The meat always stays tender and juicy.
—Suzanne Anctil, Aldergrove, BC

Prep: 10 min+ refrigerating
Bake: 3 hours + standing
Makes: 24 servings

- 1 turkey (12 to 14 lbs.)
- ⅓ cup kosher salt
- 1 onion, quartered
- 1 navel orange, quartered
- 2 bay leaves
- 1 cup maple syrup
- ¾ cup whole-berry cranberry sauce
- ¼ cup finely chopped walnuts

1. Place turkey on a rack in a shallow roasting pan, breast side up. Pat turkey dry outside and inside the cavity and loosen skin. Sprinkle salt inside cavity, under skin and over outside of turkey; tuck wings. Cover and refrigerate for 8 hours or up to 24 hours.
2. Preheat oven to 325°. Insert onion, orange and bay leaves into cavity; tie drumsticks together. In a small bowl, combine the maple syrup, cranberry sauce and walnuts. Spoon over turkey.
3. Bake, uncovered, until a thermometer inserted into thickest part of thigh reads 170° to 175°, basting occasionally with pan drippings, 3 to 3½ hours. Cover loosely with foil if turkey browns too quickly. Cover and let stand 20 minutes before carving.

5 OZ. COOKED TURKEY 320 cal., 13g fat (4g sat. fat), 123mg chol., 93mg sod., 12g carb. (10g sugars, 0 fiber), 36g pro.

MA

SPRINGTIME BEIGNETS & BERRIES

I've always loved beignets, but never thought I could make them myself. Turns out they're easy! Sometimes I'll even make a quick berry whipped cream and pipe it inside for a fun surprise.
—Kathi Hemmer, Grand Junction, CO

Prep: 25 min. + chilling • **Cook:** 25 min.
Makes: 4 dozen

- ¼ cup butter, room temperature
- ¾ cup sugar
- ½ tsp. salt
- ½ tsp. ground cinnamon
- ½ cup plus 2 Tbsp. warm water (120° to 130°), divided
- ½ cup evaporated milk
- 1 pkg. (¼ oz.) quick-rise yeast
- 1 large egg
- 3¼ to 3¾ cups all-purpose flour
- Oil for deep-fat frying
- Confectioners' sugar
- Berries and whipped topping, optional

1. Beat butter, sugar, salt and cinnamon until crumbly. Beat in ½ cup water and evaporated milk. In another bowl, dissolve yeast in remaining 2 Tbsp. water; add to milk mixture. Beat in the egg until blended.
2. Add 2 cups flour; mix until well blended. Stir in enough remaining flour to form a soft dough (dough will be sticky). Place in a greased bowl, turning once to grease the top. Cover; refrigerate 4 hours or overnight.
3. Bring dough to room temperature. On a floured surface, roll out dough into a 16x12-in. rectangle. Cut into 2-in. squares. In a deep cast-iron skillet or deep- fat fryer, heat oil to 375°. Drop beignets, a few at a time, into hot oil. Fry until golden brown, about 1 minute per side. Drain on paper towels. Dust with confectioners' sugar. If desired, serve with assorted berries and whipped topping.

1 BEIGNET 74 cal., 3g fat (1g sat. fat), 7mg chol., 36mg sod., 10g carb. (3g sugars, trace fiber), 1g pro.

ROASTED TURKEY WITH MAPLE CRANBERRY GLAZE

GRILLED ITALIAN
SAUSAGE SANDWICHES

GRILLED ITALIAN SAUSAGE SANDWICHES

Try these sausage sandwiches for a casual but hearty meal. Full of traditional Italian flavor, they're a snap to make.
—Mike Yaeger, Brookings, SD

Prep: 30 min. • **Grill:** 10 min.
Makes: 20 servings

- 4 large green peppers, thinly sliced
- ½ cup chopped onion
- 2 Tbsp. olive oil
- 4 garlic cloves, minced
- 1 can (15 oz.) tomato sauce
- 1 can (12 oz.) tomato paste
- 1 cup water
- 1 Tbsp. sugar
- 2 tsp. dried basil
- 1 tsp. salt
- 1 tsp. dried oregano
- 20 uncooked Italian sausage links
- 20 sandwich buns
- Shredded part-skim mozzarella cheese, optional

1. In a large saucepan, saute peppers and onion in oil until crisp-tender. Add garlic; cook 1 minute longer. Drain. Stir in tomato sauce, tomato paste, water, sugar, basil, salt and oregano. Bring to a boil. Reduce heat; cover and simmer for 30 minutes or until heated through.
2. Meanwhile, grill sausages, covered, over medium heat for 10-16 minutes or until a thermometer reads 160°, turning occasionally. Serve on buns with sauce and, if desired, cheese.

1 SANDWICH 525 cal., 28g fat (10g sat. fat), 60mg chol., 1327mg sod., 45g carb. (10g sugars, 2g fiber), 25g pro.

APPLE RED-HOT SLAB PIE

MA

APPLE RED-HOT SLAB PIE

This dessert is my family's absolute favorite because it holds so many memories for us. Red Hots give the filling a color that makes it an instant hit at parties.
—Linda Morten, Somerville, TX

Prep: 45 min. + chilling • **Bake:** 50 min.
Makes: 24 servings

- 5 cups all-purpose flour
- 2 Tbsp. sugar
- 2 tsp. salt
- 2 cups cold butter, cubed
- 1 to 1¼ cups ice water

FILLING

- ⅔ cup sugar
- ⅔ cup all-purpose flour
- ½ tsp. salt
- 6 cups thinly sliced peeled Granny Smith apples (about 6 medium)
- 6 cups thinly sliced peeled Gala or Jonathan apples (about 6 medium)
- 1 cup Red Hots
- ¼ cup cold butter
- Vanilla ice cream, optional

1. In a large bowl, mix flour, sugar and salt; cut in butter until crumbly. Gradually add ice water, tossing with a fork until dough holds together when pressed. Divide dough into 2 portions so that 1 portion is slightly larger than the other. Shape each into a rectangle; cover and refrigerate 1 hour or overnight.
2. Preheat oven to 375°. For filling, in a large bowl, mix sugar, flour and salt. Add apples and Red Hots; toss to coat.
3. On a lightly floured surface, roll out larger portion of dough into an 18x13-in. rectangle. Transfer to an ungreased 15x10x1-in. baking pan. Press onto the bottom and up the sides of pan. Add filling; dot with butter.
4. Roll out remaining dough; place over filling. Fold bottom crust over edge of top crust; seal and flute or press with a fork to seal. Prick top with a fork.
5. Bake 50-55 minutes or until golden brown and filling is bubbly. Cool on a wire rack. Serve warm. If desired, top with ice cream.

1 PIECE 349 cal., 18g fat (11g sat. fat), 46mg chol., 383mg sod., 45g carb. (19g sugars, 2g fiber), 3g pro.

TRES LECHES COFFEE CREAMER

Tres leches cake is one of my family's favorite cakes. I decided to make it into a coffee creamer, so I could enjoy the tres leches flavor in my morning coffee! For coconut tres leches coffee creamer, replace 1 cup of the whipping cream with coconut cream and instead of the vanilla extract add 1/2 to 1 teaspoon coconut extract.
—Marina Castle Kelley, Canyon Country, CA

Takes: 10 min. • **Makes:** 5 cups

- 2 cups heavy whipping cream
- 1 can (14 oz.) sweetened condensed milk
- 1 can (12 oz.) evaporated milk
- 1½ tsp. vanilla extract
- ½ to 1 tsp. imitation rum extract

In a small pitcher, whisk all ingredients until blended. Cover and refrigerate up to 4 days. Stir before using.
1 TBSP. 43 cal., 3g fat (2g sat. fat), 10mg chol., 12mg sod., 3g carb. (3g sugars, 0 fiber), 1g pro.

PICNIC CHICKEN WITH YOGURT DIP

I made this well-seasoned chicken one evening for dinner and served it hot from the oven. While raiding the fridge the next day, I discovered how delicious it was cold and created the yogurt dip to go with it.
—Ami Okasinski, Memphis, TN

Prep: 20 min. • **Bake:** 1 hour + chilling
Makes: 24 servings (4 cups dip)

- 3 large eggs
- 3 Tbsp. water
- 1½ cups dry bread crumbs
- 2 tsp. paprika
- 1 tsp. salt
- ½ tsp. each dried marjoram, thyme and rosemary, crushed
- ½ tsp. pepper
- 1 cup butter, melted
- 12 chicken drumsticks
- 12 bone-in chicken thighs

CREAMY LEEK DIP

- 1 cup heavy whipping cream
- 1½ cups plain yogurt
- 1 envelope leek soup mix
- 1 cup shredded Colby cheese

1. Preheat oven to 375°. In a shallow bowl, whisk eggs and water. In another shallow bowl, combine bread crumbs and seasonings. Divide butter between two 13x9-in. baking dishes.
2. Dip chicken pieces in egg mixture, then coat with crumb mixture. Place in prepared pans. Bake, uncovered, 1 hour or until a thermometer reads 170°-175°, turning once. Cool 30 minutes and then refrigerate until chilled.
3. For dip, in a small bowl, beat cream until stiff peaks form. In another bowl, combine yogurt, soup mix and cheese; fold in whipped cream. Cover and refrigerate until serving. Serve with cold chicken.
1 SERVING 321 cal., 22g fat (11g sat. fat), 129mg chol., 346mg sod., 7g carb. (2g sugars, 0 fiber), 23g pro.

ALMOND TEA CAKES

ALMOND TEA CAKES

When I have time, I love to bake. I make these tea cakes every Christmas, double the recipe and freeze half for later. Then, I simply take them out of the freezer and drop them off at charity bake sales, potlucks and the like.
—Janet Fennema Ringelberg, Troy, ON

Prep: 30 min. + chilling • **Bake:** 15 min.
Makes: 5 dozen

- 2 cups butter, softened
- ¾ cup sugar
- ¾ cup packed brown sugar
- 2 large eggs, room temperature
- 4 tsp. almond extract
- 4 cups all-purpose flour
- 1 tsp. baking powder

FILLING

- 1 large egg white
- ½ cup sugar
- ½ cup ground almonds
- ½ tsp. lemon juice
- Milk
- Sliced almonds

1. In a large bowl, cream butter and sugars until light and fluffy, 5-7 minutes. Add eggs and extract and mix well. Add flour and baking powder (dough will be soft). Chill.

2. For filling, in a small bowl, stir egg white, sugar, almonds and lemon juice. Remove a portion of the dough at a time from the refrigerator. Place 1-in. balls of dough into miniature muffin cups, pressing slightly into sides and bottom. Place ½ tsp. filling into each. Cover with quarter-sized circles of dough.

3. Brush with a little milk and top with an almond. Bake at 350° until golden, 14-16 minutes.

1 SERVING 119 cal., 7g fat (4g sat. fat), 23mg chol., 73mg sod., 13g carb. (7g sugars, 0 fiber), 1g pro.

HOMEMADE ANTIPASTO SALAD

MA

HOMEMADE ANTIPASTO SALAD

This colorful salad is a tasty crowd-pleaser. Guests love the homemade dressing, which is a nice change from bottled Italian.

—Linda Harrington, Windham, NH

Prep: 50 minutes + chilling • **Cook:** 10 min.
Makes: 32 servings

- 2 pkg. (1 lb. each) spiral pasta
- 4 to 5 large tomatoes, chopped
- 3 large onions, chopped
- 2 large green peppers, chopped
- 2 cans (15 to 16 oz. each) garbanzo beans or chickpeas, rinsed and drained
- 1 lb. thinly sliced Genoa salami, julienned
- 1 lb. sliced pepperoni, julienned
- ½ lb. provolone cheese, cubed
- 1 cup pitted ripe olives, halved

DRESSING

- 1 cup red wine vinegar
- ½ cup sugar
- 2 Tbsp. dried oregano
- 2 tsp. salt
- 1 tsp. pepper
- 1½ cups olive oil

1. Cook pasta according to package directions. Drain; rinse with cold water. In several large bowls, combine pasta with next 8 ingredients.

2. For dressing, pulse vinegar, sugar, oregano, salt and pepper in a blender. While processing, gradually add oil in a steady stream. Pour over salad; toss to coat. Refrigerate, covered, 4 hours or overnight.

¾ CUP 396 cal., 24g fat (7g sat. fat), 32mg chol., 783mg sod., 33g carb. (6g sugars, 3g fiber), 13g pro.

FARMHOUSE APPLE PIE

FARMHOUSE APPLE PIE

Apple slab pie is a terrific contribution to a covered-dish supper, picnic or potluck. It's baked in a large 15x10 baking pan, so it's easy to make and tote, too. But be prepared—people always ask for a copy of the recipe!

—Dolores Skrout, Summerhill, PA

Prep: 30 min. • **Bake:** 50 min.
Makes: 24 servings

EGG YOLK PASTRY

- 5 cups all-purpose flour
- 4 tsp. sugar
- ½ tsp. salt
- ½ tsp. baking powder
- 1½ cups shortening
- 2 large egg yolks, lightly beaten
- ¾ cup cold water

FILLING

- 5 lbs. tart apples, peeled and thinly sliced
- 4 tsp. lemon juice
- ¾ cup sugar
- ¾ cup packed brown sugar
- 1 tsp. ground cinnamon
- ½ tsp. ground nutmeg
- ¼ tsp. salt
- 2% milk
- Additional sugar

1. In a large bowl, combine the flour, sugar, salt and baking powder; cut in shortening until the mixture resembles coarse crumbs. Combine yolks and cold water. Sprinkle over dry ingredients; toss with fork. If needed, add additional water, 1 Tbsp. at a time, until mixture can be formed into a ball.

2. Divide the dough in half. On a lightly floured surface, roll out half the dough to fit a 15x10x1-in. baking pan.

3. Sprinkle apples with lemon juice; arrange half of them over dough. Combine the sugars, cinnamon, nutmeg and salt; sprinkle half over apples. Top with remaining apples; sprinkle with remaining sugar mixture.

4. Roll out remaining dough to fit pan; place on top of filling and seal edges. Brush with milk and sprinkle with sugar. Cut vents in top crust. Bake at 400° until crust is golden brown and filling is bubbly, 50 minutes.

1 PIECE 317 cal., 13g fat (3g sat. fat), 18mg chol., 86mg sod., 48g carb. (26g sugars, 3g fiber), 3g pro.

SAUSAGE-STUFFED JALAPENOS

If you like foods that pack a little kick, you'll love these jalapenos filled with sausage and cheese. The recipe is one of my favorites for parties.
—Rachel Oswald, Greenville, MI

Prep: 20 min. • **Bake:** 15 min.
Makes: 44 appetizers

- 1 lb. bulk pork sausage
- 1 pkg. (8 oz.) cream cheese, softened
- 1 cup shredded Parmesan cheese
- 22 large jalapeno peppers, halved lengthwise and seeded
- Ranch salad dressing, optional

1. In a large skillet, cook the sausage over medium heat until no longer pink; drain. In a small bowl, combine the cream cheese and Parmesan cheese; fold in sausage.
2. Spoon about 1 tablespoonful into each jalapeno half. Place in 2 ungreased 13x9-in. baking dishes. Bake, uncovered, at 425° until filling is lightly browned and bubbly, 15-20 minutes. Serve with ranch dressing if desired.
NOTE Wear disposable gloves when cutting hot peppers; the oils can burn skin. Avoid touching your face.
1 APPETIZER 56 cal., 5g fat (2g sat. fat), 13mg chol., 123mg sod., 1g carb. (0 sugars, 0 fiber), 2g pro.

SAUSAGE-STUFFED JALAPENOS

CREAMY CARAMEL DIP

Because I feed three hungry men (my husband, a member of the Royal Canadian Mounted Police, and our two boys), I love satisfying snacks that are easy to make. We all appreciate this cool, light fruit dip.
—Karen Laubman, Spruce Grove, AB

Prep: 10 min. + chilling • **Makes:** 3½ cups

- 1 pkg. (8 oz.) cream cheese, softened
- ¾ cup packed brown sugar
- 1 cup sour cream
- 2 tsp. vanilla extract
- 2 tsp. lemon juice
- 1 cup cold milk
- 1 pkg. (3.4 oz.) instant vanilla pudding mix
- Assorted fresh fruit

1. In a bowl, beat cream cheese and brown sugar until smooth. Add the sour cream, vanilla, lemon juice, milk and pudding mix, beating well after each addition.
2. Cover and chill for at least 1 hour. Serve as a dip for fruit.
2 TBSP. 87 cal., 5g fat (3g sat. fat), 16mg chol., 83mg sod., 10g carb. (9g sugars, 0 fiber), 1g pro.

CHOCOLATE SCOTCHEROOS

CHOCOLATE SCOTCHEROOS

This recipe was given to me by a student at my school. It has become one of my family's favorites and is so easy to make.
—Lois Mays, Covington, PA

Prep: 25 min. + chilling • **Makes:** 2 dozen

- 1 cup sugar
- 1 cup light corn syrup
- 1 cup creamy peanut butter
- 6 cups crisp rice cereal
- ¾ cup butterscotch chips
- ¾ cup semisweet chocolate chips
- ¾ tsp. shortening

1. In a large saucepan, bring sugar and corn syrup to a boil. Cook and stir until sugar is dissolved; stir in peanut butter.
2. Remove from the heat. Add cereal and mix well. Press into a greased 13x9-in. pan.
3. In a microwave-safe bowl, melt the chips and shortening; stir until smooth. Spread over cereal mixture. Cover and refrigerate for at least 1 hour before cutting.

1 BAR 232 cal., 9g fat (4g sat. fat), 0 chol., 98mg sod., 36g carb. (29g sugars, 1g fiber), 4g pro.

KEEP IT CHEWY

For soft, chewy bars, reduce the heat or take the pan off the burner as soon as the sugar and corn syrup start to boil. Overheating the mixture can cause it to harden over time.

SLOW-COOKER SENSATIONS

P. 230

P. 257

P. 258

CHILE BEEF DIP

No last-minute party prep needed! Just put this creamy dip together a couple of hours before your shindig and let your slow cooker do the work.
—Pat Habiger, Spearville, KS

Prep: 25 min. • **Cook:** 2 hours
Makes: 32 servings (8 cups)

- 2 lbs. lean ground beef (90% lean)
- 1 large onion, chopped
- 1 jalapeno pepper, seeded and chopped
- 2 pkg. (8 oz. each) cream cheese, cubed
- 2 cans (8 oz. each) tomato sauce
- 1 can (4 oz.) chopped green chiles
- ½ cup grated Parmesan cheese
- ½ cup ketchup
- 2 garlic cloves, minced
- 1½ tsp. chili powder
- 1 tsp. dried oregano
- Tortilla chips

1. In a large skillet, brown the beef, onion and jalapeno until the meat is no longer pink; drain. Transfer to a 3- or 4-qt. slow cooker. Stir in the cream cheese, tomato sauce, chiles, Parmesan, ketchup, garlic, chili powder and oregano.
2. Cover and cook on low for 2-3 hours or until heated through. Stir; serve with chips.

NOTE Wear disposable gloves when cutting hot peppers; the oils can burn skin. Avoid touching your face.

¼ CUP 110 cal., 8g fat (4g sat. fat), 34mg chol., 204mg sod., 3g carb. (2g sugars, 0 fiber), 7g pro.

CREAMY CHEESE POTATOES

This easy potato dish is a comfort-food classic. It's popular at gatherings.
—Greg Christiansen, Parker, KS

Prep: 10 min. • **Cook:** 3¼ hours
Makes: 10 servings

- 1 can (10¾ oz.) condensed cream of chicken soup, undiluted
- 1 can (10¾ oz.) condensed cream of mushroom soup, undiluted
- 3 Tbsp. butter, melted
- 1 pkg. (30 oz.) frozen shredded hash brown potatoes, thawed
- 2 cups shredded cheddar cheese
- 1 cup sour cream
- Minced fresh parsley, optional

1. In a 3-qt. slow cooker coated with cooking spray, combine the soups and butter. Stir in potatoes.
2. Cover and cook on low for 3-4 hours or until potatoes are tender. Stir in cheese and sour cream. Cover and cook 15-30 minutes longer or until heated through. If desired, top with additional shredded cheddar cheese and fresh parsley.

¾ CUP 278 cal., 17g fat (10g sat. fat), 52mg chol., 614mg sod., 21g carb. (2g sugars, 2g fiber), 9g pro.

COCONUT-PECAN SWEET POTATOES

COCONUT-PECAN SWEET POTATOES

These sweet potatoes cook effortlessly in the slow cooker so you can tend to other things. Coconut gives the classic dish new flavor.
—Raquel Haggard, Edmond, OK

Prep: 15 min. • **Cook:** 4 hours
Makes: 12 servings

- ½ cup chopped pecans
- ½ cup sweetened shredded coconut
- ⅓ cup sugar
- ⅓ cup packed brown sugar
- ½ tsp. ground cinnamon
- ¼ tsp. salt
- ¼ cup reduced-fat stick margarine, melted
- 4 lbs. sweet potatoes (about 6 medium), peeled and cut into 1-in. pieces
- ½ tsp. coconut extract
- ½ tsp. vanilla extract

1. In a small bowl, combine the first 6 ingredients; stir in melted margarine. Place sweet potatoes in a 5-qt. slow cooker coated with cooking spray. Sprinkle with pecan mixture.
2. Cook, covered, on low 4-4½ hours or until potatoes are tender. Stir in extracts.

⅔ CUP 269 cal., 7g fat (2g sat. fat), 0 chol., 101mg sod., 51g carb. (29g sugars, 5g fiber), 3g pro.

LOW & SLOW PORK VERDE

My family loves this versatile pork dish. We like to have it over a serving of cheesy grits, but it also goes well with rice or potatoes. Leftovers make an excellent starter for white chili.
—Val Ruble, Ava, MO

Prep: 15 min. • **Cook:** 5 hours
Makes: 8 servings

- 1 boneless pork shoulder butt roast (3½ to 4 lbs.)
- 1 large onion, chopped
- 1 jar (16 oz.) salsa verde
- 2 cans (4 oz. each) chopped green chiles
- 2 tsp. ground cumin
- 1 tsp. dried oregano
- 1 tsp. salt
- 1 tsp. pepper
- ¼ tsp. crushed red pepper flakes
- ⅛ tsp. ground cinnamon
- ¼ cup minced fresh cilantro
- Hot cooked grits
- Sour cream, optional

1. Place pork and onion in a 4-qt. slow cooker. In a small bowl, combine salsa, chiles, cumin, oregano, salt, pepper, pepper flakes and cinnamon; pour over meat. Cook, covered, on low 5-6 hours or until meat is tender.
2. Remove roast; cool slightly. Skim fat from cooking juices. Shred pork with 2 forks. Return pork to slow cooker; heat through. Stir in cilantro. Serve with grits and, if desired, sour cream.

FREEZE OPTION Freeze cooled meat mixture in freezer containers. To use, partially thaw in refrigerator overnight. Microwave, covered, on high in a microwave-safe dish until heated through, gently stirring; add broth if necessary.

1 CUP 349 cal., 20g fat (7g sat. fat), 118mg chol., 872mg sod., 8g carb. (3g sugars, 1g fiber), 34g pro.

LOW & SLOW PORK VERDE

LOW & SLOW
HUEVOS RANCHEROS

MA

LOW & SLOW HUEVOS RANCHEROS

We love Mexican food, especially for breakfast. My slow-cooker version of a favorite, huevos rancheros, is rolled into flour tortillas. It's a perfect way to serve a breakfast crowd.
—Joan Hallford, North Richland Hills, TX

Prep: 25 min. • **Cook:** 3½ hours + standing
Makes: 10 servings

- ½ lb. fresh chorizo
- ½ cup chopped onion
- ½ cup chopped sweet red pepper
- 2 jalapeno peppers, seeded and chopped
- 1 garlic clove, minced
- 3 cups frozen cubed hash brown potatoes, thawed
- 8 large eggs, beaten
- 2 cups shredded Colby-Monterey Jack cheese
- 1 cup salsa
- 4 bacon strips, cooked and crumbled
- 20 flour tortillas (6 in.), warmed
- Optional: Fresh chopped cilantro and additional salsa

1. In a large skillet, cook the chorizo, onion, pepper, jalapenos and garlic over medium-high heat until cooked through, 6-8 minutes, breaking the meat into crumbles; drain. Transfer mixture to a 3- or 4-qt. slow cooker. Stir in next 5 ingredients.
2. Cook, covered, on low until potatoes are tender and eggs are set, 3½-4 hours. Turn off slow cooker; remove insert. Let stand 10 minutes before serving. Serve with tortillas, and top with cilantro and additional salsa if desired.

NOTE Wear disposable gloves when cutting hot peppers; the oils can burn skin. Avoid touching your face.

2 TACOS 488 cal., 25g fat (11g sat. fat), 192mg chol., 1028mg sod., 41g carb. (3g sugars, 4g fiber), 21g pro.

SLOW-COOKER SPUMONI CAKE

SLOW-COOKER SPUMONI CAKE

I created this cake for a holiday potluck once. It has become one of my most requested desserts. If you prefer, you can use all semisweet chips instead of a mix.
—Lisa Renshaw, Kansas City, MO

Prep: 10 min. • **Cook:** 4 hours + standing
Makes: 10 servings

- 3 cups cold 2% milk
- 1 pkg. (3.4 oz.) instant pistachio pudding mix
- 1 pkg. white cake mix (regular size)
- ¾ cup chopped maraschino cherries
- 1 cup white baking chips
- 1 cup semisweet chocolate chips
- 1 cup pistachios, chopped

1. In a large bowl, whisk the milk and pudding mix for 2 minutes. Transfer to a greased 5-qt. slow cooker. Prepare cake mix batter according to package directions, folding cherries into batter. Pour into slow cooker.
2. Cook, covered, on low for 4 hours or until edge of cake is golden brown.
3. Remove slow cooker insert; sprinkle cake with baking chips and chocolate chips. Let cake stand, uncovered, for 10 minutes. Sprinkle with pistachios before serving.

1 SERVING 588 cal., 27g fat (9g sat. fat), 9mg chol., 594mg sod., 79g carb. (54g sugars, 3g fiber), 10g pro.

SLOW-COOKER SPANAKOPITA FRITTATA SANDWICHES

On our cruise through the Greek islands, delicious and nutritious food like this was served on our ship all day, every day.
—Laura Wilhelm, West Hollywood, CA

Prep: 20 min. • **Cook:** 2 hours + standing
Makes: 8 servings

- 12 large eggs
- ½ cup 2% milk
- 2 tsp. Greek seasoning
- 2 cups fresh baby spinach
- 1½ cups crumbled feta cheese
- 1 cup sliced fresh mushrooms
- ½ cup roasted sweet red pepper strips
- ½ cup shredded Italian cheese blend
- ¼ tsp. smoked paprika
- 8 ciabatta rolls, bagels or English muffins, split and toasted

1. In a large bowl, whisk eggs, milk and Greek seasoning until blended. Stir in spinach, feta cheese, mushrooms and pepper strips. Pour into a greased 3½-qt. slow cooker.
2. Cook, covered, on high 2-3 hours or until eggs are set and a thermometer reads 160°. Remove lid; sprinkle frittata with shredded Italian cheese blend and paprika. Turn off slow cooker; remove insert. Let stand until cheese is melted, about 10 minutes. Cut and serve on bread of your choice.

1 SANDWICH 481 cal., 14g fat (6g sat. fat), 296mg chol., 1115mg sod., 60g carb. (11g sugars, 3g fiber), 27g pro.

SLOW-COOKER SPANAKOPITA FRITTATA SANDWICHES

CORN SPOON BREAD

My spoon bread is moister than corn pudding made in the oven. The cream cheese is a nice addition. We especially enjoy this with Thanksgiving turkey or Christmas ham.
—Tamara Ellefson, Frederic, WI

Prep: 15 min. • **Cook:** 3 hours
Makes: 8 servings

- 1 pkg. (8 oz.) cream cheese, softened
- ⅓ cup sugar
- 1 cup 2% milk
- 2 large eggs
- 2 Tbsp. butter, melted
- 1 tsp. salt
- ¼ tsp. ground nutmeg
- Dash pepper
- 2⅓ cups frozen corn, thawed
- 1 can (14¾ oz.) cream-style corn
- 1 pkg. (8½ oz.) cornbread/muffin mix

1. In a large bowl, beat cream cheese and sugar until smooth. Gradually beat in milk. Beat in the eggs, butter, salt, nutmeg and pepper until blended. Stir in corn and cream-style corn. Stir in cornbread mix just until moistened.
2. Pour into a greased 3-qt. slow cooker. Cover and cook on high until center is almost set, 3-4 hours.

½ CUP 391 cal., 18g fat (10g sat. fat), 100mg chol., 832mg sod., 52g carb. (19g sugars, 2g fiber), 9g pro.

HAWAIIAN MEATBALLS

Forget takeout! Now you can get Chinese food from your slow cooker. Serve the meatballs over rice or ramen noodles for dinner, or as a tasty addition to an appetizer buffet.
—Julie Schiefer, Nappanee, IN

Prep: 20 min. • **Cook:** 6¼ hours
Makes: 8 servings

- 1 can (20 oz.) unsweetened pineapple chunks, undrained
- ½ cup packed brown sugar
- ¼ cup cornstarch
- ½ cup cider vinegar
- 1 pkg. (32 oz.) frozen fully cooked homestyle meatballs
- 2 medium green peppers, cut into 1-in. pieces
- 1 jar (10 oz.) maraschino cherries, drained
- Salt and pepper to taste
- Hot cooked rice, optional

1. Drain pineapple, reserving juice in a 2-cup measuring cup; add enough water to measure 2 cups. In a small saucepan, mix brown sugar, cornstarch, vinegar and juice mixture until blended. Bring to a boil; cook and stir until thickened.
2. In a 3-qt. slow cooker, combine meatballs, peppers, drained pineapple and sauce. Cook, covered, on low 6-8 hours or until meatballs are heated through and peppers are tender.
3. Stir in the cherries; cook, covered, on low 15-30 minutes longer or until heated through. Season with salt and pepper to taste. If desired, serve with rice.

1 CUP 520 cal., 30g fat (14g sat. fat), 47mg chol., 837mg sod., 50g carb. (36g sugars, 2g fiber), 16g pro.

TANGY BARBECUE WINGS

I took these slow-cooked wings to work, and they vanished before I even got a bite! The tangy sauce is lip-smacking good.

—Sherry Pitzer, Troy, MO

Prep: 1 hour • **Cook:** 3 hours
Makes: 2 dozen wings (2 sections each)

- 5 lbs. chicken wings
- 2½ cups ketchup
- ⅔ cup white vinegar
- ⅔ cup honey
- ½ cup molasses
- 2 to 3 Tbsp. hot pepper sauce
- 1 tsp. salt
- 1 tsp. Worcestershire sauce
- ½ tsp. onion powder
- ½ tsp. chili powder
- ½ to 1 tsp. liquid smoke, optional

1. Preheat oven to 375°. Using a sharp knife, cut through the 2 wing joints; discard wing tips. Arrange remaining wing pieces in 2 greased 15x10x1-in. baking pans. Bake 30 minutes; drain. Turn wings; bake 20-25 minutes longer or until juices run clear.
2. Meanwhile, in a large saucepan, combine next 9 ingredients and liquid smoke if desired; bring to a boil. Reduce heat; simmer, uncovered, 30 minutes, stirring occasionally.
3. Drain wings. Place a third of chicken in a 5-qt. slow cooker; top with a third of sauce. Repeat layers twice. Cook, covered, on low 3-4 hours. Stir.

NOTE Uncooked chicken wing sections (wingettes) may be substituted for whole chicken wings.

1 WING (2 SECTIONS) 178 cal., 7g fat (2g sat. fat), 30mg chol., 458mg sod., 19g carb. (19g sugars, 0 fiber), 10g pro.

TANGY BARBECUE WINGS

SLOW-COOKER SPINACH & ARTICHOKE DIP

Here's a creamy, delicious appetizer that's perfect for special occasions. It's especially good served with Asiago cheese bread for dipping.

—Diane Morrison, Bradford, PA

Prep: 10 min. • **Cook:** 2 hours
Makes: 12 servings (3 cups)

- 1 can (14 oz.) water-packed artichoke hearts, drained and chopped
- 1 cup fresh baby spinach, chopped
- ½ cup sour cream
- ½ cup mayonnaise
- ½ cup shredded part-skim mozzarella cheese
- ½ cup shredded Parmesan cheese
- ⅓ cup chopped red onion
- ¼ tsp. garlic powder
- Whole wheat baguette slices, chunks of rainbow carrots and celery

1. Place the first 8 ingredients in a 1½-qt. slow cooker; stir to combine. Cook, covered, on low 2-2½ hours or until heated through.
2. Stir to blend. Serve with whole wheat baguette slices and chunks of rainbow carrots and celery.

¼ CUP 123 cal., 11g fat (3g sat. fat), 8mg chol., 223mg sod., 3g carb. (1g sugars, 0 fiber), 4g pro.

BLUEBERRY ICED TEA

I enjoy coming up with new ways to use my slow cooker. If it's going to take up space, it needs to earn its keep! Pour this refreshing tea over plenty of ice and garnish with blueberries if desired. For extra fun, freeze blueberries in the ice cubes.
—Colleen Delawder, Herndon, VA

Prep: 10 min. • **Cook:** 3 hours + cooling
Makes: 11 servings (2¾ qt.)

- 12 cups water
- 2 cups fresh blueberries
- 1 cup sugar
- ¼ tsp. salt
- 4 family-sized tea bags
- Ice cubes
- Optional: Lemon slices and fresh mint leaves

1. In a 5-qt. slow cooker, combine water, blueberries, sugar and salt. Cover and cook on low 3 hours.
2. Turn off slow cooker; add tea bags. Cover and let stand 5 minutes. Discard tea bags; cool 2 hours. Strain tea and discard blueberries. Pour the tea into a 3-qt. pitcher; refrigerate until serving. Serve over ice cubes. If desired, top each serving with lemon slices, fresh mint leaves and additional fresh blueberries.

1 CUP 73 cal., 0 fat (0 sat. fat), 0 chol., 61mg sod., 19g carb. (18g sugars, 0 fiber), 0 pro.

READER RAVES

"Really good iced tea. I can see this recipe working for any fruit and being just as tasty. I used frozen blueberries and they worked great."

—TAMMYCOOKBLOGSBOOKS, TASTEOFHOME.COM

SLOW-COOKED PORK WITH BAKED BEANS

This is my version of my mom's baked beans. I added slow-cooked pork to transform this tangy side dish into a satisfying meal.
—Cyndy Gerken, Naples, FL

Prep: 6 hours 45 min. • **Bake:** 50 min.
Makes: 12 servings

- 2 Tbsp. olive oil, divided
- 4 Tbsp. Worcestershire sauce, divided
- 1 bone-in pork shoulder butt roast (3 to 4 lbs.)
- 1 Tbsp. garlic powder
- ½ tsp. salt
- ½ tsp. pepper
- 1 large onion, thinly sliced
- 3 garlic cloves, minced
- 1 bottle (18 oz.) honey barbecue sauce
- 1 cup chicken stock
- 6 cans (15 oz. each) pork and beans
- 1 cup molasses
- ½ cup packed brown sugar
- ¼ cup ketchup
- ¼ cup spicy brown mustard
- 6 bacon strips

1. Combine 1 Tbsp. oil and 1 Tbsp. Worcestershire sauce; rub over roast. Sprinkle with garlic powder, salt and pepper. In a large skillet, heat remaining 1 Tbsp. oil over medium heat; brown meat. Place half the onion in a 4- or 5-qt. slow cooker; add garlic. Place meat in slow cooker; top with remaining onion. In a small bowl, combine barbecue sauce and stock; pour over the meat. Cook, covered, on low until tender, 6-8 hours.
2. Preheat oven to 375°. In a large bowl, combine pork and beans, molasses, brown sugar, ketchup, mustard and remaining 3 Tbsp. Worcestershire sauce. When cool enough to handle, remove meat from bones; discard bones. Discard onion and cooking juices. Using 2 forks, shred meat into large chunks; stir into bean mixture. Transfer to 2 greased 13x9-in. baking dishes. Top with bacon.
3. Bake, uncovered, until bubbly, 50-60 minutes. Discard bacon before serving. Serve with a slotted spoon.

1⅓ CUPS 531 cal., 18g fat (5g sat. fat), 59mg chol., 1099mg sod., 71g carb. (44g sugars, 10g fiber), 26g pro.

SLOW-COOKED TURKEY SLOPPY JOES

This tangy sandwich filling is so easy to prepare in the slow cooker and it goes over well at all gatherings. I frequently take it to potlucks, and I'm always asked what my secret ingredient is.
—Marylou LaRue, Freeland, MI

Prep: 15 min. • **Cook:** 4 hours
Makes: 8 servings

- 1 lb. lean ground turkey
- 1 small onion, chopped
- ½ cup chopped celery
- ¼ cup chopped green pepper
- 1 can (10¾ oz.) reduced-sodium condensed tomato soup, undiluted
- ½ cup ketchup
- 2 Tbsp. prepared mustard
- 1 Tbsp. brown sugar
- ¼ tsp. pepper
- 8 hamburger buns, split
- Pickle slices, optional

1. In a large skillet coated with cooking spray, cook turkey, onion, celery and green pepper over medium heat until meat is no longer pink, breaking it into crumbles; drain. Stir in soup, ketchup, mustard, brown sugar and pepper.
2. Transfer to a 3-qt. slow cooker. Cover and cook on low to allow the flavors to blend, about 4 hours. Serve on buns, with pickles if desired.

1 SANDWICH 264 cal., 7g fat (2g sat. fat), 39mg chol., 614mg sod., 34g carb. (13g sugars, 2g fiber), 16g pro.

SLOW-COOKED TURKEY SLOPPY JOES

SWEET & TANGY PULLED PORK

SWEET & TANGY PULLED PORK

The slow cooker makes these terrific sandwiches a convenient option for busy weeknights. The apricot preserves lend a sweet flavor to the pork.
—Megan Klimkewicz, Kaiser, MO

Prep: 15 min. • **Cook:** 8 hours
Makes: 12 servings

- 1 jar (18 oz.) apricot preserves
- 1 large onion, chopped
- 2 Tbsp. reduced-sodium soy sauce
- 2 Tbsp. Dijon mustard
- 1 boneless pork shoulder butt roast (3 to 4 lbs.)
- Hamburger buns, split, optional

1. Mix first 4 ingredients. Place roast in a 4- or 5-qt. slow cooker; top with preserves mixture. Cook, covered, on low until meat is tender, 8-10 hours.
2. Remove pork from slow cooker. Skim fat from cooking juices. Shred pork with 2 forks; return to slow cooker and heat through. If desired, serve on buns.

½ CUP PORK MIXTURE 296 cal., 11g fat (4g sat. fat), 67mg chol., 243mg sod., 29g carb. (19g sugars, 0 fiber), 20g pro.

EVERYTHING STUFFING

EVERYTHING STUFFING

My family goes crazy for this stuffing that I make in the slow cooker. It freezes well so we can enjoy it long after Thanksgiving has passed.
—Bette Votral, Bethlehem, PA

Prep: 30 min. • **Cook:** 3 hours
Makes: 9 servings

- ½ lb. bulk Italian sausage
- 4 cups seasoned stuffing cubes
- 1½ cups crushed cornbread stuffing
- ½ cup chopped toasted chestnuts or pecans
- ½ cup minced fresh parsley
- 1 Tbsp. minced fresh sage or 1 tsp. rubbed sage
- ⅛ tsp. salt
- ⅛ tsp. pepper
- 1¾ cups sliced baby portobello mushrooms
- 1 pkg. (5 oz.) sliced fresh shiitake mushrooms
- 1 large onion, chopped
- 1 medium apple, peeled and chopped
- 1 celery rib, chopped
- 3 Tbsp. butter
- 1 can (14½ oz.) chicken broth

1. In a large skillet, cook the sausage over medium heat until no longer pink, breaking it into crumbles; drain. Transfer to a large bowl. Stir in the stuffing cubes, cornbread stuffing, chestnuts, parsley, sage, salt and pepper.
2. In the same skillet, saute mushrooms, onion, apple and celery in butter until tender. Stir into the stuffing mixture. Add enough broth to reach desired moistness. Transfer to a 4-qt. slow cooker. Cover and cook on low for 3 hours, stirring once.

¾ CUP 267 cal., 13g fat (4g sat. fat), 21mg chol., 796mg sod., 30g carb. (5g sugars, 3g fiber), 8g pro.

CHEESY SLOW-COOKED CORN

Even those who usually don't eat much corn will ask for a second helping of this creamy, cheesy side dish. Folks love the flavor, but I love how easy it is to make with ingredients I usually have on hand.
—Mary Ann Truitt, Wichita, KS

Prep: 5 min. • **Cook:** 3 hours
Makes: 12 servings

- 9½ cups (48 oz.) frozen corn
- 11 oz. cream cheese, softened
- ¼ cup butter, cubed
- 3 Tbsp. water
- 3 Tbsp. 2% milk
- 2 Tbsp. sugar
- 6 slices American cheese, cut into small pieces

In a 4- or 5-qt. slow cooker, combine all ingredients. Cook, covered, on low, until heated through and cheese is melted, 3-4 hours, stirring once.

1 CUP 265 cal., 16g fat (9g sat. fat), 39mg chol., 227mg sod., 27g carb. (6g sugars, 2g fiber), 7g pro.

SLOW-COOKER SAUSAGE & WAFFLE BAKE

Here's an easy dish that's guaranteed to create excitement at the breakfast table! Nothing is missing from this sweet and savory combination. It's so wrong, it's right!
—Courtney Lentz, Boston, MA

Prep: 20 min. • **Cook:** 5 hours + standing
Makes: 12 servings

- 2 lbs. bulk spicy breakfast pork sausage
- 1 Tbsp. rubbed sage
- ½ tsp. fennel seed
- 1 pkg. (12.3 oz.) frozen waffles, cut into bite-sized pieces
- 8 large eggs
- 1¼ cups half-and-half cream
- ¼ cup maple syrup
- ¼ tsp. salt
- ¼ tsp. pepper
- 2 cups shredded cheddar cheese
- Additional maple syrup

1. Fold two 18-in.-long pieces of foil into two 18x4-in. strips. Line the sides around the perimeter of a 5-qt. slow cooker with foil strips; spray with cooking spray.
2. In a large skillet, cook and crumble sausage over medium heat; drain. Add sage and fennel.
3. Place waffles in slow cooker; top with sausage. In a bowl, mix eggs, cream, syrup, salt and pepper. Pour over the sausage and waffles. Top with cheese. Cook, covered, on low 5-6 hours or until set. Remove insert and let stand, uncovered, 15 minutes. Serve with additional maple syrup.

1 SERVING 442 cal., 31g fat (12g sat. fat), 200mg chol., 878mg sod., 20g carb. (7g sugars, 1g fiber), 19g pro.

SLOW-COOKER FRENCH DIP SANDWICHES

SLOW-COOKER FRENCH DIP SANDWICHES

These sandwiches make a standout addition to any buffet line. Make sure to have plenty of small cups of broth for everyone to grab. Dipping perfection!
—Holly Neuharth, Mesa, AZ

Prep: 15 min. • **Cook:** 8 hours
Makes: 12 servings

- 1 beef rump or bottom round roast (about 3 lbs.)
- 1½ tsp. onion powder
- 1½ tsp. garlic powder
- ½ tsp. Creole seasoning
- 1 carton (26 oz.) beef stock
- 12 whole wheat hoagie buns, split
- 6 oz. Havarti cheese, cut into 12 slices

1. Cut roast in half. Mix onion powder, garlic powder and Creole seasoning; rub onto beef. Place in a 5-qt. slow cooker; add stock. Cook, covered, on low until meat is tender, 8-10 hours.
2. Remove beef; cool slightly. Skim fat from cooking juices. When cool enough to handle, shred beef with 2 forks and return to slow cooker.
3. Place buns on ungreased baking sheets, cut side up. Using tongs, place beef on bun bottoms. Place cheese on bun tops. Broil 3-4 in. from heat until cheese is melted, 1-2 minutes. Close sandwiches; serve with cooking juices.

NOTE If you don't have Creole seasoning in your cupboard, you can make your own using ¼ tsp. each salt, garlic powder and paprika; and a pinch each of dried thyme, ground cumin and cayenne pepper.

1 SANDWICH WITH ⅓ CUP JUICES 456 cal., 14g fat (5g sat. fat), 81mg chol., 722mg sod., 50g carb. (9g sugars, 7g fiber), 35g pro.

SLOW-COOKER MUSHROOM BEEF STROGANOFF

I love to make this for my husband and me to have on a cold night. It warms us right up! You can substitute Greek yogurt for the sour cream.

—Meg Hilton, Atlanta, GA

Prep: 15 min. • **Cook:** 6 hours 10 min.
Makes: 8 servings

- 2 lbs. boneless beef chuck steak
- 1 lb. sliced fresh mushrooms
- 2 medium onions, chopped
- 1 can (10¾ oz.) condensed golden mushroom soup, undiluted
- 2 Tbsp. reduced-sodium soy sauce
- 2 Tbsp. Dijon mustard
- 1 Tbsp. Worcestershire sauce
- 3 garlic cloves, minced
- ¾ tsp. salt
- ½ tsp. pepper
- 2 Tbsp. cornstarch
- 2 Tbsp. water
- 1 cup sour cream
- Hot cooked egg noodles
- Minced fresh parsley, optional

1. Cut steak into 3x½-in. strips. In a 5- or 6-qt. slow cooker, combine next 9 ingredients. Stir in steak strips. Cook, covered, on low until meat is tender, 6-8 hours.
2. Transfer steak to a serving dish; keep warm. Skim fat from cooking juices. Mix cornstarch and water until smooth; stir into cooking juices. Cook, covered, on high until thickened, 10-15 minutes. Stir in sour cream; pour over beef. Serve with noodles and, if desired, minced parsley.

¾ CUP 317 cal., 18g fat (8g sat. fat), 81mg chol., 736mg sod., 11g carb. (4g sugars, 1g fiber), 26g pro.

SLOW-COOKER MUSHROOM BEEF STROGANOFF

PORK CHILE VERDE

Pork slowly stews with jalapenos, onion, green enchilada sauce and spices in this flavor-packed Mexican dish. It's terrific on its own or stuffed in a warm tortilla with sour cream, grated cheese or olives on the side.

—Kimberly Burke, Chico, CA

Prep: 25 min. • **Cook:** 6½ hours
Makes: 8 servings

- 1 boneless pork sirloin roast (3 lbs.), cut into 1-in. cubes
- 4 medium carrots, sliced
- 1 medium onion, thinly sliced
- 4 garlic cloves, minced
- 3 Tbsp. canola oil
- 1 can (28 oz.) green enchilada sauce
- ¼ cup cold water
- 2 jalapeno peppers, seeded and chopped
- 1 cup minced fresh cilantro
- Hot cooked rice
- Flour tortillas, warmed

In a large skillet, saute the pork, carrots, onion and garlic in oil in batches until pork is browned. Transfer to a 5-qt. slow cooker. Add the enchilada sauce, water, jalapenos and cilantro. Cover and cook on low for 6 hours or until meat is tender. Serve with rice and tortillas.

NOTE Wear disposable gloves when cutting hot peppers; the oils can burn skin. Avoid touching your face.

1 CUP 345 cal., 18g fat (4g sat. fat), 102mg chol., 545mg sod., 12g carb. (4g sugars, 1g fiber), 35g pro.

APPLE BETTY
WITH ALMOND CREAM

APPLE BETTY WITH ALMOND CREAM

I love making this treat for friends during the peak of apple season. I plan a quick soup and bread meal so we can get right to the dessert!
—Elizabeth Godecke, Chicago, IL

Prep: 15 min. • **Cook:** 3 hours
Makes: 8 servings

- 3 lbs. tart apples, peeled and sliced
- 10 slices cinnamon-raisin bread, cubed
- ¾ cup packed brown sugar
- ½ cup butter, melted
- 1 tsp. almond extract
- ½ tsp. ground cinnamon
- ¼ tsp. ground cardamom
- ⅛ tsp. salt

ALMOND CREAM

- 1 cup heavy whipping cream
- 2 Tbsp. sugar
- 1 tsp. grated lemon zest
- ½ tsp. almond extract

1. Place apples in an ungreased 4- or 5-qt. slow cooker. In a large bowl, combine the bread, brown sugar, butter, extract, cinnamon, cardamom and salt; spoon over apples. Cover and cook on low 3-4 hours or until apples are tender.
2. In a small bowl, beat cream until it begins to thicken. Add the sugar, lemon zest and extract; beat until soft peaks form. Serve with apple mixture. If desired, sprinkle with cinnamon.

1 CUP WITH ¼ CUP ALMOND CREAM 468 cal., 23g fat (14g sat. fat), 71mg chol., 224mg sod., 65g carb. (45g sugars, 5g fiber), 5g pro.

HOISIN PORK WRAPS

HOISIN PORK WRAPS

For a casual get-together, set a buffet with pork, tortillas and red cabbage slaw, and have your guests make their own wraps.
—Linda Woo, Derby, KS

Prep: 25 min. • **Cook:** 7 hours
Makes: 15 servings

- 1 boneless pork loin roast (3 lbs.)
- 1 cup hoisin sauce, divided
- 1 Tbsp. minced fresh gingerroot
- 6 cups shredded red cabbage
- 1½ cups shredded carrots
- ¼ cup thinly sliced green onions
- 3 Tbsp. rice vinegar
- 4½ tsp. sugar
- 15 flour tortillas (8 in.), warmed

1. Cut the roast in half. Combine ⅓ cup hoisin sauce and ginger; rub over pork. Transfer to a 4- or 5-qt. slow cooker. Cover and cook on low for 7-8 hours or until pork is tender.
2. Meanwhile, in a large bowl, combine the cabbage, carrots, onions, vinegar and sugar. Refrigerate until serving.
3. Shred meat with 2 forks and return to the slow cooker; heat through. Place 2 tsp. remaining hoisin sauce down the center of each tortilla; top with ⅓ cup shredded pork and ⅓ cup coleslaw. Roll up.

1 WRAP 314 cal., 8g fat (2g sat. fat), 46mg chol., 564mg sod., 37g carb. (7g sugars, 1g fiber), 23g pro.

READER RAVES

"My family loved this! We have made it more than once. It is definitely a family favorite and really easy to make. Delicious!"

—JEANNETTEJOHNSON, TASTEOFHOME.COM

SLOW-COOKER MEATBALL SANDWICHES

SLOW-COOKER MEATBALL SANDWICHES

Our approach to meatball sandwiches is a simple one: Cook the meatballs low and slow, load them into hoagie buns, and top them with provolone and pepperoncini.
—Stacie Nicholls, Spring Creek, NV

Prep: 5 min. • **Cook:** 3 hours
Makes: 8 servings

- 2 pkg. (12 oz. each) frozen fully cooked Italian meatballs, thawed
- 2 jars (24 oz. each) marinara sauce
- 8 hoagie buns, split
- 8 slices provolone cheese
- Sliced pepperoncini, optional

1. Place meatballs and sauce in a 3- or 4-qt. slow cooker. Cook, covered, on low 3-4 hours or until meatballs are heated through.
2. On each bun bottom, layer cheese, meatballs and, if desired, pepperoncini; replace tops.

1 SANDWICH 526 cal., 20g fat (7g sat. fat), 93mg chol., 1674mg sod., 55g carb. (15g sugars, 4g fiber), 32g pro.

MA

FALL VEGETABLE SLOPPY JOES

I make this dish in the fall and sneak grated vegetables into the sloppy joe mixture, which is especially good for children who don't like to eat their vegetables! Just walk away and let the slow cooker do all the work. Top the filling with a little shredded cheese before serving.
—Nancy Heishman, Las Vegas, NV

Prep: 30 min. • **Cook:** 4 hours
Makes: 18 servings

- 8 bacon strips, cut into 1-in. pieces
- 2 lbs. lean ground beef (90% lean)
- 1 medium onion, chopped
- 2 garlic cloves, minced
- 2 cups shredded peeled butternut squash
- 2 medium parsnips, peeled and shredded
- 2 medium carrots, peeled and shredded
- 1 can (12 oz.) cola
- 1 can (8 oz.) tomato paste
- 1 cup water
- ⅓ cup honey mustard
- 1½ tsp. ground cumin
- 1¼ tsp. salt
- 1 tsp. ground allspice
- ½ tsp. pepper
- 18 hamburger buns, split

1. In a large skillet, cook bacon over medium heat until crisp, stirring occasionally. Remove with a slotted spoon; drain on paper towels. Discard drippings. In the same skillet, cook beef, onion and garlic over medium heat until the beef is no longer pink and onion is tender, 10-12 minutes, breaking meat into crumbles; drain.
2. Transfer to a 5- or 6-qt. slow cooker. Stir in the squash, parsnips, carrots, cola, tomato paste, water, mustard and seasonings. Cook, covered, on low until vegetables are tender, 4-5 hours. Stir in bacon. Serve on buns.

FREEZE OPTION Freeze cooled meat mixture in freezer containers. To use, partially thaw in refrigerator overnight. Heat through in a saucepan, stirring occasionally; add water if necessary.

1 SANDWICH 275 cal., 8g fat (3g sat. fat), 35mg chol., 526mg sod., 35g carb. (9g sugars, 3g fiber), 17g pro

MEATY SLOW-COOKED JAMBALAYA

This recipe makes a big batch of delicious meaty gumbo. Stash some away in the freezer for days you don't feel like cooking.
—Diane Atherton, Pine Mountain, GA

Prep: 25 min. • **Cook:** 7¼ hours
Makes: 12 servings (3 qt.)

- 1 can (28 oz.) diced tomatoes, undrained
- 1½ cup reduced-sodium chicken broth
- 1 large green pepper, chopped
- 1 medium onion, chopped
- 2 celery ribs, sliced
- 4 garlic cloves, minced
- 2 tsp. Cajun seasoning
- 2 tsp. dried parsley flakes
- 1 tsp. dried basil
- 1 tsp. dried oregano
- ¾ tsp. salt
- ½ to 1 tsp. cayenne pepper
- 2 lbs. boneless skinless chicken thighs, cut into 1-in. pieces
- 1 pkg. (12 oz.) fully cooked andouille or other spicy chicken sausage links
- 2 lbs. uncooked shrimp (31-40 per lb.), peeled and deveined
- 8 cups hot cooked brown rice

1. In a large bowl, combine the first 12 ingredients. Place the chicken and sausage in a 6-qt. slow cooker. Pour tomato mixture over top. Cook, covered, on low until chicken is tender, 7-9 hours.
2. Stir in shrimp. Cook, covered, until shrimp turn pink, 15-20 minutes longer. Serve with rice.

1 CUP JAMBALAYA WITH ⅔ CUP COOKED RICE 387 cal., 10g fat (3g sat. fat), 164mg chol., 674mg sod., 37g carb. (4g sugars, 4g fiber), 36g pro.

MEATY SLOW-COOKED JAMBALAYA

ROOT BEER BRATS

ROOT BEER BRATS

Here's an easy recipe that's versatile too. Serve the saucy brats over rice for one meal and then have them on buns the next. For extra punch, add a splash of root beer concentrate to the sauce.
—Pamela Thompson, Girard, IL

Prep: 15 min. • **Cook:** 6 hours
Makes: 10 servings

- 1 can (12 oz.) root beer
- 3 Tbsp. cornstarch
- 3 tsp. ground mustard
- 3 tsp. caraway seeds
- 10 uncooked bratwurst links
- 1 large onion, coarsely chopped
- 1 bottle (12 oz.) chili sauce
- 10 hoagie buns, toasted
- Optional: Thinly sliced red onion and prepared mustard

1. Whisk first 4 ingredients until blended. In a large nonstick skillet, brown the bratwursts over medium-high heat. Transfer to a 4- or 5-qt. slow cooker. Add onion, chili sauce and root beer mixture.
2. Cook, covered, on low 6-8 hours or until a thermometer inserted in sausage reads at least 160°. Serve in buns. If desired, top with onion and mustard.

1 SERVING 563 cal., 30g fat (10g sat. fat), 63mg chol., 1575mg sod., 54g carb. (16g sugars, 2g fiber), 20g pro.

READER RAVES

"Wow! This has great flavor. I used just plain brats and really enjoyed this recipe. I could not really taste the root beer but found the resulting taste very flavorful."

—BILL GARRISON JR., TASTEOFHOME.COM

SLOW-COOKER BREAKFAST CASSEROLE

SLOW-COOKER BREAKFAST CASSEROLE

Here's a breakfast casserole that's easy to cook. I can make it the night before and it's ready in the morning. It's the perfect recipe when I have weekend guests.
—Ellie Stutheit, Las Vegas, NV

Prep: 25 min. • **Cook:** 7 hours
Makes: 12 servings

- 1 pkg. (30 oz.) frozen shredded hash brown potatoes
- 1 lb. bulk pork sausage, cooked and drained
- 1 medium onion, chopped
- 1 can (4 oz.) chopped green chiles
- 1½ cups shredded cheddar cheese
- 12 large eggs
- 1 cup 2% milk
- ½ tsp. salt
- ½ tsp. pepper

In a greased 5- or 6-qt. slow cooker, layer half the potatoes, sausage, onion, chiles and cheese. Repeat layers. In a large bowl, whisk eggs, milk, salt and pepper; pour over top. Cover and cook on low for 7-9 hours or until eggs are set.

1 CUP 272 cal., 16g fat (7g sat. fat), 242mg chol., 466mg sod., 16g carb. (3g sugars, 1g fiber), 15g pro.

MA

SLOW-COOKED ITALIAN MEATBALLS

These meatballs are delectable on pasta, in a sandwich or alongside mashed potatoes. They're also wonderful served as an appetizer straight out the of the slow cooker.
—Jason Romano, Downingtown, PA

Prep: 50 min. • **Cook:** 3 hours
Makes: about 5 dozen

- 2 Tbsp. olive oil
- 1 small onion, finely chopped
- 3 garlic cloves, minced
- 1 cup Italian-style panko bread crumbs
- 2 large eggs, lightly beaten
- ½ cup grated Parmesan cheese
- ½ cup minced fresh parsley
- ¼ cup water
- ¼ cup minced fresh basil
- 2 Tbsp. Worcestershire sauce
- ½ tsp. salt
- ½ tsp. pepper
- 1 lb. ground beef
- ½ lb. ground pork
- ½ lb. ground veal
- 4 cups spaghetti sauce
- Minced fresh parsley, optional

1. Preheat oven to 400°. In a small skillet, heat oil over medium heat. Add onion and garlic; cook until onion is tender and golden brown, 5-9 minutes. Cool slightly.
2. In a large bowl, combine the bread crumbs, eggs, cheese, parsley, water, basil, Worcestershire sauce, salt, pepper and onion mixture. Add ground meats; mix lightly but thoroughly. Shape into 1-in. balls. Place on greased racks in shallow baking pans. Bake meatballs until browned, 20-25 minutes.
3. Transfer meatballs to a 4- or 5-qt. slow cooker. Pour the spaghetti sauce over top. Cook, covered, on low for 3-4 hours or until meatballs are cooked through. If desired, serve with minced parsley.

FREEZE OPTION Freeze cooled meatballs and sauce in freezer containers. To use, partially thaw in refrigerator overnight. Heat through in a covered saucepan, stirring gently; add water or broth if necessary. Serve as directed.

1 MEATBALL 54 cal., 3g fat (1g sat. fat), 16mg chol., 146mg sod., 3g carb. (1g sugars, 0 fiber), 3g pro.

SLOW-COOKED SHORT RIBS

Smothered in a finger-licking barbecue sauce, these meaty ribs are a winner everywhere I take them. The recipe is great for a busy cook because once everything is combined, the slow cooker does all the work.
—Pam Halfhill, Wapakoneta, OH

Prep: 25 min. • **Cook:** 9 hours
Makes: 12 servings

- ⅔ cup all-purpose flour
- 2 tsp. salt
- ½ tsp. pepper
- 4 to 4½ lbs. boneless beef short ribs
- ¼ to ⅓ cup butter
- 1 large onion, chopped
- 1½ cups beef broth
- ¾ cup red wine vinegar
- ¾ cup packed brown sugar
- ½ cup chili sauce
- ⅓ cup ketchup
- ⅓ cup Worcestershire sauce
- 5 garlic cloves, minced
- 1½ tsp. chili powder

1. In a bowl or shallow dish, combine the flour, salt and pepper. Add ribs in batches and turn to coat. In a large skillet over medium heat, brown ribs in the butter.
2. Transfer to a 6-qt. slow cooker. In the same skillet, combine the remaining ingredients. Cook and stir until mixture comes to a boil; pour over ribs.
3. Cover and cook on low until meat is tender, 9-10 hours.

3 OZ. COOKED PORK 342 cal., 16g fat (8g sat. fat), 71mg chol., 899mg sod., 28g carb. (19g sugars, 1g fiber), 22g pro.

SLOW-COOKED
SHORT RIBS

LOUISIANA
RED BEANS & RICE

LOUISIANA RED BEANS & RICE

Smoked turkey sausage and red pepper flakes add zip to this tasty slow-cooked version of the New Orleans classic. For extra heat, add red pepper sauce.
—Julia Bushree, Menifee, CA

Prep: 20 min. • **Cook:** 3 hours
Makes: 8 servings (2 qt.)

- 4 cans (16 oz. each) kidney beans, rinsed and drained
- 1 can (14½ oz.) diced tomatoes, undrained
- 1 pkg. (14 oz.) smoked turkey sausage, sliced
- 3 celery ribs, chopped
- 1 large onion, chopped
- 1 cup chicken broth
- 1 medium green pepper, chopped
- 1 small sweet red pepper, chopped
- 6 garlic cloves, minced
- 1 bay leaf
- ½ tsp. crushed red pepper flakes
- 2 green onions, chopped
- Hot cooked rice

1. In a 4- or 5-qt. slow cooker, combine the first 11 ingredients. Cook, covered, on low 3-4 hours or until vegetables are tender.
2. Stir before serving. Remove bay leaf. Serve with green onions and rice.

FREEZE OPTION Discard bay leaf and freeze cooled bean mixture in freezer containers. To use, partially thaw in refrigerator overnight. Heat through in a saucepan, stirring occasionally; add broth or water if necessary. Serve as directed.

1 CUP 291 cal., 3g fat (1g sat. fat), 32mg chol., 1070mg sod., 44g carb. (8g sugars, 13g fiber), 24g pro.

RICH & CREAMY MASHED POTATOES

RICH & CREAMY MASHED POTATOES

It's a cinch to jazz up instant mashed potatoes with sour cream and cream cheese, then cook and serve them from a slow cooker. For an extra-special touch, sprinkle the perfect-for-a-party potatoes with some chopped fresh chives, canned french-fried onions or fresh grated Parmesan cheese.
—Donna Bardocz, Howell, MI

Prep: 15 min. • **Cook:** 2 hours
Makes: 10 servings

- 3¾ cups boiling water
- 1½ cups 2% milk
- 1 pkg. (8 oz.) cream cheese, softened
- ½ cup butter, cubed
- ½ cup sour cream
- 4 cups mashed potato flakes
- 1 tsp. garlic salt
- ¼ tsp. pepper
- Minced fresh parsley, optional

In a greased 4-qt. slow cooker, whisk the boiling water, milk, cream cheese, butter and sour cream until smooth. Stir in the potato flakes, garlic salt and pepper. Cook, covered, on low 2-3 hours or until heated through. Sprinkle with parsley if desired.

¾ CUP 299 cal., 20g fat (13g sat. fat), 60mg chol., 390mg sod., 25g carb. (2g sugars, 1g fiber), 6g pro.

TEST KITCHEN TIP

If your mashed potatoes are too creamy, you can add a thickening agent, such as cornstarch or flour, to the mix. You could also add more potatoes to thicken up your mashed potatoes.

SLOW-COOKED BLUEBERRY FRENCH TOAST

Your slow cooker can be your best friend on a busy morning. Just get this recipe going, run some errands and come back to the aroma of French toast ready to eat.
—Elizabeth Lorenz, Peru, IN

Prep: 30 min. + chilling • **Cook:** 3 hours
Makes: 12 servings (2 cups syrup)

- 8 large eggs
- ½ cup plain yogurt
- ⅓ cup sour cream
- 1 tsp. vanilla extract
- ½ tsp. ground cinnamon
- 1 cup 2% milk
- ⅓ cup maple syrup
- 1 loaf (1 lb.) French bread, cubed
- 1½ cups fresh or frozen blueberries
- 12 oz. cream cheese, cubed

BLUEBERRY SYRUP

- 1 cup sugar
- 2 Tbsp. cornstarch
- 1 cup cold water
- ¾ cup fresh or frozen blueberries, divided
- 1 Tbsp. butter
- 1 Tbsp. lemon juice

1. In a large bowl, whisk eggs, yogurt, sour cream, vanilla and cinnamon. Gradually whisk in milk and maple syrup until blended.
2. Place half of the bread in a greased 5- or 6-qt. slow cooker; layer with half the blueberries, cream cheese and egg mixture. Repeat layers. Refrigerate, covered, overnight.
3. Remove from refrigerator 30 minutes before cooking. Cook, covered, on low 3-4 hours or until a knife inserted in the center comes out clean.
4. For syrup, in a small saucepan, mix sugar and cornstarch; stir in water until smooth. Stir in ¼ cup blueberries. Bring to a boil; cook and stir until berries pop, about 3 minutes. Remove from heat; stir in butter, lemon juice and remaining berries. Serve warm, with French toast.

NOTE If using frozen blueberries, use without thawing to avoid discoloring the batter.

1 CUP WITH ABOUT 2 TBSP. SAUCE 390 cal., 17g fat (9g sat. fat), 182mg chol., 371mg sod., 49g carb. (28g sugars, 2g fiber), 12g pro.

SLOW-COOKED BLUEBERRY FRENCH TOAST

SLOW-COOKED HAM

Entertaining doesn't get much easier than when you serve this tasty five-ingredient ham from the slow cooker. Plus, the leftovers are delicious in casseroles!
—Heather Spring, Sheppard Air Force Base, TX

Prep: 5 min. • **Cook:** 6 hours
Makes: 20 servings

- ½ cup packed brown sugar
- 1 tsp. ground mustard
- 1 tsp. prepared horseradish
- 2 Tbsp. plus ¼ cup cola, divided
- 1 fully cooked boneless ham (5 to 6 lbs.), cut in half

In a small bowl, combine the brown sugar, mustard, horseradish and 2 Tbsp. cola. Rub over ham. Transfer to a 5-qt. slow cooker; add remaining cola to slow cooker. Cover and cook on low until a thermometer reads 140°, 6-8 hours.

3 OZ. COOKED HAM 143 cal., 4g fat (1g sat. fat), 58mg chol., 1180mg sod., 6g carb. (6g sugars, 0 fiber), 21g pro.

HOT WING DIP

HOT WING DIP

Since I usually have all the ingredients on hand for this recipe, this is a terrific go-to snack when entertaining friends and family.
—Coleen Corner, Grove City, PA

Prep: 10 min. • **Cook:** 1 hour
Makes: 4½ cups

- 2 cups shredded cooked chicken
- 1 pkg. (8 oz.) cream cheese, cubed
- 2 cups shredded cheddar cheese
- 1 cup ranch salad dressing
- ½ cup Louisiana-style hot sauce
- Minced fresh parsley, optional
- Tortilla chips and celery sticks

In a 3- or 4-qt. slow cooker, mix the first 5 ingredients. Cook, covered, on low for 1-2 hours or until cheese is melted. If desired, sprinkle with parsley. Serve with tortilla chips and celery.

¼ CUP 186 cal., 16g fat (7g sat. fat), 43mg chol., 235mg sod., 2g carb. (1g sugars, 0 fiber), 8g pro.

TEST KITCHEN TIP

To make Baked Hot Wing Dip, preheat oven to 350°. Spread the dip mixture into an ungreased 9-in. square baking dish. Bake, uncovered, until heated through, 20-25 minutes.

MA

PULLED PORK NACHOS

While home from college, my daughter made these tempting pork nachos—her first recipe ever. My son and I couldn't get enough.
—Carol Kurpjuweit, Humansville, MO

Prep: 30 min. • **Cook:** 8 hours
Makes: 16 servings

- 1 tsp. garlic powder
- 1 tsp. mesquite seasoning
- ¼ tsp. pepper
- ⅛ tsp. celery salt
- 3 lbs. boneless pork shoulder butt roast
- 1 medium green pepper, chopped
- 1 medium sweet red pepper, chopped
- 1 medium onion, chopped
- 1 can (16 oz.) baked beans
- 1 cup barbecue sauce
- 1 cup shredded cheddar cheese
- Corn or tortilla chips
- Optional toppings: Chopped tomatoes, shredded lettuce and chopped green onions

1. In a small bowl, mix the seasoning ingredients. Place roast in a 5- or 6-qt. slow cooker; rub with seasonings. Add peppers and onion. Cook, covered, on low 8-10 hours.
2. Remove roast; cool slightly. Strain cooking juices, reserving vegetables and ½ cup juices; discard remaining juices. Skim fat from reserved juices. Shred pork with 2 forks.
3. Return pork, reserved juices and vegetables to slow cooker. Stir in the beans, barbecue sauce and cheese; heat through. Serve over chips with toppings as desired.

FREEZE OPTION Freeze cooled pork mixture in freezer containers. To use, partially thaw in refrigerator overnight. Heat through in a saucepan, stirring occasionally; add broth or water if necessary.

½ CUP PORK MIXTURE 233 cal., 11g fat (5g sat. fat), 60mg chol., 416mg sod., 14g carb. (6g sugars, 2g fiber), 18g pro.

SIMMERED SMOKED LINKS

No one can resist the sweet and spicy glaze on these bite-sized sausages. They are so effortless to prepare, and they make the perfect party nibbler. Serve them on frilled toothpicks to make them extra fancy.
—Maxine Cenker, Weirton, WV

Prep: 5 min. • **Cook:** 4 hours
Makes: about 6½ dozen

- 2 pkg. (16 oz. each) miniature smoked sausage links
- 1 cup packed brown sugar
- ½ cup ketchup
- ¼ cup prepared horseradish

Place sausages in a 3-qt. slow cooker. Combine the brown sugar, ketchup and horseradish; pour over sausages and stir. Cover and cook on low for 4 hours.

1 SAUSAGE 46 cal., 3g fat (1g sat. fat), 7mg chol., 136mg sod., 3g carb. (3g sugars, 0 fiber), 1g pro.

GRANOLA APPLE CRISP

Tender apple slices are tucked beneath a sweet crunchy topping in my comforting dessert. For variety, replace the apples with your favorite fruit.

—Barbara Schindler, Napoleon, OH

Prep: 20 min. • **Cook:** 5 hours
Makes: 8 servings

- 8 medium tart apples, peeled and sliced
- ¼ cup lemon juice
- 1½ tsp. grated lemon zest
- 2½ cups granola with fruit and nuts
- 1 cup sugar
- 1 tsp. ground cinnamon
- ½ cup butter, melted
- Vanilla ice cream, optional

1. In a large bowl, toss apples, lemon juice and zest. Transfer to a greased 3-qt. slow cooker. Combine granola, sugar and cinnamon; sprinkle over apples. Drizzle with butter.
2. Cover and cook on low until apples are tender, 5-6 hours. Serve warm; if desired, top with vanilla ice cream and additional cinnamon.

1 SERVING 382 cal., 17g fat (8g sat. fat), 31mg chol., 153mg sod., 58g carb. (44g sugars, 4g fiber), 3g pro.

SLOW-COOKER CHEESE DIP

SLOW-COOKER CHEESE DIP

I brought this slightly spicy cheese dip to a gathering with friends and it was a huge hit. The spicy pork sausage provides the zip!
—Marion Bartone, Conneaut, OH

Prep: 15 min. • **Cook:** 4 hours
Makes: 32 servings (2 qt.)

- 1 lb. ground beef
- ½ lb. bulk spicy pork sausage
- 2 lbs. cubed Velveeta
- 2 cans (10 oz. each) diced tomatoes and green chiles
- Tortilla chip scoops, red pepper and cucumber sticks

1. In a large skillet, cook beef and sausage over medium heat until no longer pink; drain. Transfer to a 3- or 4-qt. slow cooker. Stir in cheese and tomatoes.
2. Cover and cook on low for 4-5 hours or until the cheese is melted, stirring occasionally. Serve with tortilla chips, and red pepper and cucumber sticks.

¼ CUP 139 cal., 10g fat (5g sat. fat), 40mg chol., 486mg sod., 3g carb. (2g sugars, 0 fiber), 8g pro.

READER RAVES

"Is it bad that I can almost eat the whole dish by myself? It is so delicious. I use a milder sausage (my family's preference), but still is delish!"

—RENA55, TASTEOFHOME.COM

TERIYAKI CHICKEN THIGHS

Here's a real slow-cooker sensation: Asian-style chicken and rice. It always goes over big with my family.
—Gigi Miller, Stoughton, WI

Prep: 15 min. • **Cook:** 4 hours
Makes: 8 servings

- 3 lbs. boneless skinless chicken thighs
- ¾ cup sugar
- ¾ cup reduced-sodium soy sauce
- ⅓ cup cider vinegar
- 1 garlic clove, minced
- ¾ tsp. ground ginger
- ¼ tsp. pepper
- 4 tsp. cornstarch
- 4 tsp. cold water
- Hot cooked rice, optional

1. Place chicken in a 4- or 5-qt. slow cooker. In a small bowl, mix sugar, soy sauce, vinegar, garlic, ginger and pepper; pour over chicken. Cook, covered, on low 4-5 hours or until chicken is tender.
2. Remove chicken to a serving platter; keep warm. Transfer cooking juices to a small saucepan; skim fat. Bring cooking juices to a boil. In a small bowl, mix the cornstarch and cold water until smooth; stir into cooking juices. Return to a boil; cook and stir for 1-2 minutes or until thickened. Serve with chicken and, if desired, rice.

5 OZ. COOKED CHICKEN WITH ¼ CUP SAUCE 342 cal., 12g fat (3g sat. fat), 113mg chol., 958mg sod., 22g carb. (19g sugars, 0 fiber), 33g pro.

MA

HONEY PULLED PORK SUBS

Honey and ground ginger are the big flavor boosters behind my no-stress sandwiches. A bottle of barbecue sauce quickly ties it all together.
—Denise Davis, Porter, ME

Prep: 15 min. • **Cook:** 5 hours
Makes: 16 servings

- 1 small onion, finely chopped
- 1 boneless pork shoulder butt roast (2½ lbs.)
- 1 bottle (18 oz.) barbecue sauce
- ½ cup water
- ¼ cup honey
- 6 garlic cloves, minced
- 1 tsp. seasoned salt
- 1 tsp. ground ginger
- 8 submarine buns, split

1. Place onion and roast in a 5-qt. slow cooker. In a small bowl, combine the barbecue sauce, water, honey, garlic, seasoned salt and ginger; pour over meat. Cover and cook on high 5-6 hours or until meat is tender.
2. Remove meat; cool slightly. Shred meat with 2 forks and return to the slow cooker; heat through. Serve on buns. Cut sandwiches in half.

FREEZE OPTION Place individual portions of the cooled meat mixture in freezer containers. To use, partially thaw in the refrigerator overnight. Microwave, covered, on high in a microwave-safe dish until heated through, gently stirring; add water if necessary. Serve on buns.

½ SANDWICH 417 cal., 13g fat (4g sat. fat), 81mg chol., 867mg sod., 44g carb. (12g sugars, 2g fiber), 29g pro.

TEST KITCHEN TIP

To make Italian Pulled Pork, omit all ingredients except the roast and buns. Combine 1 Tbsp. crushed fennel seed, 1 Tbsp. steak seasoning and ½ tsp. cayenne; rub mixture over the roast. In a skillet, brown the roast on all sides in 1 Tbsp. olive oil. Place the roast in a slow cooker. Add 2 thinly sliced medium green or sweet red peppers, 2 thinly sliced medium onions and 1 can (14½ oz.) diced tomatoes with liquid. Proceed as the recipe directs.

SLOW-COOKER CHICKEN STROGANOFF

This recipe is creamy, warm, satisfying and fairly inexpensive—and it needs just a few ingredients! Who could ask for more on a cold winter evening? I will admit, though, that I have been known to make it during summer too.
—Jason Kretzer, Grants Pass, OR

Prep: 15 min. • **Cook:** 4½ hours
Makes: 8 servings

- 3 lbs. boneless skinless chicken thighs
- 2 cans (10½ oz. each) condensed cream of chicken with herbs soup, undiluted
- ½ cup chicken broth
- ½ lb. sliced baby portobello mushrooms
- 2 cups sour cream
- ¾ tsp. salt
- Hot cooked egg noodles
- Pepper
- Chopped fresh parsley, optional

1. Place chicken, soup and broth in a 5- or 6-qt. slow cooker. Cook, covered, on high until a thermometer inserted into chicken reads at least 165°, about 3 hours. Cut chicken into bite-sized pieces; return to slow cooker.
2. Add mushrooms. Cook, covered, on high until mushrooms are tender, 1½-2 hours longer. Stir in sour cream and salt. Serve with egg noodles; sprinkle with pepper and, if desired, parsley.

1⅓ CUPS 447 cal., 29g fat (12g sat. fat), 133mg chol., 877mg sod., 9g carb. (3g sugars, 2g fiber), 36g pro.

SLOW-COOKER CHICKEN STROGANOFF

SLOW-COOKER LAVA CAKE

SLOW-COOKER LAVA CAKE

I love chocolate. Perhaps that's why this decadent slow-cooker cake has long been a family favorite. The cake can also be served cold.
—Elizabeth Farrell, Hamilton, MT

Prep: 15 min. • **Cook:** 2 hours + standing
Makes: 8 servings

- 1 cup all-purpose flour
- 1 cup packed brown sugar, divided
- 5 Tbsp. baking cocoa, divided
- 2 tsp. baking powder
- ¼ tsp. salt
- ½ cup fat-free milk
- 2 Tbsp. canola oil
- ½ tsp. vanilla extract
- ⅛ tsp. ground cinnamon
- 1¼ cups hot water

1. In a large bowl, whisk flour, ½ cup brown sugar, 3 Tbsp. cocoa, baking powder and salt. In another bowl, whisk milk, oil and vanilla until blended. Add to flour mixture; stir just until moistened.
2. Spread into a 3-qt. slow cooker coated with cooking spray. In a small bowl, mix cinnamon and remaining brown sugar and cocoa; stir in hot water. Pour over batter (do not stir).
3. Cook, covered, on high 2-2½ hours or until a toothpick inserted in cake portion comes out clean. Turn off slow cooker; let stand 15 minutes before serving.

1 SERVING 207 cal., 4g fat (0 sat. fat), 0 chol., 191mg sod., 41g carb. (28g sugars, 1g fiber), 3g pro.

EASY SLOW-COOKER MAC & CHEESE

EASY SLOW-COOKER MAC & CHEESE

"You're the best mom in the world!" my sons cheer whenever I make this creamy mac and cheese perfection. You can't beat a response like that!
—Heidi Fleek, Hamburg, PA

Prep: 25 min. • **Cook:** 1 hour
Makes: 8 servings

- 2 cups uncooked elbow macaroni
- 1 can (10¾ oz.) condensed cheddar cheese soup, undiluted
- 1 cup 2% milk
- ½ cup sour cream
- ¼ cup butter, cubed
- ½ tsp. onion powder
- ¼ tsp. white pepper
- ⅛ tsp. salt
- 1 cup shredded cheddar cheese
- 1 cup shredded fontina cheese
- 1 cup shredded provolone cheese

1. Cook macaroni according to package directions for al dente. Meanwhile, in a large saucepan, combine soup, milk, sour cream, butter and seasonings; cook and stir over medium-low heat until blended. Stir in cheeses until melted.
2. Drain macaroni; transfer to a greased 3-qt. slow cooker. Stir in cheese mixture. Cook, covered, on low 1-2 hours or until heated through.

¾ CUP 346 cal., 23g fat (14g sat. fat), 71mg chol., 712mg sod., 20g carb. (4g sugars, 1g fiber), 15g pro.

BUTTERSCOTCH FRUIT DIP

If you like the sweetness of butterscotch chips, you'll definitely enjoy this warm rum-flavored fruit dip. I serve it with apple and pear wedges. It holds up for up to two hours in the slow cooker.
—Jeaune Hadl Van Meter, Lexington, KY

Prep: 5 min. • **Cook:** 45 min.
Makes: about 3 cups

- 2 pkg. (10 to 11 oz. each) butterscotch chips
- ⅔ cup evaporated milk
- ⅔ cup chopped pecans
- 1 Tbsp. imitation rum extract
- Apple and pear wedges

In a 1½-qt. slow cooker, combine the butterscotch chips and milk. Cover and cook on low for 45-50 minutes or until chips are softened; stir until smooth. Stir in pecans and extract. Serve warm with apple and pear wedges.

¼ CUP 197 cal., 13g fat (7g sat. fat), 6mg chol., 32mg sod., 17g carb. (16g sugars, 1g fiber), 2g pro.

MA

PIZZA SOUP WITH GARLIC TOAST CROUTONS

This comforting soup satisfies our pizza cravings. I sometimes substitute Italian sausage for the chicken or add a little Parmesan cheese. Go nuts and add all your favorite pizza toppings!
—Joan Hallford, North Richland Hills, TX

Prep: 10 min. • **Cook:** 6 hours
Makes: 10 servings (about 4 qt.)

- 1 can (28 oz.) diced tomatoes, drained
- 1 can (15 oz.) pizza sauce
- 1 lb. boneless skinless chicken breasts, cut into 1-in. pieces
- 1 pkg. (3 oz.) sliced pepperoni, halved
- 1 cup sliced fresh mushrooms
- 1 small onion, chopped
- ½ cup chopped green pepper
- ¼ tsp. pepper
- 2 cans (14½ oz. each) chicken broth
- 1 pkg. (11¼ oz.) frozen garlic Texas toast
- 1 pkg. (10 oz.) frozen chopped spinach, thawed and squeezed dry
- 1 cup shredded part-skim mozzarella cheese

1. In a 6-qt. slow cooker, combine first 9 ingredients. Cook, covered, on low for 6-8 hours or until chicken is tender.
2. For croutons, cut Texas toast into cubes; bake according to package directions. Add spinach to soup; heat through, stirring occasionally. Top servings with cheese and warm croutons.

FREEZE OPTION Freeze cooled soup in freezer containers. To use, partially thaw in refrigerator overnight. Heat through in a saucepan, stirring occasionally. Prepare croutons as directed. Top soup with cheese and croutons.

1½ CUPS 292 cal., 13g fat (5g sat. fat), 46mg chol., 1081mg sod., 24g carb. (7g sugars, 4g fiber), 20g pro.

PIZZA SOUP WITH GARLIC TOAST CROUTONS

SLOW-COOKER BERRY COBBLER

Even during warm weather, you can still enjoy the amazing flavor of homemade cobbler without heating up the kitchen.
—Karen Jarocki, Yuma, AZ

Prep: 15 min. • **Cook:** 1¾ hours
Makes: 8 servings

- 1¼ cups all-purpose flour, divided
- 2 Tbsp. plus 1 cup sugar, divided
- 1 tsp. baking powder
- ¼ tsp. ground cinnamon
- 1 large egg, room temperature
- ¼ cup fat-free milk
- 2 Tbsp. canola oil
- ⅛ tsp. salt
- 2 cups fresh or frozen raspberries, thawed
- 2 cups fresh or frozen blueberries, thawed
- Low-fat vanilla frozen yogurt, optional

1. Whisk together 1 cup flour, 2 Tbsp. sugar, baking powder and cinnamon. In another bowl, whisk together egg, milk and oil; add to dry ingredients, stirring just until moistened (batter will be thick). Spread onto bottom of a 5-qt. slow cooker coated with cooking spray.
2. Mix salt and remaining ¼ cup flour and 1 cup sugar; toss with berries. Spoon over batter. Cook, covered, on high until berry mixture is bubbly, 1¾-2 hours. If desired, serve with frozen yogurt.

1 SERVING 260 cal., 5g fat (1g sat. fat), 23mg chol., 110mg sod., 53g carb. (34g sugars, 3g fiber), 4g pro.

SLOW-COOKER BERRY COBBLER

BARBECUED PARTY STARTERS

These sweet and tangy bites are sure to tide everyone over until dinner. At the buffet, set out some fun toothpicks to make for easy nibbling.
—Anastasia Weiss, Punxsutawney, PA

Prep: 30 min. • **Cook:** 2¼ hours
Makes: 16 servings

- 1 lb. ground beef
- ¼ cup finely chopped onion
- 1 pkg. (16 oz.) miniature hot dogs, drained
- 1 jar (12 oz.) apricot preserves
- 1 cup barbecue sauce
- 1 can (20 oz.) pineapple chunks, drained

1. In a large bowl, combine beef and onion, mixing lightly but thoroughly. Shape into 1-in. balls. In a large skillet over medium heat, cook meatballs in 2 batches until cooked through, turning occasionally.
2. Using a slotted spoon, transfer the meatballs to a 3-qt. slow cooker. Add hot dogs; stir in preserves and barbecue sauce. Cook, covered, on high or until heated through, 2-3 hours.
3. Stir in pineapple; cook, covered, until heated through, 15-20 minutes longer.

⅓ CUP 237 cal., 11g fat (4g sat. fat), 36mg chol., 491mg sod., 26g carb. (20g sugars, 0 fiber), 9g pro.

HOT SPICED CRANBERRY DRINK

I serve this rosy spiced beverage at parties and family gatherings during the winter. Friends like the tangy twist it gets from Red Hots. It's a nice change from the usual hot chocolate.
—*Laura Burgess, Ballwin, MO*

Prep: 10 min. • **Cook:** 2 hours
Makes: 14 servings (3½ qt.)

- 8 cups hot water
- 1½ cups sugar
- 4 cups cranberry juice
- ¾ cup orange juice
- ¼ cup lemon juice
- 12 whole cloves, optional
- ½ cup Red Hots

In a 5-qt. slow cooker, combine water, sugar and juices; stir until sugar is dissolved. If desired, place cloves in a double thickness of cheesecloth; bring up corners of cloth and tie with string to form a bag. Add spice bag and Red Hots to slow cooker. Cover and cook on low until heated through, 2-3 hours. Before serving, discard spice bag and stir punch.

1 CUP 155 cal., 0 fat (0 sat. fat), 0 chol., 2mg sod., 40g carb. (37g sugars, 0 fiber), 0 pro.

READER RAVES

"Served this at my work's Christmas potluck and I had requests for the recipe. I kept it on warm in the Crock-Pot after it heated through. I'll definitely make this again."

—MISSKARLA, TASTEOFHOME.COM

THE SWEETEST TREATS

P. 293

P. 266

P. 267

MISSISSIPPI MUD PIE

MISSISSIPPI MUD PIE

This southern favorite is one my family can never get enough of, and there are never any leftovers. My grandmother, mother and aunts always made this dish for family gatherings. Now I make it for just about every event because it's so easy to prepare and everyone loves it!
—Elizabeth Williston, Thibodaux, LA

Prep: 30 min. • **Bake:** 15 min. + cooling
Makes: 12 servings

- 1 cup all-purpose flour
- 1 cup chopped pecans
- ½ cup butter, softened
- 1 pkg. (5.9 oz.) instant chocolate pudding mix
- 1 pkg. (8 oz.) cream cheese, softened
- 1 cup confectioners' sugar
- 1 container (16 oz.) frozen whipped topping, thawed, divided
- Optional: Toasted chopped pecans and chocolate curls

1. Preheat oven to 350°. In a large bowl, beat the flour, pecans and butter until blended. Press into bottom of a 13x9-in. baking dish. Bake until golden brown, about 15 minutes. Remove to a wire rack; cool completely.
2. Make chocolate pudding according to package directions; let stand 5 minutes. In a bowl, beat the cream cheese and confectioners' sugar until smooth; fold in 1 cup whipped topping. Spread cream cheese mixture over cooled crust. Spread pudding over cream cheese layer; top with remaining whipped topping. If desired, top with additional pecans and chocolate curls.

1 PIECE 466 cal., 29g fat (17g sat. fat), 46mg chol., 214mg sod., 44g carb. (28g sugars, 2g fiber), 5g pro.

GERMAN SPICE COOKIES

These chewy spice cookies are fantastic with coffee and taste even better the next day. The recipe has been a family favorite for more than 40 years.
—Joan Tyson, Bowling Green, OH

Takes: 20 min. • **Makes:** 3½ dozen

- 3 large eggs, room temperature
- 2 cups packed brown sugar
- 1 tsp. ground cloves
- 1 tsp. ground cinnamon
- ½ tsp. pepper
- 2 cups all-purpose flour
- ½ tsp. baking soda
- ½ tsp. salt
- 1 cup raisins
- 1 cup chopped walnuts

1. In a large bowl, beat eggs. Add the brown sugar, cloves, cinnamon and pepper. Combine the flour, baking soda and salt; gradually add to egg mixture. Stir in raisins and walnuts.
2. Drop by tablespoonfuls 2 in. apart onto lightly greased baking sheets. Bake at 400° for 8-10 minutes or until surface cracks. Remove to wire racks to cool.

1 COOKIE 96 cal., 2g fat (0 sat. fat), 13mg chol., 52mg sod., 18g carb. (12g sugars, 1g fiber), 2g pro.

READER RAVES

"These cookies were so good. They have very intense spice flavor and the perfect texture."

—EMILY357, TASTEOFHOME.COM

PUMPKIN PIE BARS

MA

PUMPKIN PIE BARS

These bars taste like a cross between pumpkin pie and pecan pie—yum! If you can't find butter cake mix, yellow cake mix works.
—Sue Draheim, Waterford, WI

Prep: 15 min. • **Bake:** 50 min. + chilling
Makes: 16 servings

- 1 can (29 oz.) pumpkin
- 1 can (12 oz.) evaporated milk
- 1½ cups sugar
- 4 large eggs
- 2 tsp. ground cinnamon
- 1 tsp. ground ginger
- ½ tsp. ground nutmeg
- 1 pkg. butter recipe golden cake mix (regular size)
- 1 cup butter, melted
- 1 cup chopped pecans
- Whipped topping, optional

1. Preheat oven to 350°. In a large bowl, combine the first 7 ingredients; beat on medium speed until smooth. Pour into an ungreased 13x9-in. baking pan. Sprinkle with dry cake mix. Drizzle butter over top; sprinkle with pecans.
2. Bake 50-60 minutes or until a toothpick inserted in center comes out clean. Cool 1 hour on a wire rack.
3. Refrigerate 3 hours or overnight. Remove from refrigerator 15 minutes before serving. Cut into bars. If desired, serve with whipped topping.

1 BAR 419 cal., 22g fat (10g sat. fat), 91mg chol., 360mg sod., 53g carb. (38g sugars, 3g fiber), 5g pro.

EASY COCONUT CREAM PIE

EASY COCONUT CREAM PIE

This is my own recipe for a pie that I make often. It's been a family-favorite dessert for decades. I even made several of these pies to serve a threshing crew of 21 men!
—Vera Moffitt, Oskaloosa, KS

Prep: 20 min. + chilling
Cook: 10 min. + cooling
Makes: 8 servings

- 1 sheet refrigerated pie crust
- ¾ cup sugar
- 3 Tbsp. all-purpose flour
- ⅛ tsp. salt
- 3 cups whole milk
- 3 large eggs, beaten
- 1½ cups sweetened shredded coconut, toasted, divided
- 1 Tbsp. butter
- 1½ tsp. vanilla extract

1. Unroll crust into a 9-in. pie plate; flute edge. Refrigerate 30 minutes. Preheat oven to 400°.
2. Line crust with a double thickness of foil. Fill with pie weights, dried beans or uncooked rice. Bake on a lower oven rack or until edge is golden brown, 15-20 minutes. Remove foil and weights; bake 3-6 minutes longer or until bottom is golden brown. Cool on a wire rack.
3. In a medium saucepan, combine sugar, flour and salt. Stir in milk; cook and stir over medium-high heat until thickened and bubbly. Reduce heat; cook and stir 2 minutes longer.
4. Remove from the heat; gradually stir about 1 cup of hot mixture into beaten eggs. Return all to the saucepan; cook and stir over medium heat until nearly boiling. Reduce heat; cook and stir about 2 minutes more (do not boil). Remove from heat; stir in 1 cup coconut, butter and vanilla.
5. Pour into crust; sprinkle with the remaining coconut. Refrigerate for several hours before serving.

1 PIECE 389 cal., 19g fat (12g sat. fat), 88mg chol., 260mg sod., 47g carb. (32g sugars, 1g fiber), 7g pro.

SOFT TRIED & TRUE PEANUT BUTTER COOKIES

When I want to offer friends and family soft and chewy peanut butter cookies, this is the recipe I turn to. Use either creamy or crunchy peanut butter with delicious results. These are the best, and my family can't get enough.
—Emma Lee Granger, La Pine, OR

Prep: 15 min. • **Bake:** 15 min./batch
Makes: about 5 dozen

- 1 cup butter-flavored shortening
- 1 cup creamy peanut butter
- ¾ cup sugar
- ¾ cup packed brown sugar
- 2 large eggs, room temperature
- 1 tsp. vanilla extract
- ½ tsp. water
- 2¼ cups all-purpose flour
- 1 tsp. baking soda
- 1 tsp. salt

1. In a large bowl, cream the shortening, peanut butter and sugars until light and fluffy, 5-7 minutes. Add eggs, 1 at a time, beating well after each addition. Beat in vanilla and water. Combine the flour, baking soda and salt; gradually add to the creamed mixture and mix well.
2. Drop by tablespoonfuls 2 in. apart onto ungreased baking sheets. Flatten with a fork. Bake at 350° until golden brown, 12-15 minutes. Remove to wire racks to cool.

1 COOKIE 105 cal., 6g fat (1g sat. fat), 7mg chol., 91mg sod., 11g carb. (6g sugars, 0 fiber), 2g pro.

TEST KITCHEN TIP

Wondering whether to use shortening or butter in recipes? Shortening melts at a higher temperature than butter. Hence, it is useful for baking cookies that you want to have a nice uniform shape.

SOFT TRIED & TRUE PEANUT BUTTER COOKIES

ITALIAN CHOCOLATE-HAZELNUT CHEESECAKE PIE

ITALIAN CHOCOLATE-HAZELNUT CHEESECAKE PIE

I first prepared an Italian-style cheese pie years ago. When I changed it up by adding a chocolate-hazelnut topping, it proved so popular that I had to give out copies of the recipe.

—Steve Meredith, Streamwood, IL

Prep: 25 min. • **Bake:** 30 min. + chilling
Makes: 8 servings

- 2 pkg. (8 oz. each) cream cheese, softened
- ½ cup sugar
- ½ cup mascarpone cheese
- ¼ cup sour cream
- 1 tsp. lime juice
- 1 tsp. vanilla extract
- 2 large eggs, room temperature, lightly beaten
- 1 chocolate crumb crust (9 in.)

TOPPING

- ½ cup semisweet chocolate chips
- ⅓ cup heavy whipping cream
- ½ tsp. vanilla extract
- Whole or chopped hazelnuts, toasted

1. Preheat oven to 350°. In a large bowl, beat cream cheese and sugar until smooth. Beat in mascarpone cheese, sour cream, lime juice and vanilla. Add the eggs; beat on low speed just until blended. Pour into crust. Place on a baking sheet.
2. Bake 30-35 minutes or until center is almost set. Cool 1 hour on a wire rack.
3. Meanwhile, for topping, place chocolate chips in a small bowl. In a small saucepan, bring cream just to a boil. Pour over chips; stir with a whisk until smooth. Stir in vanilla. Cool to room temperature or until mixture thickens to a spreading consistency, stirring occasionally.
4. Spread chocolate topping over pie; refrigerate overnight. Just before serving, top with hazelnuts.

NOTE To toast nuts, bake in a shallow pan in a 350° oven for 5-10 minutes or cook in a skillet over low heat until lightly browned, stirring occasionally.

1 PIECE 590 cal., 47g fat (25g sat. fat), 152mg chol., 319mg sod., 38g carb. (28g sugars, 1g fiber), 9g pro.

ORANGE BAVARIAN

This refreshing treat is perfect after a hearty meal.

—Adeline Piscitelli, Sayreville, NJ

Prep: 15 min. + chilling
Makes: 14 servings

- 3 pkg. (3 oz. each) orange gelatin
- 2¼ cups boiling water
- 1 cup sour cream
- 1 qt. orange sherbet, softened
- 1 can (11 oz.) mandarin oranges, drained and halved
- Red and green grapes, optional

Dissolve gelatin in water. Stir in sour cream until smooth. Mix in sherbet until melted. Refrigerate until partially set. Fold in oranges. Pour into a 7-cup ring mold coated with cooking spray. Cover and refrigerate 8 hours or overnight. Just before serving, unmold onto a platter; fill the center with grapes if desired.

1 PIECE 126 cal., 4g fat (2g sat. fat), 13mg chol., 43mg sod., 22g carb. (20g sugars, 0 fiber), 2g pro.

BANANA CREAM PIE

BANANA CREAM PIE

Made from our farm-fresh dairy products, this pie was a sensational creamy treat any time Mom served it. Her recipe is a real treasure, and I've never found one that tastes better!
—Bernice Morris, Marshfield, MO

Prep: 35 min. + cooling
Cook: 10 min. + chilling
Makes: 8 servings

Dough for single-crust pie
¾ cup sugar
⅓ cup all-purpose flour
¼ tsp. salt
2 cups whole milk
3 large egg yolks, lightly beaten
2 Tbsp. butter
1 tsp. vanilla extract
3 firm medium bananas
Whipped cream, optional

1. On a lightly floured surface, roll dough to a ⅛-in.-thick circle; transfer to a 9-in. pie plate. Trim to ½ in. beyond rim of plate; flute edge. Refrigerate 30 minutes. Preheat oven to 425°.
2. Line crust with a double thickness of foil. Fill with pie weights, dried beans or uncooked rice. Bake on a lower oven rack until the edge is golden brown, 20-25 minutes. Remove foil and weights; bake until the bottom is golden brown, 3-6 minutes longer. Cool on a wire rack.
3. Meanwhile, in a saucepan, combine sugar, flour and salt; stir in milk and mix well. Cook over medium-high heat until mixture is thickened and bubbly. Cook and stir 2 minutes longer. Remove from the heat. Stir a small amount of hot mixture into egg yolks; return all to saucepan. Bring to a gentle boil. Cook and stir 2 minutes; remove from the heat. Add butter and vanilla; cool slightly.
4. Slice bananas into crust; pour filling over top. Cover and refrigerate until set, about 2 hours. If desired, garnish with whipped cream and additional sliced bananas.

DOUGH FOR SINGLE-CRUST PIE Combine 1¼ cups all-purpose flour and ¼ tsp. salt; cut in ½ cup cold butter until crumbly. Gradually add 3-5 Tbsp. ice water, tossing with a fork until dough holds together when pressed. Shape into a disk; wrap and refrigerate 1 hour.

1 PIECE 338 cal., 14g fat (7g sat. fat), 101mg chol., 236mg sod., 49g carb. (30g sugars, 1g fiber), 5g pro.

FLUFFY RAISIN PUMPKIN BARS

The chocolate-covered raisins inside are a fun surprise. The traditional cream cheese frosting never fails to please.
—Margaret Wilson, San Bernardino, CA

Prep: 20 min. • **Bake:** 25 min. + cooling
Makes: 4 dozen

2 cups sugar
¾ cup canola oil
4 large eggs, room temperature
2 cups canned pumpkin
2 cups all-purpose flour
2 tsp. baking powder
1 tsp. baking soda
1 tsp. ground cinnamon
1 tsp. ground nutmeg
½ tsp. ground ginger
¼ tsp. ground cloves
1 cup chopped walnuts
1 cup chocolate-covered raisins for baking

FROSTING

⅓ cup butter, softened
3 oz. cream cheese, softened
2 cups confectioners' sugar
1 Tbsp. 2% milk
1 tsp. orange extract

1. In a large bowl, beat sugar and oil. Add eggs, 1 at a time, beating well after each addition. Add pumpkin; mix well. Combine the flour, baking powder, baking soda and spices; gradually add to the pumpkin mixture. Stir in walnuts and chocolate-covered raisins.
2. Pour into a greased 15x10x1-in. baking pan. Bake at 350° for 25-30 minutes or until a toothpick inserted in the center comes out clean. Cool on a wire rack.
3. For frosting, in a large bowl, cream the butter, cream cheese and confectioners' sugar. Add milk and orange extract; beat until smooth. Frost bars. Sprinkle with additional cinnamon if desired. Cut into bars. Store in the refrigerator.

1 PIECE 162 cal., 8g fat (2g sat. fat), 23mg chol., 67mg sod., 21g carb. (15g sugars, 1g fiber), 2g pro.

FLUFFY RAISIN PUMPKIN BARS

MA

LAYERED TURTLE CHEESECAKE

After receiving a request for a special turtle cheesecake and not finding a good recipe, I created my own. Everyone is thrilled with the results and this remains a favorite treat at the coffee shop where I work.

—Sue Gronholz, Beaver Dam, WI

Prep: 40 min. • **Bake:** 1¼ hours + chilling
Makes: 16 servings

- 1 cup all-purpose flour
- ⅓ cup packed brown sugar
- ¼ cup finely chopped pecans
- 6 Tbsp. cold butter, cubed

FILLING

- 4 pkg. (8 oz. each) cream cheese, softened
- 1 cup sugar
- ⅓ cup packed brown sugar
- ¼ cup plus 1 tsp. all-purpose flour, divided
- 2 Tbsp. heavy whipping cream
- 1½ tsp. vanilla extract
- 4 large eggs, room temperature, lightly beaten
- ½ cup milk chocolate chips, melted and cooled
- ¼ cup caramel ice cream topping
- ⅓ cup chopped pecans

GANACHE

- ½ cup milk chocolate chips
- ¼ cup heavy whipping cream
- 2 Tbsp. chopped pecans
- Additional caramel ice cream topping, optional

1. Place a greased 9-in. springform pan on a double thickness of heavy-duty foil (about 18 in. square). Securely wrap foil around pan.
2. In a small bowl, combine the flour, brown sugar and pecans; cut in butter until crumbly. Press onto the bottom of prepared pan. Place pan on a baking sheet. Bake at 325° for 12-15 minutes or until set. Cool on a wire rack.
3. In a large bowl, beat cream cheese and sugars until smooth. Beat in ¼ cup flour, cream and vanilla. Add eggs; beat on low speed just until blended. Remove 1 cup batter to a small bowl; stir in the melted chocolate. Spread over crust.
4. In another bowl, mix caramel topping and remaining 1 tsp. flour; stir in pecans. Drop by tablespoonfuls over chocolate batter. Top with remaining batter. Place springform pan in a large baking pan; add 1 in. hot water to larger pan.
5. Bake at 325° until center is just set and top appears dull, 1¼-1½ hours. Remove springform pan from water bath; remove foil. Cool cheesecake on a wire rack for 10 minutes. Loosen side from pan with a knife; cool 1 hour longer. Refrigerate overnight.
6. For ganache, place chocolate chips in a small bowl. In a small saucepan, bring cream just to a boil. Pour over the chips; whisk until smooth. Cool slightly, stirring occasionally.
7. Spread ganache over cheesecake; sprinkle with pecans. Refrigerate until set. Remove side of springform pan. If desired, drizzle cheesecake with additional caramel topping before serving.

1 PIECE 495 cal., 34g fat (18g sat. fat), 124mg chol., 260mg sod., 42g carb. (32g sugars, 1g fiber), 8g pro.

LAYERED TURTLE CHEESECAKE

MINI PEANUT BUTTER SANDWICH COOKIES

Peanut butter lovers go nuts for these rich little sandwich cookies. To cool down on a hot day, sandwich ice cream between the cookies instead of frosting.
—Keri Wolfe, Nappanee, IN

Prep: 25 min.
Bake: 15 min./batch + cooling
Makes: about 3½ dozen

- 1 cup shortening
- 1 cup creamy peanut butter
- 1 cup sugar
- 1 cup packed brown sugar
- 3 large eggs, room temperature
- 1 tsp. vanilla extract
- 3½ cups all-purpose flour
- 2 tsp. baking soda
- ½ tsp. salt

FILLING

- ¾ cup creamy peanut butter
- ½ cup 2% milk
- 1½ tsp. vanilla extract
- 4 cups confectioners' sugar

1. Preheat oven to 350°. In a large bowl, cream shortening, peanut butter and sugars until blended. Beat in eggs and vanilla. In another bowl, whisk flour, baking soda and salt; gradually beat into creamed mixture.
2. Shape into 1-in. balls; place 2 in. apart on ungreased baking sheets. Bake until set, 11-13 minutes. Remove from pans to wire racks to cool completely.
3. In a small bowl, beat peanut butter, milk and vanilla until blended. Beat in confectioners' sugar until smooth. Spread filling on bottoms of half of the cookies; cover with remaining cookies.

FREEZE OPTION Freeze unfilled cookies in freezer containers. To use, thaw cookies and fill as directed.

NOTE Reduced-fat peanut butter is not recommended for this recipe.

1 SANDWICH COOKIE 240 cal., 11g fat (2g sat. fat), 14mg chol., 145mg sod., 33g carb. (23g sugars, 1g fiber), 4g pro.

MAMAW EMILY'S STRAWBERRY CAKE

MAMAW EMILY'S STRAWBERRY CAKE

My husband loved his Mamaw's strawberry cake. He thought no one could duplicate it. I made it and it's just as scrumptious as he remembers.
—Jennifer Bruce, Manitou, KY

Prep: 15 min. • **Bake:** 25 min. + cooling
Makes: 12 servings

- 1 pkg. white cake mix (regular size)
- 1 pkg. (3 oz.) strawberry gelatin
- 3 Tbsp. sugar
- 3 Tbsp. all-purpose flour
- 1 cup water
- ½ cup canola oil
- 2 large eggs, room temperature
- 1 cup finely chopped strawberries

FROSTING

- ½ cup butter, softened
- ½ cup crushed strawberries
- 4½ to 5 cups confectioners' sugar

1. Preheat oven to 350°. Line the bottoms of 2 greased 8-in. round baking pans with parchment; grease parchment.
2. In a large bowl, combine cake mix, gelatin, sugar and flour. Add water, oil and eggs; beat on low speed 30 seconds. Beat on medium 2 minutes. Fold in the chopped strawberries. Transfer to the prepared pans.
3. Bake until a toothpick inserted in center comes out clean, 25-30 minutes. Cool in pans 10 minutes before removing to wire racks; remove paper. Cool cake layers completely.
4. For frosting, in a small bowl, beat butter until creamy. Beat in crushed strawberries. Gradually beat in enough confectioners' sugar to reach desired consistency. Spread frosting between layers and over top and side of cake.

1 PIECE 532 cal., 21g fat (7g sat. fat), 51mg chol., 340mg sod., 85g carb. (69g sugars, 1g fiber), 4g pro.

RAISIN DATE BREAD PUDDING

RAISIN DATE BREAD PUDDING

I put all my leftover bread and buns in the freezer, and when I've stashed away enough, I whip up a batch of this delicious pudding. It's the perfect dish for any occasion.
—Dawn Green, Hopkins, MI

Prep: 15 min. • **Bake:** 55 min.
Makes: 12 servings

- 4 cups 2% milk
- 5 cups cubed day-old bread
- 1 cup sugar
- 8 large eggs, room temperature, beaten
- ½ cup butter, melted
- ¼ cup chopped dates
- ¼ cup raisins
- 1 tsp. vanilla extract
- ½ tsp. ground cinnamon
- Dash salt
- Dash ground nutmeg
- Optional: Additional sugar, cinnamon and nutmeg, and whipped cream

1. In a large bowl, pour milk over bread. Add sugar, eggs, butter, dates, raisins, vanilla, cinnamon, salt and nutmeg; stir to mix well. Pour into a greased 13x9-in. baking dish. If desired, sprinkle with additional sugar, cinnamon and nutmeg.
2. Bake at 350° until top is golden brown and a knife inserted in the center comes out clean, about 55 minutes. If desired, serve warm with whipped cream.

1 PIECE 290 cal., 14g fat (8g sat. fat), 173mg chol., 250mg sod., 33g carb. (25g sugars, 1g fiber), 8g pro.

CONTEST-WINNING FRESH BLUEBERRY PIE

I've been making this dessert for decades since blueberries are readily available in Michigan. Nothing says summer like a piece of fresh blueberry pie!
—Linda Kernan, Mason, MI

Prep: 25 min. + cooling
Cook: 15 min. + chilling
Makes: 8 servings

- 1 sheet refrigerated pie crust
- ¾ cup sugar
- 3 Tbsp. cornstarch
- ⅛ tsp. salt
- ¼ cup cold water
- 5 cups fresh blueberries, divided
- 1 Tbsp. butter
- 1 Tbsp. lemon juice

1. Preheat oven to 425°. Unroll crust into a 9-in. pie plate. Trim and flute edge. Refrigerate 30 minutes. Line crust with a double thickness of foil. Fill with pie weights, dried beans or uncooked rice. Bake on a lower oven rack until golden brown, 20-25 minutes. Remove foil and weights; bake until bottom is golden brown, 3-6 minutes. Cool on a wire rack.
2. In a saucepan over medium heat, combine the sugar, cornstarch, salt and water until smooth. Add 3 cups blueberries. Bring to a boil; cook and stir for 2 minutes or until thickened and bubbly.
3. Remove from the heat. Add butter, lemon juice and remaining 2 cups berries; stir until butter is melted. Cool. Pour into crust. Refrigerate until serving.

1 PIECE 269 cal., 9g fat (4g sat. fat), 9mg chol., 150mg sod., 48g carb. (29g sugars, 2g fiber), 2g pro.

CONTEST-WINNING FRESH BLUEBERRY PIE

KEY LIME CREAM PIE

I am very proud of this luscious no-bake beauty. It's so cool and refreshing—just perfect for any summer get-together or potluck. Wherever I take this pie, it quickly disappears and everyone asks for the recipe.
—Shirley Rickis, The Villages, FL

Prep: 40 min. + chilling
Makes: 12 servings

- 1 pkg. (11.3 oz.) pecan shortbread cookies, crushed (about 2 cups)
- ⅓ cup butter, melted
- 4 cups heavy whipping cream
- ¼ cup confectioners' sugar
- 1 tsp. coconut extract
- 1 pkg. (8 oz.) cream cheese, softened
- 1 can (14 oz.) sweetened condensed milk
- ½ cup Key lime juice
- ¼ cup sweetened shredded coconut, toasted
- Sliced Key limes, optional

1. In a small bowl, mix crushed cookies and butter. Press onto bottom and up side of a greased 9-in. deep-dish pie plate. In a large bowl, beat cream until it begins to thicken. Add confectioners' sugar and extract; beat until stiff peaks form. In another large bowl, beat cream cheese, condensed milk and lime juice until blended. Fold in 2 cups whipped cream. Spoon into prepared crust.
2. Top with the remaining whipped cream; sprinkle with toasted coconut. Refrigerate for at least 4 hours before serving. If desired, garnish with sliced Key limes.

1 PIECE 646 cal., 52g fat (30g sat. fat), 143mg chol., 252mg sod., 41g carb. (29g sugars, 0 fiber), 8g pro.

HOLIDAY CORNFLAKE COOKIES

I can't seem to make enough of these cornflake wreaths around the holidays. The cookies firm up quickly, so you'll need to place the Red Hots right away.
—Kathleen Hedger, Godfrey, IL

Takes: 15 min. • **Makes:** 16 cookies

- ½ cup butter, cubed
- 40 large marshmallows
- 4 cups frosted cornflakes
- Red Hots
- Assorted sprinkles

1. In a 6-qt. stockpot, melt butter over medium heat. Add marshmallows; cook and stir until melted. Remove from heat.
2. Fold in cornflakes. Working quickly, fill 16 greased muffin cups two-thirds full. Using the end of a wooden spoon, make holes in centers to resemble wreaths. Decorate immediately with Red Hots and sprinkles.

1 COOKIE 147 cal., 6g fat (4g sat. fat), 15mg chol., 109mg sod., 24g carb. (14g sugars, 0 fiber), 1g pro.

RHUBARB MANDARIN CRISP

An attractive and unique dessert, this crisp is also a popular breakfast dish at our house, served with a glass of milk rather than topped with ice cream. Since it calls for lots of rhubarb, it's a great use for the bounty you harvest.
—Rachael Vandendool, Barry's Bay, ON

Prep: 20 min. + standing • **Bake:** 40 min.
Makes: 12 servings

- 6 cups chopped fresh or frozen rhubarb
- 1½ cups sugar
- 5 Tbsp. quick-cooking tapioca
- 1 can (11 oz.) mandarin oranges, drained
- 1 cup packed brown sugar
- 1 cup quick-cooking oats
- ½ cup all-purpose flour
- ½ tsp. salt
- ½ cup cold butter, cubed
- Ice cream, optional

1. In a large bowl, toss the rhubarb, sugar and tapioca; let stand 15 minutes, stirring occasionally. Pour into a greased 13x9-in. baking pan. Top with oranges.
2. In a large bowl, combine the brown sugar, oats, flour and salt. Cut in butter until mixture resembles coarse crumbs; sprinkle evenly over oranges.
3. Bake at 350° for 40 minutes or until top is golden brown. Serve with ice cream if desired.

NOTE If using frozen rhubarb, measure rhubarb while still frozen, then thaw completely. Drain in a colander, but do not press liquid out.

1 SERVING 323 cal., 8g fat (5g sat. fat), 20mg chol., 187mg sod., 62g carb. (48g sugars, 2g fiber), 2g pro.

RHUBARB MANDARIN CRISP

CHOCOLATE GANACHE PEANUT BUTTER CUPCAKES

CHOCOLATE GANACHE PEANUT BUTTER CUPCAKES

I've been baking cakes for years and enjoy trying new combinations of flavors and textures. Well, I blended two popular flavors: peanut butter and chocolate. As soon as I took the first bite of these rich cupcakes, I knew I had created something divine! Most people who try them say they are the best thing they've ever eaten. They are definitely worth the time it takes to make them.
—Ronda Schabes, Vicksburg, MI

Prep: 55 min. • **Bake:** 20 min. + cooling
Makes: 2 dozen

- 2 cups sugar
- 1¾ cups all-purpose flour
- ¾ cup baking cocoa
- ½ tsp. salt
- ½ tsp. baking soda
- ½ tsp. baking powder
- 1 cup buttermilk
- 1 cup strong brewed coffee, room temperature
- ½ cup canola oil
- 2 large eggs, room temperature
- 1 tsp. vanilla extract

FILLING

- ½ cup creamy peanut butter
- 3 Tbsp. unsalted butter, softened
- 1 cup confectioners' sugar
- 2 to 4 Tbsp. 2% milk

GANACHE

- 2 cups semisweet chocolate chips
- ½ cup heavy whipping cream

PEANUT BUTTER FROSTING

- 1 cup packed brown sugar
- 4 large egg whites, room temperature
- ¼ tsp. salt
- ¼ tsp. cream of tartar
- 1 tsp. vanilla extract
- 2 cups unsalted butter, softened
- ⅓ cup creamy peanut butter
- Chocolate curls, optional

1. Preheat oven to 350°. In a large bowl, combine the first 6 ingredients. Whisk buttermilk, coffee, oil, eggs and vanilla until blended; add to the dry ingredients until combined. (Batter will be very thin.) Fill paper-lined muffin cups two-thirds full.
2. Bake 18-20 minutes or until a toothpick inserted in the center comes out clean. Cool 10 minutes before removing from pans to wire racks to cool completely.
3. In a small bowl, cream peanut butter, butter, confectioners' sugar and enough milk to reach piping consistency. Cut a small hole in the corner of a pastry bag; insert a small round tip. Fill with peanut butter filling. Insert tip into the top center of each cupcake; pipe about 1 Tbsp. filling into each.
4. Place chocolate chips in a small bowl. In a small saucepan, bring cream just to a boil. Pour over chocolate; whisk until smooth. Dip the top of each cupcake into ganache; place on wire racks to set.
5. In a large heavy saucepan, combine the brown sugar, egg whites, salt and cream of tartar over low heat. With a hand mixer, beat on low speed 1 minute. Continue beating on low over low heat until frosting reaches 160°, 8-10 minutes. Pour into a large bowl; add vanilla. Beat on high until stiff peaks form, about 5 minutes.
6. Add butter, 1 Tbsp. at a time, beating well after each addition. If mixture begins to look curdled, place frosting bowl in another bowl filled with hot water for a few seconds. Continue adding butter and beating until smooth. Beat in the peanut butter 1-2 minutes or until smooth.
7. Place frosting in a pastry bag with large star tip; pipe onto each cupcake. If desired, top with chocolate curls. Store in an airtight container in the refrigerator. Let stand at room temperature before serving.

1 CUPCAKE 498 cal., 33g fat (16g sat. fat), 69mg chol., 196mg sod., 50g carb. (39g sugars, 2g fiber), 6g pro.

LEMON-BLUEBERRY POUND CAKE

LEMON-BLUEBERRY POUND CAKE

Pair a slice of this moist cake with a scoop of vanilla ice cream. It's a staple at our family barbecues.
—Rebecca Little, Park Ridge, IL

Prep: 25 min. • **Bake:** 55 min. + cooling
Makes: 12 servings

- ⅓ cup butter, softened
- 4 oz. cream cheese, softened
- 2 cups sugar
- 3 large eggs, room temperature
- 1 large egg white, room temperature
- 1 Tbsp. grated lemon zest
- 2 tsp. vanilla extract
- 2 cups fresh or frozen unsweetened blueberries
- 3 cups all-purpose flour, divided
- 1 tsp. baking powder
- ½ tsp. baking soda
- ½ tsp. salt
- 1 cup lemon yogurt

GLAZE

- 1¼ cups confectioners' sugar
- 2 Tbsp. lemon juice

1. Preheat oven to 350°. Grease and flour a 10-in. fluted tube pan. In a large bowl, cream the butter, cream cheese and sugar until blended. Add eggs and egg white, 1 at a time, beating well after each addition. Beat in lemon zest and vanilla.
2. Toss blueberries with 2 Tbsp. flour. In another bowl, mix the remaining flour with baking powder, baking soda and salt; add to creamed mixture alternately with yogurt, beating after each addition just until combined. Fold in blueberry mixture.
3. Transfer batter to prepared pan. Bake for 55-60 minutes or until a toothpick inserted in center comes out clean. Cool in pan 10 minutes before removing to wire rack; cool completely.
4. In a small bowl, mix confectioners' sugar and lemon juice until smooth. Drizzle over cake.

NOTE To remove cakes easily, use solid shortening to grease plain and fluted tube pans.

1 PIECE 434 cal., 10g fat (6g sat. fat), 78mg chol., 281mg sod., 80g carb. (54g sugars, 1g fiber), 7g pro.

ICEBOX CAKE

You don't have to bake to serve a lovely dessert! This unique cake is made from chocolate wafers and whipping cream.
—Cindy Hawkins, New York, NY

Prep: 15 min. + chilling
Makes: 8 servings

- 3 cups heavy whipping cream
- ¼ cup confectioners' sugar
- 1 tsp. vanilla extract
- 1 pkg. (11.78 oz.) Oreo Thins (about 48 cookies)
- Optional: chocolate curls and cocoa powder

1. In a large bowl, beat cream until soft peaks form. Add confectioners' sugar and vanilla; beat until stiff. Spread heaping teaspoons on the cookies. Make 8 stacks of cookies; turn stacks on edge and place on a serving platter, forming a 14-in.-long cake.
2. Frost top and sides with remaining whipped cream. If desired, dust with cocoa powder and top with chocolate curls. Refrigerate before serving, 4-6 hours.

1 PIECE 488 cal., 38g fat (23g sat. fat), 103mg chol., 266mg sod., 33g carb. (18g sugars, 1g fiber), 5g pro.

TEST KITCHEN TIP

Having trouble assembling your icebox cake? Line a 9×5-in. loaf pan with plastic wrap, letting it hang over the edges. Spread a layer of whipped cream on the bottom, stand the cookie stacks on their edges without pressing them down, then cover with the remaining cream. Wrap and refrigerate for 4-6 hours. Then invert onto a platter, and top with chocolate curls.

ICEBOX CAKE

ELEGANT ORANGE BLOSSOM CHEESECAKE

This cheesecake tastes heavenly. Gingersnap cookie crumbs make a distinctive crust, while glazed orange slices become a blossomlike topping.
—Sharon Delaney-Chronis, South Milwaukee, WI

Prep: 40 min. • **Bake:** 70 min. + chilling
Makes: 16 servings

- 3 cups crushed gingersnap cookies (about 60 cookies)
- 2 tsp. plus 2 Tbsp. grated orange zest, divided
- ⅓ cup butter, melted
- 1½ cups orange juice
- ⅓ cup sliced fresh gingerroot
- 4 pkg. (8 oz. each) cream cheese, softened
- ⅔ cup sugar
- 6 oz. white baking chocolate, melted
- 1 Tbsp. vanilla extract
- 4 large eggs, lightly beaten, room temperature

CANDIED ORANGE SLICES

- 3 cups water
- 1½ cups sugar
- 2 small navel oranges, thinly sliced

1. Place a greased 9-in. springform pan on a double thickness of heavy-duty foil (about 18 in. square). Securely wrap foil around pan.

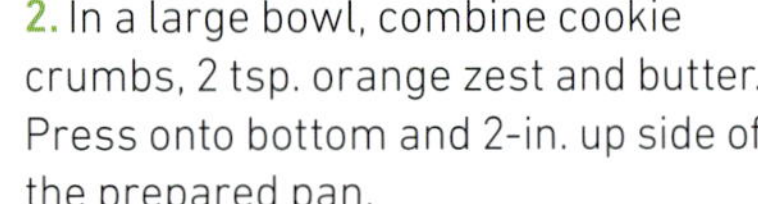

2. In a large bowl, combine cookie crumbs, 2 tsp. orange zest and butter. Press onto bottom and 2-in. up side of the prepared pan.
3. In a large saucepan, combine orange juice and ginger; bring to a boil. Reduce heat and simmer, stirring occasionally, until syrupy and reduced to about 3 Tbsp. Strain mixture, discarding ginger.
4. In a large bowl, beat cream cheese and sugar until smooth. Beat in ginger syrup, melted chocolate, vanilla and remaining orange zest. Add eggs; beat on low speed just until combined. Pour into crust. Place springform pan in a large baking pan; add 1 in. of hot water to larger pan.
5. Bake at 325° for 70-80 minutes or until center is just set and top appears dull. Remove springform pan from water bath; remove foil. Cool on a wire rack for 10 minutes. Carefully run a knife around edge of pan to loosen; cool 1 hour longer. Refrigerate overnight.
6. For candied orange slices, in a large skillet, combine water and sugar. Cook and stir over medium heat until sugar is completely dissolved. Add orange slices. Bring to a boil. Reduce heat; simmer for 45 minutes or until translucent. Drain oranges on a wire rack; arrange in a single layer on waxed paper to dry.
7. Remove side of pan. Top cheesecake with candied orange slices. Refrigerate leftovers.

1 PIECE 752 cal., 35g fat (18g sat. fat), 119mg chol., 660mg sod., 101g carb. (55g sugars, 2g fiber), 10g pro.

ELEGANT ORANGE BLOSSOM CHEESECAKE

READER RAVES

"The flavor was excellent. The crust was a little crumbly but still good."

—ALICE827, TASTEOFHOME.COM

CHERRY RHUBARB CRUNCH

My husband's grandmother gave me this recipe, along with a bundle of rhubarb, when we were first married. I had never cared for rhubarb, but after trying this dessert, I changed my mind. Now my children dig in too!
—Sharon Wasikowski, Middleville, MI

Prep: 20 min. • **Bake:** 40 min.
Makes: 15 servings

- 1 cup rolled oats
- 1 cup packed brown sugar
- 1 cup all-purpose flour
- ¼ tsp. salt
- ½ cup cold butter, cubed
- 4 cups diced rhubarb
- 1 cup sugar
- 2 Tbsp. cornstarch
- 1 cup water
- 1 tsp. almond extract
- 1 can (21 oz.) cherry pie filling
- ½ cup finely chopped walnuts
- Vanilla ice cream, optional

1. Preheat oven to 350°. In a large bowl, combine oats, brown sugar, flour and salt; stir well. Cut in butter until crumbly. Pat 2 cups mixture into a greased 13x9-in. baking dish; cover with rhubarb. Set aside remaining crumb mixture.
2. In a saucepan, combine sugar and cornstarch. Stir in water; cook until mixture is thickened and clear. Stir in extract and cherry pie filling; spoon over rhubarb. Combine nuts with reserved crumb mixture; sprinkle over cherries. Bake until filling is bubbly and topping is lightly browned, 40-45 minutes. If desired, serve with ice cream.

1 SERVING 294 cal., 9g fat (4g sat. fat), 16mg chol., 116mg sod., 52g carb. (38g sugars, 2g fiber), 3g pro.

REESE'S CHOCOLATE SNACK CAKE

REESE'S CHOCOLATE SNACK CAKE

This cake is constantly requested by my family. With its yellow and orange toppings, it's the perfect dessert for a Halloween party.
—Eileen Travis, Ukiah, CA

Prep: 15 min. • **Bake:** 30 min.
Makes: 20 servings

- 3⅓ cups all-purpose flour
- ⅔ cup sugar
- ⅔ cup packed brown sugar
- ½ cup baking cocoa
- 2 tsp. baking soda
- 1 tsp. salt
- 2 cups water
- ⅓ cup canola oil
- ⅓ cup unsweetened applesauce
- 2 tsp. white vinegar
- 1 tsp. vanilla extract
- 1 cup Reese's Pieces
- ½ cup coarsely chopped salted peanuts

1. Preheat oven to 350°. Coat a 13x9-in. pan with cooking spray.
2. Whisk together first 6 ingredients. In another bowl, whisk together water, oil, applesauce, vinegar and vanilla. Add to flour mixture, stirring just until blended. Transfer to prepared pan. Sprinkle with Reese's Pieces and peanuts.
3. Bake until a toothpick inserted in the center comes out clean, 30-35 minutes. Cool on a wire rack.

1 PIECE 240 cal., 8g fat (2g sat. fat), 0 chol., 280mg sod., 38g carb. (19g sugars, 2g fiber), 5g pro.

READER RAVES

"This is a keeper recipe. So easy and good love this recipe!"

—BONITO15, TASTEOFHOME.COM

CHEWY GOOD OATMEAL COOKIES

CHEWY GOOD OATMEAL COOKIES

Here's a classic oatmeal cookie with all my favorite extras: dried cherries, white chocolate chips and macadamia nuts.
—Sandy Harz, Spring Lake, MI

Prep: 20 min. • **Bake:** 10 min./batch
Makes: 3½ dozen

- 1 cup butter, softened
- 1 cup packed brown sugar
- ½ cup sugar
- 2 large eggs, room temperature
- 1 Tbsp. honey
- 2 tsp. vanilla extract
- 2½ cups quick-cooking oats
- 1½ cups all-purpose flour
- 1 tsp. baking soda
- ½ tsp. salt
- ½ tsp. ground cinnamon
- 1⅓ cups dried cherries
- 1 cup white baking chips
- 1 cup chopped macadamia nuts

1. Preheat oven to 350°. In a large bowl, cream butter and sugars until light and fluffy, 5-7 minutes. Beat in the eggs, honey and vanilla. In another bowl, mix the oats, flour, baking soda, salt and cinnamon; gradually beat into creamed mixture. Stir in remaining ingredients.
2. Drop by rounded tablespoonfuls 2 in. apart onto greased baking sheets. Bake 10-12 minutes or until golden brown. Cool on pan 2 minutes; remove to wire racks to cool.

1 COOKIE 161 cal., 8g fat (4g sat. fat), 22mg chol., 105mg sod., 20g carb. (13g sugars, 1g fiber), 2g pro.

CHEWY CRANBERRY OATMEAL COOKIES Substitute dried cranberries for the dried cherries.

CHEWY OATMEAL CHIP COOKIES Omit the cinnamon, dried cherries and macadamia nuts. Add 1 cup each semisweet chocolate chips and butterscotch chips with white baking chips.

BUTTERSCOTCH PIE

This creamy pudding-like pie filling is crowned with golden peaks of meringue.
—Cary Letsche, Brandenton, FL

Prep: 30 min. + chilling
Bake: 15 min. + cooling
Makes: 8 servings

Dough for single-crust pie
6 Tbsp. butter
6 Tbsp. all-purpose flour
1½ cup packed brown sugar
2 cups whole milk
¼ tsp. salt
3 large egg yolks, room temperature, beaten
1 tsp. vanilla extract

MERINGUE
3 large egg whites, room temperature
¼ tsp. cream of tartar
½ cup sugar

1. On a lightly floured surface, roll dough to a ⅛-in.-thick circle; transfer to a 9-in. pie plate. Trim to ½ in. beyond rim of plate; flute edge. Refrigerate 30 minutes. Preheat oven to 425°.
2. Line unpricked crust with a double thickness of foil. Fill with pie weights, dried beans or uncooked rice. Bake on a lower oven rack until edge is light golden brown, 15-20 minutes. Remove foil and weights; bake until bottom is golden brown, 3-6 minutes longer. Cool on a wire rack. Reduce oven setting to 350°.
3. In a saucepan, melt butter. Remove from the heat; add flour and stir until smooth. Stir in brown sugar. Return to heat; stir in milk and salt until blended. Cook and stir over medium-high heat until thickened and bubbly. Reduce heat; cook and stir 2 minutes longer. Remove from the heat. Stir about 1 cup hot filling into egg yolks; return all to pan, stirring constantly. Bring to a gentle boil; cook and stir for 2 minutes longer. Remove from the heat. Gently stir in vanilla. Pour into crust.
4. For meringue, beat the egg whites and cream of tartar in a small bowl on medium speed until soft peaks form. Gradually beat in sugar, about 1 Tbsp. at a time, on high until stiff glossy peaks form and sugar is dissolved. Spread evenly over hot filling, sealing edge to crust.
5. Bake until meringue is golden brown, 12-15 minutes. Cool on a wire rack for 1 hour. Refrigerate at least 3 hours before serving. Refrigerate leftovers.

DOUGH FOR SINGLE-CRUST PIE Combine 1¼ cups all-purpose flour and ¼ tsp. salt; cut in ½ cup cold butter until crumbly. Gradually add 3-5 Tbsp. ice water, tossing with a fork until dough holds together when pressed. Shape into a disk; wrap and refrigerate 1 hour.

1 PIECE 541 cal., 24g fat (14g sat. fat), 128mg chol., 359mg sod., 76g carb. (56g sugars, 1g fiber), 7g pro.

BUTTERSCOTCH PIE

READER RAVES

"This was an excellent pie. Butterscotch pie is my dad's favorite and I recently made this for him while visiting—he loved it. It looked and tasted great. Excellent recipe!"

—LVARNER, TASTEOFHOME.COM

CARAMEL TOFFEE BROWNIES

I love to make up recipes for foods that I am craving, such as chocolate, toffee and caramel. They came together in this brownie for one sensational treat. I frequently bake these to add to care packages for family and friends.
—Brenda Caughell, Durham, NC

Prep: 30 min. • **Bake:** 40 min.
Makes: 2 dozen

CARAMEL LAYER
- ½ cup butter, softened
- ⅓ cup sugar
- ⅓ cup packed brown sugar
- 1 large egg, room temperature
- ½ tsp. vanilla extract
- 1 cup all-purpose flour
- ½ tsp. baking soda
- ¼ tsp. salt
- ½ cup caramel ice cream topping
- 2 Tbsp. 2% milk
- 1 cup toffee bits

BROWNIE LAYER
- 1 cup butter, cubed
- 4 oz. unsweetened chocolate
- 4 large eggs, lightly beaten, room temperature
- 2 cups sugar
- 2 tsp. vanilla extract
- 2 cups all-purpose flour

1. Preheat oven to 350°. For the caramel layer, in a large bowl, cream butter and sugars until light and fluffy, 5-7 minutes; beat in egg and vanilla. Combine flour, baking soda and salt; gradually add to creamed mixture and mix well. In a small bowl, combine caramel topping and milk. Add to batter; mix well. Fold in the toffee bits; set aside.
2. For brownie later, in a microwave, melt butter and chocolate. Beat in the eggs, sugar and vanilla; gradually beat in flour.
3. Spread half of the brownie batter into a greased 13x9-in. baking pan. Drop the caramel batter by spoonfuls onto the brownie batter; swirl to combine. Drop remaining brownie batter on top.
4. Bake for 40-45 minutes or until a toothpick inserted in center comes out clean. Cool on a wire rack.
1 BROWNIE 355 cal., 18g fat (10g sat. fat), 78mg chol., 230mg sod., 46g carb. (29g sugars, 1g fiber), 4g pro.

LEMON LIME DESSERT

This make-ahead treat offers a wonderfully refreshing blend of citrus flavors. Topped with a smooth lemon sauce, it's the perfect ending to any meal. Using an electric mixer makes it easy to combine the lime sherbet and vanilla ice cream.
—Marsha Schindler, Fort Wayne, IN

Prep: 20 min. • **Cook:** 10 min. + freezing
Makes: 15 servings

- 1½ cups graham cracker crumbs
- 14 Tbsp. butter, melted ,divided
- 1¼ cups sugar, divided
- ½ gallon vanilla ice cream, softened
- 1 qt. lime sherbet, softened
- 2 large eggs, lightly beaten
- ¼ cup lemon juice

1. In a large bowl, combine cracker crumbs, 7 Tbsp. butter and ¼ cup sugar. Press into an ungreased 13x9-in. dish; freeze until firm. In a large bowl, combine ice cream and sherbet; pour over the crust. Freeze until firm.
2. In a heavy saucepan, combine the eggs and remaining sugar. Stir in the lemon juice and remaining butter. Cook and stir until mixture reaches 160° and coats the back of a spoon. Transfer to a bowl; refrigerate until cooled.
3. Spread over ice cream mixture. Cover and freeze for 3 hours or overnight. May be frozen for up to 2 months.
4. Just before serving, remove from the freezer and cut into squares.
1 PIECE 401 cal., 21g fat (12g sat. fat), 90mg chol., 242mg sod., 52g carb. (40g sugars, 0 fiber), 4g pro.

HEAVENLY FILLED STRAWBERRIES

These luscious stuffed berries are the perfect bite-sized dessert.
—Stephen Munro, Beaverbank, NS

Takes: 20 min. • **Makes:** 3 dozen

- 3 dozen large fresh strawberries
- 11 oz. cream cheese, softened
- ½ cup confectioners' sugar
- ¼ tsp. almond extract
- Grated chocolate, optional

1. Remove stems from strawberries. Cut a deep "X" in the tip of each berry. Gently spread berries open.
2. In a small bowl, beat cream cheese, confectioners' sugar and extract until light and fluffy, 3-4 minutes. Pipe or spoon about 2 tsp. into each berry; if desired, sprinkle with chocolate. Chill until serving.

1 FILLED STRAWBERRY 41 cal., 3g fat (2g sat. fat), 9mg chol., 27mg sod., 3g carb. (3g sugars, 0 fiber), 1g pro.

CHILL AND FILL

These cheesecake-stuffed strawberries are best eaten the day they are made. If you have a few minutes to assemble them right before serving, you can prepare the strawberries and the filling ahead of time, stored separately in the fridge. Then, pipe the filling into the berries right as guests arrive. If you need to have your cheesecake-filled strawberries fully assembled and complete before the gathering, you can store them in the fridge, lightly covered, for up to a day.

HEAVENLY FILLED STRAWBERRIES

PEACH PIE

I acquired this delicious peach pie filling recipe some 40 years ago, when my husband and I first moved to southern Iowa and had peach trees growing in our backyard. It's been a family favorite since then and always brings back memories of both summer and those happy early years in Iowa.

—June Mueller, Sioux City, IA

Prep: 35 min. + standing
Bake: 50 min. + cooling
Makes: 8 servings

- ½ cup sugar
- ¼ cup packed brown sugar
- 4½ cups sliced peeled peaches
- Dough for double-crust pie
- 3 Tbsp. cornstarch
- ¼ tsp. ground nutmeg
- ¼ tsp. ground cinnamon
- ⅛ tsp. salt
- 2 tsp. lemon juice
- 1 Tbsp. butter
- Vanilla ice cream, optional

1. In a large bowl, combine sugars; add peaches and toss gently. Cover and let stand for 1 hour. On a lightly floured surface, roll 1 half of dough to a ⅛-in.-thick circle; transfer to a 9-in. pie plate or iron skillet. Trim even with rim. Refrigerate while preparing filling.
2. Preheat oven to 400°. Drain peaches, reserving juice. In a small saucepan, combine cornstarch, nutmeg, cinnamon and salt; gradually stir in the reserved juice. Bring to a boil; cook and stir until thickened, about 2 minutes. Remove from the heat; stir in lemon juice and butter. Gently fold in peaches. Pour into crust.
3. Roll the remaining dough to a ⅛-in.-thick circle; cut into 1½-in.-wide strips. Arrange over filling in a lattice pattern. Trim and seal strips to edge of bottom crust; flute edge. Cover edge loosely with foil. Bake 40 minutes; remove foil. Bake until crust is golden brown and filling is bubbly, 10-20 minutes longer. Cool on a wire rack. If desired, serve with vanilla ice cream.

DOUGH FOR DOUBLE-CRUST PIE Combine 2½ cups all-purpose flour and ½ tsp. salt; cut in 1 cup cold butter until crumbly. Gradually add ⅓-⅔ cup ice water, tossing with a fork until the dough holds together when pressed. Divide the dough in half. Shape each into a disk; wrap disks and refrigerate 1 hour.

1 PIECE 477 cal., 25g fat (15g sat. fat), 64mg chol., 360mg sod., 60g carb. (27g sugars, 2g fiber), 5g pro.

PEELS INTACT

You don't always need to peel peaches for pie. The skins are edible, and they'll add a nice rustic look to desserts. Just be sure to wash the peaches well before use.

NANTUCKET CRANBERRY TART

NANTUCKET CRANBERRY TART

While everyone is enjoying a bountiful meal, this eye-catching tart can be baking to perfection in the oven. This holiday dessert calls for very few ingredients and it's a snap to assemble.
—Jackie Zack, Riverside, CT

Prep: 15 min. • **Bake:** 40 min. + cooling
Makes: 12 servings

- 1 pkg. (12 oz.) fresh or frozen cranberries, thawed
- 1 cup sugar, divided
- ½ cup sliced almonds
- 2 large eggs, room temperature
- ¾ cup butter, melted
- 1 tsp. almond extract
- 1 cup all-purpose flour
- 1 Tbsp. confectioners' sugar

1. In a small bowl, combine cranberries, ½ cup sugar and almonds. Transfer to a greased 11-in. fluted tart pan with a removable bottom. Place tart pan on a baking sheet.
2. In a small bowl, beat the eggs, butter, extract and remaining sugar. Beat in flour just until moistened (batter will be thick). Spread evenly over berries.
3. Bake at 325° for 40-45 minutes or until a toothpick inserted in the center comes out clean. Cool in pan on a wire rack. Dust with the confectioners' sugar. Refrigerate leftovers.

1 PIECE 255 cal., 14g fat (8g sat. fat), 65mg chol., 93mg sod., 30g carb. (19g sugars, 2g fiber), 3g pro.

STRAWBERRY POKE CAKE

STRAWBERRY POKE CAKE

Strawberry shortcake takes on a wonderful new twist with this super simple recipe. Strawberries liven up each pretty slice.
—Mary Jo Griggs, West Bend, WI

Prep: 25 min. • **Bake:** 25 min. + chilling
Makes: 12 servings

- 1 pkg. white cake mix (regular size)
- 1¼ cups water
- 2 large eggs, room temperature
- ¼ cup canola oil
- 2 pkg. (10 oz. each) frozen sweetened sliced strawberries, thawed
- 2 pkg. (3 oz. each) strawberry gelatin
- 1 carton (12 oz.) frozen whipped topping, thawed, divided
- Fresh strawberries, optional

1. Preheat oven to 350°. In a large bowl, combine the cake mix, water, eggs and oil; beat on low speed for 30 seconds. Beat on medium speed for 2 minutes.
2. Pour into 2 greased and floured 9-in. round baking pans. Bake 25-35 minutes or until a toothpick inserted in center comes out clean. Cool for 10 minutes; remove from pans to wire racks to cool completely.
3. Using a serrated knife, level tops of cakes if necessary. Return layers, top side up, to 2 clean 9-in. round baking pans. Pierce cakes with a meat fork or wooden skewer at ½-in. intervals.
4. Drain juice from strawberries into a 2-cup glass measuring cup; refrigerate berries. Add water to juice to measure 2 cups; pour into a small saucepan. Bring to a boil; stir in gelatin until dissolved. Refrigerate for 30 minutes. Gently spoon over each cake layer. Refrigerate for 2-3 hours.
5. Dip bottom of 1 pan into warm water for 10 seconds. Invert cake onto a serving platter. Top with chilled strawberries and 1 cup whipped topping. Place the second cake layer over topping.
6. Frost cake with remaining whipped topping. Refrigerate for at least 1 hour. Serve with fresh berries if desired. Refrigerate leftovers.

1 PIECE 376 cal., 14g fat (7g sat. fat), 35mg chol., 301mg sod., 56g carb. (37g sugars, 1g fiber), 4g pro.

LEMON RASPBERRY BUCKLE

I've given a fresh summery twist to the classic blueberry buckle everyone loves by swapping out the blueberries for raspberries (my favorite) and adding sweet and tart lemon curd. This berry buckle cake tastes great with vanilla ice cream!
—Jenna Fleming, Lowville, NY

Prep: 30 min. • **Bake:** 45 min. + standing
Makes: 15 servings

- ½ cup butter, softened
- 1 cup sugar
- 2 large eggs plus 1 large egg yolk, room temperature
- 1 tsp. vanilla extract
- 1½ cups all-purpose flour
- 1½ tsp. baking powder
- ¼ tsp. salt
- ⅔ cup buttermilk
- 4 cups fresh raspberries
- ¼ cup sugar
- 1 jar (10 oz.) lemon curd

LEMON RASPBERRY BUCKLE

TOPPING

- ½ cup sugar
- ½ cup all-purpose flour
- ¼ cup butter, melted
- ½ tsp. ground cinnamon
- Optional: Whipped cream and additional raspberries

1. Preheat oven to 350°. In a large bowl, cream butter and sugar until light and fluffy, 5-7 minutes. Add eggs and egg yolk, 1 at a time, beating well after each addition. Beat in vanilla. In another bowl, whisk together flour, baking powder and salt; add to creamed mixture alternately with buttermilk, beating well after each addition. Transfer to a greased 13x9-in. baking dish.

2. In a bowl, combine raspberries and sugar; sprinkle over batter. Drop lemon curd by tablespoonfuls over raspberries. Combine the 4 topping ingredients; sprinkle over batter. Bake until fruit is bubbly and a toothpick inserted into cake comes out clean, 45-50 minutes. Let stand 20 minutes before serving. If desired, serve with whipped cream and more fresh raspberries.

NOTE To substitute for each cup of buttermilk, use 1 Tbsp. white vinegar or lemon juice plus enough milk to measure 1 cup. Stir, then let stand 5 minutes. Or use 1 cup plain yogurt. Or use 1¾ tsp. cream of tartar plus 1 cup milk.

1 PIECE 335 cal., 12g fat (7g sat. fat), 76mg chol., 206mg sod., 54g carb. (38g sugars, 3g fiber), 4g pro.

PISTACHIO CAKE WITH WALNUTS

It didn't take long for this dessert to become my husband's favorite birthday cake.
—Patty LaNoue Stearns, Traverse City, MI

Prep: 20 min. • **Bake:** 40 min. + cooling
Makes: 12 servings

- 1 pkg. white cake mix (regular size)
- 1 pkg. (3.4 oz.) instant pistachio pudding mix
- 3 large eggs, room temperature
- 1 cup club soda
- ¾ cup canola oil
- 1 cup chopped walnuts

FROSTING

- 1 pkg. (3.4 oz.) instant pistachio pudding mix
- 1 cup 2% milk
- 1 carton (8 oz.) frozen whipped topping, thawed

1. Preheat oven to 350°. Grease and flour a 10-in. fluted tube pan.
2. In a large bowl, combine the first 5 ingredients; beat on low speed for 30 seconds. Beat on medium 2 minutes. Fold in walnuts. Transfer to prepared pan. Bake 40-45 minutes or until a toothpick inserted in center comes out clean. Cool in the pan for 10 minutes before removing to a wire rack to cool completely.
3. For frosting, in a large bowl, combine pudding mix and milk; beat on low speed for 1 minute. Fold in whipped topping. Spread over cake. Refrigerate leftovers.
NOTE To remove cakes easily, use solid shortening to grease plain and fluted tube pans.
1 PIECE 476 cal., 27g fat (6g sat. fat), 54mg chol., 534mg sod., 51g carb. (31g sugars, 1g fiber), 5g pro.

SPECIAL CHOCOLATE TREATS

I serve these lovely cookies to guests. They freeze well.
—Walter Max, Wabasha, MN

Prep: 35 min. + chilling
Bake: 15 min. + cooling
Makes: about 3½ dozen servings

- ¾ cup butter, softened
- ¾ cup packed brown sugar
- 1½ tsp. vanilla extract
- ½ tsp. salt
- 1¾ cups all-purpose flour

FILLING/GLAZE

- 1 cup semisweet chocolate chips
- 1 Tbsp. shortening
- ⅔ cup finely chopped pecans
- ½ cup sweetened condensed milk
- 1 tsp. vanilla extract
- ⅛ tsp. salt
- 1 Tbsp. light corn syrup
- 1 tsp. water

1. In a large bowl, cream butter and sugar until light and fluffy, 5-7 minutes. Beat in vanilla and salt. Gradually add flour and mix well. Cover and refrigerate for 2 hours or until easy to handle.
2. For filling, melt chocolate chips and shortening in a microwave-safe bowl; stir until smooth. Set aside ¼ cup for glaze. To remaining chocolate, stir in the pecans, milk, vanilla and salt. Cover and refrigerate until cool, about 15 minutes.
3. Place a 16x12-in. piece of foil on a greased baking sheet; lightly sprinkle with flour. Divide dough in half; place 1 portion on foil. Roll into a 14x5-in. rectangle. Spread half of the filling lengthwise on half of the dough to within ½ in. of edges. Using foil, fold dough over filling; seal edges. Repeat with remaining dough and filling. Bake at 350° until golden brown, 15-20 minutes. Cool on a wire rack for 10 minutes.
4. For glaze, warm reserved chocolate; stir in corn syrup and water. Spread over cookies. Cool completely. Cut widthwise into ¾-in. strips.
1 PIECE 111 cal., 6g fat (3g sat. fat), 10mg chol., 75mg sod., 13g carb. (9g sugars, 1g fiber), 1g pro.

CARROT LAYER CAKE

My sister calls this her ultimate carrot cake, and it lives up to the name. Everyone loves the tender cake and unexpected pecan filling.
—Linda Van Holland, Innisfail, AB

Prep: 55 min. • **Bake:** 35 min. + cooling
Makes: 20 servings

- 1 cup sugar
- 2 Tbsp. all-purpose flour
- ¼ tsp. salt
- 1 cup heavy whipping cream
- ½ cup butter
- 1 cup chopped pecans
- 1 tsp. vanilla extract

CAKE

- 1¼ cups canola oil
- 2 cups sugar
- 2 cups all-purpose flour
- 2 tsp. ground cinnamon
- 2 tsp. baking powder
- 1 tsp. baking soda
- 1 tsp. salt
- 4 large eggs, room temperature
- 4 cups finely shredded carrots
- 1 cup raisins
- 1 cup chopped pecans

FROSTING

- ¾ cup butter, softened
- 6 oz. cream cheese, softened
- 1 tsp. vanilla extract
- 3 cups confectioners' sugar

1. Preheat oven to 350°. In a large heavy saucepan, combine sugar, flour and salt. Stir in cream; add butter. Cook and stir over medium heat until butter is melted; bring to a boil. Reduce heat. Simmer, uncovered, for 30 minutes, stirring occasionally. Stir in nuts and vanilla. Cool.
2. In a large bowl, beat oil and sugar until well blended. In another bowl, whisk the flour, cinnamon, baking powder, baking soda and salt; add to creamed mixture alternately with eggs, beating well after each addition. Stir in carrots, raisins and nuts.
3. Pour into 3 greased and floured 9-in. round baking pans. Bake until a toothpick inserted in center comes out clean, 35-40 minutes. Cool in pans 10 minutes before removing to wire racks to cool completely.
4. For frosting, in a bowl, beat butter, cream cheese and vanilla until fluffy. Gradually beat in confectioners' sugar until smooth. Spread filling between layers. Frost side and top of cake. Store in refrigerator. Remove from refrigerator 30 minutes before serving.

1 PIECE 641 cal., 41g fat (14g sat. fat), 94mg chol., 405mg sod., 68g carb. (53g sugars, 3g fiber), 5g pro.

TEST KITCHEN TIP

For a tender, golden cake, use aluminum pans with a dull rather than shiny or dark finish. If using glass baking dishes, reduce the oven temperature 25°. Fill the pans half to three-fourths full. A thin batter will rise more than a heavy batter, so allow more room for thin batters to rise.

STRAWBERRY CRUNCH ICE CREAM CAKE

STRAWBERRY CRUNCH ICE CREAM CAKE

Growing up, I loved treats from the ice cream truck that rolled through my neighborhood. This ice cream cake is inspired by one of those crunchy strawberry novelties.
—Lisa Kaminski, Wauwatosa, WI

Prep: 20 min. + freezing
Bake: 15 min. + cooling
Makes: 9 servings

- 36 Golden Oreo cookies, divided
- 4 Tbsp. butter, melted
- 3 cups vanilla ice cream, softened
- 5 cups strawberry ice cream, softened
- 1 carton (8 oz.) frozen whipped topping, thawed
- 1 pkg. (1 oz.) freeze-dried strawberries, coarsely crushed
- Fresh strawberries, optional

1. Line a 9x9-in. baking pan with parchment, allowing ends to extend past sides of pan. Preheat oven to 350°. Finely crush 24 cookies. In a small bowl, mix cookie crumbs and butter. Press onto the bottom of prepared pan. Bake until firm, 15-20 minutes. Cool completely on a wire rack.
2. Spread vanilla ice cream onto crust; freeze, covered, until firm. Spread with strawberry ice cream and then whipped topping; freeze, covered, until firm.
3. Coarsely crush remaining cookies. Combine cookie crumbs and freeze-dried strawberries; sprinkle over the whipped topping. Freeze, covered, until firm, 8 hours or overnight. Remove cake from freezer. Lifting with parchment, remove from pan. Gently peel off the parchment. Let stand 10 minutes before cutting. If desired, garnish with fresh strawberries.

1 PIECE 584 cal., 30g fat (16g sat. fat), 54mg chol., 280mg sod., 72g carb. (33g sugars, 2g fiber), 6g pro.

MA

ORANGE-CRANBERRY NUT TARTS

My friend gave me a recipe for orange cookies. I just had to embellish it. Now my friends and family crave these tarts.
—Nancy Bruce, Big Timber, MT

Prep: 50 min. + chilling
Bake: 10 min./batch + cooling
Makes: 4 dozen

- ½ cup butter, softened
- 1 cup sugar
- 1 large egg, room temperature
- 4 tsp. grated orange zest
- ¼ cup orange juice
- 2 Tbsp. evaporated milk or 2% milk
- 3 cups all-purpose flour
- 3 tsp. baking powder
- ¼ tsp. salt

FILLING

- 1 can (14 oz.) whole-berry cranberry sauce
- ½ cup sugar
- 2 Tbsp. orange juice
- 1 cup chopped walnuts
- 4 oz. white baking chocolate, melted

ORANGE-CRANBERRY NUT TARTS

1. In a large bowl, cream butter and sugar until light and fluffy, 5-7 minutes. Beat in egg until blended. Beat in orange zest, orange juice and milk. In another bowl, whisk flour, baking powder and salt; gradually beat into the creamed mixture.
2. Divide dough into 3 portions. On a lightly floured surface, shape each into a 10-in.-long roll. Wrap the rolls securely; refrigerate overnight or until firm.
3. For filling, in a small saucepan, combine cranberry sauce, sugar and orange juice. Bring to a boil, stirring constantly; cook and stir 2 minutes. Remove from heat; cool completely. Stir in walnuts.
4. Preheat oven to 375°. Unwrap each portion of dough and cut crosswise into 16 slices. Press onto bottoms and up the sides of 48 greased mini-muffin cups. Fill each with 2 tsp. cranberry mixture.
5. Bake 8-10 minutes or until edges are light golden. Cool in pans 10 minutes. Remove to wire racks to cool completely. Drizzle with melted white chocolate; let stand until set.

1 TART 113 cal., 4g fat (2g sat. fat), 9mg chol., 60mg sod., 18g carb. (10g sugars, 1g fiber), 2g pro.

READER RAVES

"Oh my! These are delicious. Light, sweet and tangy with a refreshing taste. I'll add them to my holiday baking rotation."

—DIANE4812, TASTEOFHOME.COM

FRESH STRAWBERRY PIE

FRESH STRAWBERRY PIE

Each year we can hardly wait for the strawberry season because we believe our strawberries are the best in the country! After plucking them from the bushes at a nearby farm, I fill my homemade pie crust.
—Mary Egan, Carney, MI

Prep: 50 min. + chilling
Makes: 8 servings

- Dough for single-crust pie
- 2 cups sliced fresh strawberries
- 2 cups halved fresh strawberries, mashed
- 1 cup sugar
- 3 Tbsp. cornstarch

TOPPING

- 2 cups halved fresh strawberries
- 1 cup heavy whipping cream
- 2 Tbsp. sugar
- ¼ tsp. almond extract, optional

1. On a lightly floured surface, roll dough to a ⅛-in.-thick circle; transfer to a 9-in. pie plate. Trim to ½ in. beyond rim of plate; flute edge. Refrigerate 30 minutes. Preheat oven to 425°.
2. Line crust with a double thickness of foil. Fill with pie weights, dried beans or uncooked rice. Bake on a lower oven rack until the edge is golden brown, 20-25 minutes. Remove the foil and weights; bake until bottom is golden brown, 3-6 minutes longer. Cool on a wire rack.
3. Arrange sliced strawberries over crust. In a saucepan over medium heat, combine mashed strawberries, sugar and cornstarch. Bring to a boil; cook and stir until thickened, 1-2 minutes. Cool for 15 minutes; pour over sliced strawberries. Arrange strawberry halves over pie. Refrigerate until chilled, 2-3 hours.
4. Just before serving, in a large bowl, beat cream until it begins to thicken. Add the sugar and, if desired, almond extract; beat until stiff peaks form. Serve with pie.

DOUGH FOR SINGLE-CRUST PIE Combine 1¼ cups all-purpose flour and ¼ tsp. salt; cut in ½ cup cold butter until crumbly. Gradually add 3-5 Tbsp. ice water, tossing with a fork until dough holds together when pressed. Shape into a disk; wrap and refrigerate 1 hour.

1 PIECE 378 cal., 18g fat (10g sat. fat), 46mg chol., 113mg sod., 53g carb. (35g sugars, 3g fiber), 2g pro.

CARAMEL CHOCOLATE TRIFLE

A highlight of our annual family reunion is the dessert competition. The judges take their jobs very seriously! Last year's first-place winner was this tempting trifle.
—Barb Hausey, Independence, MO

Prep: 20 min. • **Bake:** 20 min. + cooling
Makes: 16 servings

- 1 pkg. (9 oz.) devil's food cake mix
- 2 pkg. (3.9 oz. each) instant chocolate pudding mix
- 1 carton (12 oz.) frozen whipped topping, thawed
- 1 jar (12¼ oz.) caramel ice cream topping
- 1 pkg. (7½ or 8 oz.) English toffee bits or almond brickle chips

1. Prepare and bake cake according to package directions for an 8-in. square baking pan. Cool on a wire rack. Prepare chocolate pudding according to package directions.
2. Cut cake into 1½-in. cubes. Place half the cubes in a 3-qt. trifle bowl or large glass serving bowl; lightly press down to fill in gaps. Top cake with half each of the whipped topping, pudding, caramel topping and toffee bits; repeat layers. Cover and refrigerate until serving.

1 SERVING 349 cal., 11g fat (7g sat. fat), 21mg chol., 533mg sod., 61g carb. (29g sugars, 1g fiber), 3g pro.

BONUS: NO-BAKE COOKIES & TREATS

P. 301

P. 304

P. 317

EASY VANILLA FUDGE

This creamy, dreamy homemade fudge is a nostalgic addition to any sweets tray. Use pure vanilla extract to let the rich, classic vanilla flavor shine through.
—Julie Andrews, Rockford, MI

Takes: 15 min. + chilling
Makes: 32 servings

- 6 Tbsp. butter
- 3½ cups confectioners' sugar
- 3 Tbsp. heavy whipping cream
- 1 Tbsp. vanilla extract
- ⅛ tsp. salt

1. Line an 8x4-in. loaf pan with parchment.
2. In a medium saucepan, melt butter over medium heat. Stir in confectioners' sugar, cream, vanilla and salt until the mixture is smooth, 3-4 minutes. Transfer to prepared loaf pan. Cover; refrigerate until fudge is set, at least 2 hours.
3. Use edges of parchment to transfer fudge layer to a cutting board. Cut into 1-in. squares.

1 PIECE 76 cal., 3g fat (2g sat. fat), 7mg chol., 27mg sod., 13g carb. (13g sugars, 0 fiber), 0 pro.

FLAVOR TWIST

This recipe calls for classic vanilla, but feel free to use other flavors of extract instead, such as almond, lemon, orange, peppermint, coconut, cherry or raspberry. If desired, add a little food coloring to help hint at the flavor.

NO-BAKE BUTTERSCOTCH COOKIES

More like a candy than a cookie, these little butterscotch treats are delightful. You could even substitute chocolate fudge flavor pudding mix for the butterscotch and use semisweet chocolate chips in place of the butterscotch chips.
—Andrea Price, Grafton, WI

Prep: 20 min. + standing
Makes: about 3 dozen

- 2 cups sugar
- ¾ cup butter, cubed
- 1 can (5 oz.) evaporated milk
- 1 pkg. (3.4 oz.) instant butterscotch pudding mix
- 3½ cups old-fashioned oats
- ¾ cup butterscotch chips
- ½ cup chopped pecans

In a large saucepan, combine sugar, butter and milk. Bring to a boil; boil 1 minute. Remove from heat. Stir in pudding mix and oats until blended. Stir in chips and pecans. Drop by tablespoonfuls 1 in. apart onto parchment-lined baking sheets. Let stand until set.

1 COOKIE 150 cal., 7g fat (4g sat. fat), 11mg chol., 77mg sod., 21g carb. (16g sugars, 1g fiber), 2g pro.

CHOCOLATE HAZELNUT THUMBPRINTS

This recipe is so easy! Years ago, a friend gave me a recipe for chocolate peanut treats that didn't require baking. I thought it was a quick and clever way to whip up a batch of sweet snacks without heating up the kitchen, and I started making different variations. This one includes luscious chocolate-hazelnut spread and crunchy hazelnuts.
—Lisa Speer, Palm Beach, FL

Prep: 30 min. + chilling
Makes: about 3½ dozen

- 1 carton (8 oz.) spreadable cream cheese
- 1 cup semisweet chocolate chips, melted
- ½ cup Nutella
- 2¼ cups graham cracker crumbs
- 1 cup finely chopped hazelnuts, toasted
- 1 cup whole hazelnuts, toasted

1. Beat cream cheese, melted chocolate chips and Nutella until blended. Stir in graham cracker crumbs. Refrigerate until firm enough to roll, about 30 minutes.
2. Shape mixture into 1-in. balls; roll in chopped hazelnuts. Make an indentation in the center of each with the end of a wooden spoon handle. Fill with a hazelnut. Store between layers of waxed paper in an airtight container in the refrigerator.

NOTE To toast nuts, bake in a shallow pan in a 350° oven for 5-10 minutes or cook in a skillet over low heat until lightly browned, stirring occasionally.

1 COOKIE 111 cal., 8g fat (2g sat. fat), 3mg chol., 46mg sod., 10g carb. (6g sugars, 1g fiber), 2g pro.

BUCKEYES

These chocolate peanut butter balls are always popular at my church's annual Christmas fundraiser. They resemble chestnuts or buckeyes—hence the name.
—Merry Kay Opitz, Elkhorn, WI

Prep: 30 min. + chilling
Makes: 5½ dozen

- 5½ cups confectioners' sugar
- 1⅔ cups peanut butter
- 1 cup butter, melted
- 4 cups semisweet chocolate chips
- 1 tsp. shortening

1. In a large bowl, beat sugar, peanut butter and melted butter until smooth. Shape into 1-in. balls; refrigerate for at least 20 minutes.
2. Microwave the chocolate chips and shortening on high until melted; stir until smooth. Insert toothpick into the peanut butter ball. Holding toothpick, dip peanut butter ball three-quarters of the way in chocolate, allowing excess to drip off. Place on a waxed paper-lined baking sheet; remove toothpick. Repeat with the remaining peanut butter balls. Refrigerate 15 minutes or until firm. Cover and store in the refrigerator.

1 PIECE 127 cal., 6g fat (2g sat. fat), 0 chol., 29mg sod., 18g carb. (16g sugars, 1g fiber), 2g pro.

CHOCOLATE HAZELNUT THUMBPRINTS

TRIPLE-CHOCOLATE CRISPY BARS

TRIPLE-CHOCOLATE CRISPY BARS

These bars are crowd-pleasers! I've made them with chocolate hazelnut peanut butter spread and also with Biscoff cookie spread. The secret to making them soft and chewy is bringing the sugar mixture just to a boil and then cooking for only one minute. If it boils too long, they tend to be firmer and can become crumbly.
—Dawn Lowenstein, Huntingdon Valley, PA

Prep: 20 min. + chilling • **Makes:** 4 dozen

- ½ cup butter, cubed
- ¾ cup sugar
- ¾ cup packed brown sugar
- ½ cup baking cocoa
- ½ cup 2% milk or half-and-half cream
- ½ tsp. salt
- 1 jar (13 oz.) Nutella
- 1 jar (7 oz.) marshmallow creme
- ½ tsp. almond extract
- 3 cups Rice Krispies
- 1 cup milk chocolate English toffee bits

1. In a large saucepan, melt butter over low heat. Add the sugars, baking cocoa, milk and salt; bring to a boil. Cook and stir over medium heat for 1 minute. Remove from heat. Stir in Nutella, marshmallow creme and extract until smooth. Stir in Rice Krispies.
2. Press into a greased 15x10x1-in. pan; cool slightly. Sprinkle with toffee bits; refrigerate until set. Cut into bars; store in an airtight container.

1 BAR 132 cal., 6g fat (2g sat. fat), 7mg chol., 74mg sod., 19g carb. (17g sugars, 0 fiber), 1g pro.

RASPBERRY COCONUT BALLS

RASPBERRY COCONUT BALLS

My family loves Hostess Zingers, especially the raspberry flavor coated with coconut, inspiring this treat for school bake sales. We can make about four dozen in 30 minutes, and they sell out fast!
—Pam Clark, Wheaton, IL

Prep: 30 min. • **Makes:** about 4 dozen

- 1 pkg. (12 oz.) vanilla wafers, crushed
- 3⅓ cups sweetened shredded coconut, divided
- 1 can (14 oz.) sweetened condensed milk
- 3 tsp. raspberry extract
- 1 tsp. imitation rum extract
- ¼ cup pink sanding sugar

Mix wafer crumbs and 1⅓ cups coconut. Stir in milk and extracts. In a shallow bowl, combine sugar and remaining 2 cups coconut. Shape dough into 1-in. balls; roll in coconut mixture. Refrigerate in airtight containers.

1 COOKIE 93 cal., 4g fat (3g sat. fat), 4mg chol., 52mg sod., 13g carb. (11g sugars, 1g fiber), 1g pro.

READER REVIEW

"The recipe couldn't be any easier. I threw my coconut in the food processor for finer flakes. My guests rated it tasty, so I will make them again."

—LAURIE731 TASTEOFHOME.COM

S'MORES CRISPY BARS

My aunt always brought s'mores-style bars to our family's summer cottage. Plain or frosted, they are perfect for eating on the run.
—Elizabeth King, Duluth, MN

Prep: 15 min. + cooling • **Makes:** 2 dozen

- ¼ cup butter, cubed
- 1 pkg. (10 oz.) miniature marshmallows
- 6 cups Rice Krispies
- 1½ cups crushed graham crackers
- 1 cup milk chocolate chips

FROSTING

- ¾ cup butter, softened
- 1 cup confectioners' sugar
- 1 jar (7 oz.) marshmallow creme

TOPPING

- ¼ cup crushed graham crackers
- 2 milk chocolate candy bars (1.55 oz. each)

1. In a 6-qt. stockpot, melt the butter over medium heat. Add marshmallows; cook and stir until melted. Remove from heat. Stir in the cereal and crushed crackers. Fold in chocolate chips. Press into a greased 13x9-in. baking pan. Cool to room temperature.
2. For frosting, in a small bowl, beat butter and confectioners' sugar until smooth. Beat in marshmallow creme on low speed just until blended. Spread over bars. Sprinkle crushed crackers over frosting. Cut into bars. Break each candy bar into 12 pieces; place a piece on each bar.

1 BAR 270 cal., 12g fat (7g sat. fat), 23mg chol., 158mg sod., 40g carb. (26g sugars, 1g fiber), 2g pro.

BLACK & WHITE CEREAL TREATS

When my daughter was just 7 years old, she had the brilliant idea of adding Oreo cookies to cereal treats. Now an adult, she still asks for them on occasion; they're that good.
—Tammy Phoenix, Ava, IL

Prep: 10 min. • **Cook:** 10 min. + cooling
Makes: 2 dozen

- ¼ cup butter, cubed
- 8 cups miniature marshmallows
- 6 cups Rice Krispies
- 2½ cups double-stuffed Oreo cookies (about 16), chopped, divided
- 1⅓ cups white baking chips, melted

1. In a Dutch oven, melt the butter over medium heat. Add marshmallows; cook and stir until melted. Remove from heat. Stir in the cereal and 2 cups Oreos. Press into a greased 13x9-in. baking pan.
2. Spread the melted baking chips over the top; sprinkle with remaining ½ cup Oreos, pressing gently to adhere. Cool to room temperature. Cut into bars.

1 BAR 189 cal., 7g fat (4g sat. fat), 6mg chol., 123mg sod., 31g carb. (19g sugars, 0 fiber), 2g pro.

HOLIDAY PECAN LOGS

HOLIDAY PECAN LOGS

For 50 years, I've turned to this beloved recipe to make candy to give away at Christmas. Of the many types I have tried, these pecan logs continue to be the most popular.
—Maxine Ruhl, Fort Scott, KS

Prep: 25 min. + chilling
Cook: 10 min. + cooling
Makes: about 3¼ lbs.

- 2 tsp. plus ½ cup butter, softened, divided
- 3¾ cups confectioners' sugar
- ½ cup nonfat dry milk powder
- ½ cup sugar
- ½ cup light corn syrup
- 1 tsp. vanilla extract
- 1 pkg. (14 oz.) caramels
- 1 Tbsp. milk or half-and-half cream
- 2 cups chopped pecans

1. Butter an 8-in. square pan with 2 tsp. butter. Combine confectioners' sugar and milk powder. In a heavy saucepan, combine remaining ½ cup butter, sugar and corn syrup; cook and stir over medium heat until sugar is dissolved and mixture comes to a boil. Stir in the confectioners' sugar mixture, about a third at a time, until blended.
2. Remove from heat; stir in the vanilla. Continue stirring until mixture mounds slightly when dropped from a spoon. Spread into prepared pan. Cool.
3. Cut candy into 4 strips; cut each strip in half. Shape each into a log; wrap in waxed paper and twist ends to seal. Freeze or refrigerate until firm.
4. Meanwhile, in a microwave, melt the caramels with milk, stirring often. Roll logs in caramel mixture, then in pecans. Wrap in waxed paper. Store at room temperature in airtight containers. Cut into slices with a serrated knife.

2 OZ. 264 cal., 12g fat (4g sat. fat), 12mg chol., 96mg sod., 40g carb. (35g sugars, 1g fiber), 2g pro.

MA

FRIED ICE CREAM DESSERT BARS

Fried ice cream is such a delicious treat, but it can be a hassle to make the individual servings. This recipe gives you the same fabulous flavor in an easy and convenient bar form.
—Andrea Price, Grafton, WI

Prep: 25 min. + freezing
Cook: 5 min. + cooling
Makes: 16 servings

- ½ cup butter, cubed
- 2 cups crushed cornflakes
- 1½ tsp. ground cinnamon
- 3 Tbsp. sugar
- 1¾ cups heavy whipping cream
- ¼ cup evaporated milk
- ⅛ tsp. salt
- 1 can (14 oz.) sweetened condensed milk
- 2 tsp. vanilla extract
- Optional: Honey, whipped cream and maraschino cherries

1. In a large skillet, melt butter over medium heat. Add cornflakes and cinnamon; cook and stir until golden brown, about 5 minutes. Remove from heat; stir in sugar. Cool completely.
2. In a large bowl, beat heavy cream, evaporated milk and salt until mixture begins to thicken. Gradually beat in condensed milk and vanilla until thickened.
3. Sprinkle half the cornflakes onto bottom of a greased 9-in. square baking pan. Pour creamy filling over the crust; sprinkle with the remaining cornflakes. Cover; freeze overnight. Cut into bars. If desired, serve with honey, whipped cream and cherries.

1 BAR 276 cal., 18g fat (11g sat. fat), 55mg chol., 187mg sod., 27g carb. (18g sugars, 0 fiber), 4g pro.

FRIED ICE CREAM DESSERT BARS

CHOCOLATE MALT CRISPY BARS

These chunky, chewy squares are a feast for the eyes. Malted milk flavor coats this treat from top to bottom.
—Taste of Home *Test Kitchen*

Takes: 25 min. • **Makes:** 2 dozen

- 1 pkg. (10 oz.) large marshmallows
- 3 Tbsp. butter
- 5 cups Rice Krispies
- 1 cup malted milk powder, divided
- 4 cups malted milk balls, chopped, divided
- 2 cups semisweet chocolate chips

1. In a Dutch oven, combine the marshmallows and butter. Cook and stir over medium-low heat until melted. Remove from heat; stir in cereal, ¾ cup malt powder and 2½ cups malted milk balls. Press into a greased 13x9-in. pan.
2. In a microwave-safe bowl, melt the chocolate chips; stir until smooth. Stir in remaining ¼ cup malt powder. Spread mixture over cereal bars. Sprinkle with remaining 1½ cups malted milk balls; press into chocolate. Let stand until set. Using a serrated knife, cut into squares.

1 BAR 256 cal., 10g fat (6g sat. fat), 7mg chol., 118mg sod., 42g carb. (29g sugars, 1g fiber), 3g pro.

READER REVIEW

"I used bittersweet chocolate (in place of the semisweet) and thought the overall sweetness of the bars was just right."

—SMFELDNER TASTEOFHOME.COM

MA

CHOCOLATE CREAM BONBONS

My grandmother gave me this recipe when I was a girl. Some of my fondest childhood memories are of her enormous kitchen and all the delicious treats she made.
—Joan Lewis, Reno, NV

Prep: 20 min. + chilling
Makes: about 6 dozen

- 4 cups confectioners' sugar
- 1 cup ground pecans or walnuts
- ½ cup plus 2 Tbsp. sweetened condensed milk
- ¼ cup butter, softened
- 3 cups semisweet chocolate chips
- 2 Tbsp. shortening

1. In a large bowl, combine the confectioners' sugar, pecans, milk and butter. Roll into 1-in. balls. Place on waxed paper-lined baking sheets. Cover and refrigerate overnight.
2. In a microwave, melt the chocolate chips and shortening; stir until smooth. Dip balls in the chocolate; allow excess to drip off. Place on waxed paper; let stand until set. (If balls are too soft to dip, freeze until firm, 3-5 minutes.)

1 BONBON 84 cal., 4g fat (2g sat. fat), 3mg chol., 11mg sod., 13g carb. (12g sugars, 0 fiber), 1g pro.

GRAB-AND-GO FREEZER CHEESECAKES

GRAB-AND-GO FREEZER CHEESECAKES

I love the elegant serving style of individual cheesecakes. I never have to worry if surprise guests stop by because these can be pulled from the freezer in a flash. They're also a blue ribbon-winner at our local county fair!
—Kristyne Mcdougle Walter, Lorain, OH

Prep: 20 min. + freezing • **Makes:** 2 dozen

- 1 pkg. (8.8 oz.) Biscoff cookies
- 6 Tbsp. butter, melted
- 1 Tbsp. sugar
- ¼ tsp. salt

FILLING

- 12 oz. cream cheese, softened
- ½ cup sugar
- ½ cup sour cream
- 1 tsp. lemon juice
- 1 Tbsp. vanilla extract
- 1 carton (8 oz.) frozen whipped topping, thawed (3 cups)
- Sweetened whipped cream, optional

1. Pulse cookies in a food processor until fine crumbs form. Add the butter, sugar and salt; pulse just until combined. Press the mixture gently onto the bottoms of 24 foil-lined muffin cups.
2. For filling, beat the cream cheese in a large bowl until smooth. Add sugar, sour cream, lemon juice and vanilla. Fold in whipped topping. Spoon over crusts; freeze until firm, at least 6 hours.
3. Transfer to freezer containers; return to freezer. To use, thaw in refrigerator for 30 minutes before serving. If desired, top with whipped cream and additional cookies.

1 CHEESECAKE 181 cal., 12g fat (8g sat. fat), 25mg chol., 132mg sod., 16g carb. (12g sugars, 0 fiber), 2g pro.

BUNNY BARK

My kids love to help make this adorable bunny bark every year for Easter. Swirling the candy with festive colors is their favorite part.
—Lauren Habermehl, Pewaukee, WI

Prep: 20 min. • **Cook:** 10 min. + chilling
Makes: 16 servings

- 30 oz. white vanilla-flavored melting wafers
- Gel food coloring (3 colors)
- Assorted sprinkles in pastel colors
- Optional toppings: Chocolate Easter eggs, Easter M&M candies, marshmallow Peeps, pretzel pieces, bunny-shaped graham crackers and jelly beans

1. Line a 15x10x1-in. sheet pan with parchment. Add candy melts to the top pan of a double boiler. Position over a few inches of gently simmering water; melt over low heat, stirring until it's completely smooth, 2-3 minutes. Remove from heat.
2. Divide ½ cup melted wafers among 3 small bowls. Add 1 small drop of different colored food coloring to each. Stir into each portion, adding more dye as needed, until desired colors are achieved.
3. Spread the remaining melted candy wafers onto prepared parchment-lined sheet pan into an even layer, about ¼-in. thick. Spoon dollops of each color over the surface. Use a sharp knife to swirl the colors through the initial layer until well-marbled.
4. While candy is still tacky, sprinkle the surface with assorted sprinkles, candies and other toppings of your choice. Chill in the refrigerator until fully set, at least 30 minutes.
5. Break bunny bark into large pieces and serve.

1 PIECE 266 cal., 15g fat (11g sat. fat), 0 chol., 38mg sod., 34g carb. (34g sugars, 0 fiber), 4g pro.

CHERRY NO-BAKE COOKIES

I always loved my no-bake cookie recipe, but I was never able to place at the fair with it. So I mixed in some maraschino cherries and added almond extract, and voila! I won a blue ribbon at the county fair a few years ago.
—Denise Wheeler, Newaygo, MI

Prep: 30 min. + chilling
Makes: about 5½ dozen

- 2 cups sugar
- ½ cup butter, cubed
- 6 Tbsp. 2% milk
- 3 Tbsp. baking cocoa
- 1 cup peanut butter
- ½ tsp. vanilla extract
- ¼ tsp. almond extract
- 3 cups quick-cooking oats
- 1 jar (10 oz.) maraschino cherries, well drained and finely chopped

1. In a large saucepan, combine sugar, butter, milk and cocoa. Bring to a boil, stirring constantly. Cook and stir for 3 minutes.
2. Remove from heat; stir in peanut butter and extracts until blended. Stir in oats and cherries. Drop mixture by tablespoonfuls onto waxed paper-lined baking sheets. Refrigerate until set. Store in airtight containers.

1 COOKIE 81 cal., 4g fat (1g sat. fat), 4mg chol., 29mg sod., 11g carb. (8g sugars, 1g fiber), 2g pro.

CRUNCHY APRICOT-COCONUT BALLS

My mom gave me this recipe years ago when she had them on her Christmas buffet. I can't believe how simple they are to make.
—Jane Whittaker, Pensacola, FL

Takes: 30 min. • **Makes:** 2 dozen

- 1¼ cups sweetened shredded coconut
- 1 cup dried apricots, finely chopped
- ⅔ cup chopped pecans
- ½ cup fat-free sweetened condensed milk
- ½ cup confectioners' sugar

1. In a small bowl, combine coconut, apricots and pecans. Add condensed milk; mix well (mixture will be sticky).
2. Shape into 1¼-in. balls and roll in the confectioners' sugar. Store in an airtight container in the refrigerator.

1 BALL 87 cal., 4g fat (2g sat. fat), 1mg chol., 19mg sod., 12g carb. (10g sugars, 1g fiber), 1g pro.

NO-BAKE PEANUT BUTTER TREATS

This quick and tasty dessert is perfect for a road trip. Keep them in the refrigerator for an easy snack.
—Sonia Rohda, Waverly, NE

Takes: 10 min. • **Makes:** 15 treats

- ⅓ cup chunky peanut butter
- ¼ cup honey
- ½ tsp. vanilla extract
- ⅓ cup nonfat dry milk powder
- ⅓ cup quick-cooking oats
- 2 Tbsp. graham cracker crumbs

In a small bowl, combine the peanut butter, honey and vanilla. Stir in milk powder, oats and graham cracker crumbs. Shape into 1-in. balls. Cover and refrigerate until serving.

1 SERVING 70 cal., 3g fat (1g sat. fat), 1mg chol., 46mg sod., 9g carb. (6g sugars, 1g fiber), 3g pro.

CRUNCHY APRICOT-COCONUT BALLS

SHAMROCK CRISPY BARS

These sweet snacks are like the pot of gold at the end of your family's feast. With their yummy peppermint and marshmallow flavor, they will make even those without Irish hearts happy. These Rice Krispie bars will have the cook smiling, too, because they are so easy to assemble.
—Taste of Home *Test Kitchen*

Prep: 30 min. + cooling
Makes: 15 servings

- 3 Tbsp. butter
- 4 cups large marshmallows (about 40 pieces)
- ¼ tsp. peppermint extract
- 6 cups Rice Krispies
- 6 oz. white candy coating, coarsely chopped
- 4 drops green food coloring, optional
- Green sprinkles

1. In a large saucepan, melt butter. Add the marshmallows; cook and stir over low heat until melted. Remove from heat; stir in extract and cereal. With buttered hands, press mixture into a greased foil-lined 13-in. x 9-in. pan. Cool completely on a wire rack.
2. Turn out onto a cutting board; remove foil. Cut with a 3-in. shamrock cookie cutter; reshape shamrock stem if needed (save scraps for another use).
3. In a microwave, melt candy coating at 70% power for 1 minute; stir. Microwave in additional 10-to-20-second intervals, stirring until smooth.
4. If desired, stir in food coloring. Spoon over cutouts; spread evenly. Decorate with sprinkles. Let stand until set.

1 SERVING 156 cal., 5g fat (4g sat. fat), 5mg chol., 71mg sod., 28g carb. (17g sugars, 0 fiber), 1g pro.

SHAMROCK CRISPY BARS

NO-BAKE COOKIE BALLS

I go for these quick bites when I'm short on time or don't want to turn on the oven. I make them a day or two ahead to let the flavors blend.
—Carmeletta Dailey, Winfield, TX

Takes: 25 min. • **Makes:** about 5 dozen

- 1 cup semisweet chocolate chips
- 3 cups confectioners' sugar
- 1¾ cups crushed vanilla wafers (about 55 wafers)
- 1 cup chopped walnuts, toasted
- ⅓ cup orange juice
- 3 Tbsp. light corn syrup
- Additional confectioners' sugar

1. In a microwave, melt chocolate chips; stir until smooth. Stir in confectioners' sugar, vanilla wafers, walnuts, orange juice and corn syrup.
2. Shape into 1-in. balls; roll in additional confectioners' sugar. Store in an airtight container.

1 BALL 69 cal., 3g fat (1g sat. fat), 1mg chol., 12mg sod., 12g carb. (9g sugars, 0 fiber), 1g pro.

READER REVIEW

"My family has made these every year for over 40 years, they're so good. We roll them in white, red and green sprinkles. They can sit for over a week for flavor-blending and this is suggested. Great make-ahead, great gift!"

—MARCIAK49 TASTEOFHOME.COM

MINT CHOCOLATE COOKIES

At our house, everyone lends a hand to make these simple chocolate-covered cookies. Decorate them with sprinkles to match any occasion.
—Lily Julow, Lawrenceville, GA

Prep: 15 min. + freezing
Makes: about 3 dozen

- 3 cups crushed chocolate wafers (about 65 wafers)
- 6 oz. cream cheese, softened
- Sugar
- 1 lb. chocolate mint candy coating disks, chopped
- 2 Tbsp. shortening
- Green and white sprinkles, optional

1. In a large bowl, combine the chocolate wafer crumbs and cream cheese. Shape into 1-in. balls. Coat the bottom of a glass with cooking spray, then dip in the sugar; flatten balls to ¼-in. thickness. (Dip the glass in sugar again as needed.) Freeze 30 minutes or until firm.
2. In a microwave, melt candy coating disks and shortening; stir until smooth. Dip cookies in the coating mixture; allow excess to drip off. Place on waxed paper; if desired, decorate immediately with sprinkles. Store cookies between layers of waxed paper in an airtight container in the refrigerator.

1 COOKIE 113 cal., 6g fat (4g sat. fat), 5mg chol., 78mg sod., 14g carb. (10g sugars, 1g fiber), 1g pro.

BANANA CREAM CHOCOLATE TRUFFLES

This truffle recipe was created from ripe bananas and my imagination, and the outcome blew my family and friends away! I don't particularly like bananas, but I could eat these truffles all day long.
—Michele Lassuy, Orlando, FL

Prep: 35 min. + freezing
Makes: about 4 dozen

- 1 pkg. (14.3 oz.) Golden Oreo cookies
- 1 pkg. (8 oz.) cream cheese, softened
- 2 tsp. banana extract
- ⅓ cup mashed ripe banana
- 1 lb. milk chocolate candy coating, melted
- Dried banana chips, coarsely crushed

1. Pulse the cookies in a food processor until fine crumbs form. In a bowl, beat cream cheese and extract until blended. Beat in banana. Stir in cookie crumbs. Freeze, covered, until firm enough to shape, about 2 hours.
2. Shape mixture into 1-in. balls. Dip the cookie balls in candy coating; place on waxed paper-lined baking sheets. Top immediately with banana chips.
3. Refrigerate until set, about 30 minutes. Store in a covered container in the refrigerator.

1 TRUFFLE 110 cal., 6g fat (4g sat. fat), 5mg chol., 45mg sod., 13g carb. (9g sugars, 0 fiber), 1g pro.

BANANA CREAM CHOCOLATE TRUFFLES

EASY CANDIED FRUIT COOKIES

Family and friends always want me to make these for Christmas, so I make lots of them. They're easy to handle and store.
—Nan Bush, Morganton, NC

Prep: 25 min. + chilling • **Makes:** 5 dozen

- 1 pkg. (10 to 12 oz.) vanilla wafers, crushed
- 2 cups chopped pecans or walnuts
- 1 can (14 oz.) sweetened condensed milk
- 1 cup chopped candied pineapple
- 1 cup red and green candied cherries, chopped
- ¼ cup confectioners' sugar

1. In a large bowl, mix first 5 ingredients until blended. Divide the mixture into 3 portions. Shape each portion into a 10x2-in. rectangle. Roll each rectangle in confectioners' sugar to coat. Wrap; refrigerate for 2 hours or until firm.
2. Unwrap and cut logs crosswise into ½-in. slices. Refrigerate in airtight containers.

1 COOKIE 86 cal., 4g fat (1g sat. fat), 3mg chol., 33mg sod., 12g carb. (9g sugars, 0 fiber), 1g pro.

READER RAVES

"A no-bake cookie is always welcome! I imagine you could use whatever dried fruits you liked. I am thinking a mixture of chopped apricots, raisins and dried cherries would be nice."

—ALICE934, TASTEOFHOME.COM

NO-BAKE PEANUT BROWNIES

NO-BAKE PEANUT BROWNIES

You can enlist the kids to help make these chocolaty peanut butter brownies. I like the fact that I can enjoy them but keep my kitchen cool, especially in summer.
—Connie Ward, Mount Pleasant, IA

Prep: 25 min. + chilling
Makes: 16 servings

- 4 cups graham cracker crumbs
- 1 cup chopped peanuts
- ½ cup confectioners' sugar
- ¼ cup peanut butter
- 2 cups semisweet chocolate chips
- ¾ cup evaporated milk
- 1 tsp. vanilla extract

1. In a large bowl, combine the crumbs, peanuts, confectioners' sugar and peanut butter until crumbly. In a small saucepan, melt the chocolate chips and milk over low heat, stirring constantly until smooth. Remove from heat; add vanilla.
2. Pour chocolate mixture over crumb mixture and stir until well blended. Spread evenly in a greased 9-in. square dish. Cover and refrigerate for 1 hour.

1 BROWNIE 169 cal., 9g fat (3g sat. fat), 2mg chol., 78mg sod., 22g carb. (12g sugars, 2g fiber), 3g pro.

MA

CATHEDRAL COOKIES

Children love the colorful marshmallows in these festive confections, which look like stained glass when they're sliced. They practically light up the room from the serving platter at our holiday parties.
—Carol Shaffer, Cape Girardeau, MO

Prep: 10 min. + freezing
Cook: 10 min. + chilling
Makes: about 5 dozen

- 1 cup semisweet chocolate chips
- 2 Tbsp. butter
- 1 large egg, room temperature, lightly beaten
- 3 cups pastel miniature marshmallows
- ½ cup chopped pecans or walnuts
- 1 cup sweetened shredded coconut

1. On top of a double boiler or in a metal bowl over simmering water, melt the chocolate chips and butter over low heat, stirring occasionally. Stir a small amount into the egg, then return all to pan. Cook and stir over low heat for 2 minutes. Pour into a bowl; let cool 15 minutes. Gently stir in marshmallows and nuts. Refrigerate for 30 minutes.
2. On a sheet of waxed paper, shape mixture into a 1½-in. log. Place coconut on another sheet of waxed paper. Gently roll log over coconut to coat all sides. Wrap up tightly in waxed paper, twisting ends to seal.
3. Freeze for 4 hours or overnight. Remove waxed paper. Cut the dough into ¼-in. slices. Store in an airtight container in the refrigerator.

1 COOKIE 40 cal., 3g fat (1g sat. fat), 4mg chol., 11mg sod., 5g carb. (4g sugars, 0 fiber), 0 pro.

GOOEY CARAMEL-TOPPED GINGERSNAPS

Making these cookies is therapeutic for me. The gingersnaps are quite popular at fundraisers. You can also make variations by changing the cookie base or nuts.
—Deirdre Cox, Kansas City, MO

Prep: 30 min. + chilling
Makes: 3½ dozen

- 42 gingersnap cookies
- 1 pkg. (14 oz.) caramels
- 2 Tbsp. 2% milk or heavy whipping cream
- 1 cup chopped honey-roasted peanuts
- 12 oz. white or dark chocolate candy coating, melted
- Sprinkles or finely chopped honey-roasted peanuts

1. Arrange cookies in a single layer on waxed paper-lined baking sheets. In a microwave, melt caramels with milk in a microwave-safe bowl; stir until smooth. Stir in 1 cup chopped peanuts. Spoon about 1 tsp. caramel mixture over each cookie; refrigerate until set.
2. Dip each cookie halfway into candy coating; allow excess to drip off. Return to baking sheet; top with sprinkles or finely chopped peanuts. Refrigerate until set.

1 COOKIE 128 cal., 5g fat (3g sat. fat), 1mg chol., 70mg sod., 19g carb. (14g sugars, 0 fiber), 2g pro.

READER REVIEW

"These cookies were so fun to make and very tasty as well. Thanks for sharing them!"

—JEANNA, TASTEOFHOME.COM

GOOEY CARAMEL-TOPPED GINGERSNAPS

COPYCAT
SAMOA COOKIES

COPYCAT SAMOA COOKIES

We love Girl Scout cookies, especially Samoas, but they're available only once a year. Taking another no-bake recipe, I added ingredients to mimic the Samoa flavor. It's a wonderful recipe to make with the kids!
—Donna Gribbins, Shelbyville, KY

Prep: 35 min. + freezing
Makes: about 7½ dozen

- 1 pkg. (11 oz.) vanilla wafers, finely crushed
- 1 pkg. (7 oz.) sweetened shredded coconut, toasted
- 1 can (13.4 oz.) dulce de leche
- 1 can (14 oz.) sweetened condensed milk
- 2 cups milk chocolate chips
- 2 cups semisweet chocolate chips
- 2 Tbsp. shortening

1. In a large bowl, combine the first 4 ingredients (mixture will be thick and sticky). Roll mixture into 1-in. balls. Place on parchment-lined baking sheets. Freeze until firm, 30-45 minutes.
2. Combine the chocolate chips and shortening in a microwave-safe bowl. In a microwave, melt the chocolate mixture; stir until smooth. Dip cookies into the chocolate; allow excess to drip off. Return to parchment-lined baking sheets; let stand until set. Store the cookies in refrigerator.

1 COOKIE 93 cal., 5g fat (3g sat. fat), 4mg chol., 35mg sod., 13g carb. (11g sugars, 0 fiber), 1g pro.

PEANUT BUTTER RICE KRISPIES TREATS

This is a recipe that my mom used to make when we were little. She would never share the recipe with anyone; she wanted it to be her little secret. We found it when we cleaned out her house after she passed away. Every time I make these, people go crazy over them.
—Laura Wilkey, Jeffersonville, IN

Takes: 20 min. + standing
Makes: 24 bars

- ¼ cup butter
- 1 pkg. (10 oz.) miniature marshmallows
- ½ cup creamy peanut butter
- 2 Tbsp. light corn syrup
- 1 tsp. vanilla extract
- 6 cups Rice Krispies

1. In a large saucepan or stock pot, melt the butter over low heat. Stir in the marshmallows until melted, 2-3 minutes. Stir in peanut butter and corn syrup; stir until mixture is melted and smooth, 2-3 minutes. Stir in vanilla extract. Remove from heat, stir in Rice Krispies until incorporated.
2. Transfer mixture to a 13x9-in. baking dish. Coat fingers with cooking spray; press mixture down into an even layer. Let sit 1 hour; slice into bars.

1 BAR 120 cal., 5g fat (2g sat. fat), 5mg chol., 87mg sod., 18g carb. (10g sugars, 0 fiber), 2g pro.

INDEX

P

Q

R

S

T

V

W

Y

Z